Nikolaos Papakostas
Nikolaos Pasamitros
(Eds.)

An Agenda for the Western Balkans

From Elite Politics to Social Sustainability

Nikolaos Papakostas
Nikolaos Pasamitros
(Eds.)

AN AGENDA FOR THE WESTERN BALKANS

From Elite Politics to Social Sustainability

ibidem-Verlag
Stuttgart

Bibliografische Information der Deutschen Nationalbibliothek
Die Deutsche Nationalbibliothek verzeichnet diese Publikation in der Deutschen Nationalbibliografie; detaillierte bibliografische Daten sind im Internet über http://dnb.d-nb.de abrufbar.

Bibliographic information published by the Deutsche Nationalbibliothek
Die Deutsche Nationalbibliothek lists this publication in the Deutsche Nationalbibliografie; detailed bibliographic data are available in the Internet at http://dnb.d-nb.de.

Cover design: Revekka Vitsaxaki, revekkav@gmail.com.

∞

Gedruckt auf alterungsbeständigem, säurefreien Papier
Printed on acid-free paper

ISBN: 978-3-8382-0668-4

© *ibidem*-Verlag
Stuttgart 2015

Alle Rechte vorbehalten

Das Werk einschließlich aller seiner Teile ist urheberrechtlich geschützt. Jede Verwertung außerhalb der engen Grenzen des Urheberrechtsgesetzes ist ohne Zustimmung des Verlages unzulässig und strafbar. Dies gilt insbesondere für Vervielfältigungen, Übersetzungen, Mikroverfilmungen und elektronische Speicherformen sowie die Einspeicherung und Verarbeitung in elektronischen Systemen.

All rights reserved. No part of this publication may be reproduced, stored in or introduced into a retrieval system, or transmitted, in any form, or by any means (electronic, mechanical, photocopying, recording or otherwise) without the prior written permission of the publisher. Any person who does any unauthorized act in relation to this publication may be liable to criminal prosecution and civil claims for damages.

Printed in Germany

Table of Contents

Acknowledgements   7

List of Abbreviations   9

NIKOLAOS PAPAKOSTAS & NIKOLAOS PASAMITROS
An Agenda for the Western Balkans—Foreword   11

BILGE YABANCI
The EU Democratization and State-Building in Kosovo:
An Analysis Through the Fragmented Local Agency   23

JENNIFER L. TITANSKI-HOOPER
(B)ordering in the EU: Croatia's Path Toward Becoming 'European'   53

STEFAN ĆETKOVIĆ
The Challenge of Promoting Green Sectors in Serbia: Between
International Demands, National Controversies and Sectoral Struggles   71

MIRUNA TRONCOTA
Still "Waiting for Godot" in Sarajevo? Europeanization of Bosnia and
Herzegovina—Between the Contradictions of EU Conditionality and
Local Ownership   95

NICHOLAS ROSSIS
Macedonia: The Consequences of the Political Focus on Identity and
How This Affects Balkan Politics and the European Integration Process.   119

TONKA KOSTADINOVA
Reinventing the Past: Politics of Memory in the Post-Conflict
Reconstruction of Cultural Heritage in Bosnia and Herzegovina   133

ANASTAS VANGELI
On the Growing Cooperation Between China and the Western Balkans   157

ALMA VARDARI-KESLER
Statehood Without Sovereignty: Risky Negotiations
in Post-Independence Kosovo   191

TOM PHILLIPS
Western Europe, Western Balkans: Barriers to Cross-Cultural Encounter   225

Acknowledgements

An Agenda for the Western Balkans, evolved from the original idea of Nikos Papakostas to re-boost the dialogue on the Western Balkans region and its future. The response to the call of *INTER ALIA* for a multidisciplinary scientific collection was unexpectedly dynamic. And as all quality work derives from teamwork, *An Agenda for the Western Balkans* was no exception to the rule. The gratitude of the editing team has many recipients and whoever does not see his/her name or a sketch of him/herself in this passage can rest assured that our neglect is solely based on our eagerness not to forget anyone.

Dr. Stefan Ćetković, Dr. Tonka Kostadinova, Dr. Tom Philips, Dr. Nicholas Rossis, Jennifer Titanski-Hooper, Dr. Miruna Troncota, Anastas Vangeli, Alma Vardari Kesler and Dr. Bilge Yabanci are rightfully the first to receive our gratitude because their contribution constitutes the core of the publication.

A special mention should be made to Boyka Boneva, Inter Alia's third founding member who, while not being officially part of the editorial team, provided her energy, skills and expertise in every step of the way. From the conception of the volume and the arrangement of the first meeting with **ibidem** to the final editing she always eagerly shared her useful opinions and insights.

Many potential contributors submitted their quality abstracts and articles but their work is not included in this volume. To ease any possible bitterness we can responsibly state that we had so many quality texts in our hands that it was impossible to include them all. Anyways, we are deeply grateful for their participation.

We hold many debts of gratitude to Alba Ferreri and Lorena Pullumbi; our skilful co-reviewers that joined forces with the editing team, shared their opinions on their fields of expertise and managed to do a fine job and meet strict deadlines.

One cannot accuse us of a Balkan Babel because of the valuable contribution of our proof-readers. Alexia Eastwood and Catherine Walton did the dirty job of refining the articles and letting them exhibit their essence.

An Agenda for the Western Balkans could have never been realized without Max Jakob Horstmann of **ibidem**-Verlag whose positive energy, support and enthusiasm from day one led to the result you hold in your hands.

We also wish to thank the people who anonymously communicated our call and helped us build the "*Agenda*" team through the *INTER ALIA* network. You all demonstrated that civic action has infinite potentiality and we are confident that you will support the volume.

Finally, we cannot express the true extent of our gratitude to everybody involved in this effort-come-true and putting up with our constant needs, unscheduled demands and exhaustive meticulosity.

Change was the basic element of the creative process of this edition as change is in the epicentre of the research of social phenomena. So, as according to Heraclitus "*all entities move and nothing remains still*" we attempt to grasp and harness this change.

Nikos Papakostas and Nikos Pasamitros, May 2014

List of Abbreviations

BiH:	Bosnia & Herzegovina
BIT(s):	Bilateral Investment Agreement(s)
CCP:	China Communist Party
CEE:	Central & Eastern Europe
CEFTA:	Central European Free Trade Agreement
CFSP:	Common Foreign and Security Policy
DoI:	Declaration of Independence
DOP:	Department for Organic Production
DPA:	Dayton Peace Agreement
EBRD:	European Bank for Reconstruction and Development
EC:	European Commission
ECFR:	European Council on Foreign Relations
ECHR:	European Court of Human Rights
ECLO:	European Commission Liaison Office
EEAS:	EU External Action Service
EPS:	Electric Power Industry of Serbia
EU:	European Union
EUFOR:	European Union Force
EULEX:	European Union Rule of Law Mission in Kosovo
EUPK:	EU Perspective in Kosovo
EUPM:	EU Police Mission in Bosnia-Herzegovina
EUSR:	European Union Special Representative
F.Y.R. Macedonia:	Former Yugoslav Republic of Macedonia
FBiH:	Federation of Bosnia and Herzegovina
FIQ:	Forum for Civic Initiatives
FIT:	Feed-in Tariff
FRY or FR Yugoslavia:	Federal Republic of Yugoslavia
GAC:	General Affairs Council
GDP:	Gross Domestic Product
GIZ:	German Society for International Cooperation
ha:	Hectares
ICJ:	International Court of Justice
ICO:	International Civilian Office
ICTY:	International Criminal Tribunal for the Former Yugoslavia
KFOR:	Kosovo Force
KIPRED:	Kosovar Institute for Policy Research and Development
KLA:	Kosovo Liberation Army
KSF:	Kosovo Security Forces
LDK:	Democratic League of Kosovo
LDK:	Lidhja Demokratike e Kosoves (Democratic League of Kosovo)
MAFWM:	Ministry of Agriculture, Forestry and Water Management

NATO:	North Atlantic Treaty Organization
NMBH:	National Museum of Bosnia and Herzegovina
OFDI:	Outward Foreign Direct Investment
OHR:	Office of the High Representative
OSCE:	Organization for Security and Cooperation in Europe
OZNA:	Department for the Protection of the People
PASOS:	Policy Association for an Open Society
PDK:	Partia Demokratike e Kosoves (Democratic Party of Kosovo)
PIC:	Peace Implementation Council
PIC-SB:	Peace Implementation Council Steering Board
PISG:	Provisional Institutions of Self-Government
POS:	Political Opportunity Structure
PRC:	Peoples Republic of China
RC:	Republic of Croatia
RES:	Renewable Energy Sources
ROSU:	Special Police Forces
RS:	Republika Srspska
SAA:	Stabilisation and Association Agreement
SAP:	Stabilisation and Association Process
SE:	South-East
SEWEA:	Serbian Wind Energy Association
SITF:	Special Investigative Task Force
SOE:	Special Operations Executive
SOE:	State Owned Enterprises
UCK:	Ushtria Clirimtare e Kosoves (Kosovo Liberation Army)
UDB:	Secret Police Organization
UK:	United Kingdom
UNCTAD:	United Nations Conference on Trade and Development
UNDP:	United Nations Development Programme
UNESCO:	United Nations Educational, Scientific and Cultural Organization
UNEP:	United Nations Environment Programme
UNMBH:	United Nations Mission in Bosnia and Herzegovina
UNMIK:	United Nations Interim Administration Mission in Kosovo
UNSCR:	United Nations Security Council Resolution
UNSG:	United Nations Secretary General
VMRO-DMPNE:	Internal Macedonian Revolutionary Organization— Democratic Party for Macedonian National Unity
VV:	Levizja Vetevendosje!
WB:	Western Balkans
WMO:	World Meteorological Organization

NIKOLAOS PAPAKOSTAS & NIKOLAOS PASAMITROS

An Agenda for the Western Balkans—Foreword

Introduction

Southeast Europe has diachronically been a favorite subject-matter for stereotypes and misreading. Popular perceptions and narratives related to the exotic harshness and backwardness of the region and its peoples have played a role in creating and maintaining a dividing line between the core of Europe and the area often referred to as "the Balkans". In recent years, while this imagined region has contracted and is mostly identified with the Western part of the peninsula, the perceptions that come with its infamous brand name hardly differ. The remaining group of states is considered by the mainstream "Western" imaginary to be a place of low development and inherent instability, commonly identified with the conflicts of the 1990s.

Conversely, the post-Cold War domination in political, economic and cultural terms brought about an exaggerated notion of "the West" as a singular and elusive concept. The reunification of the two parts of the Iron Curtain and the disintegration of the Soviet Union fostered a unipolar international environment that called for continuous integration of markets, states and people and growing detestation for statism, nationalism and populism. In that context, the Western Balkans habitually abided to the narrative of being a problematic region that needed restructuring and of the "West", primarily the European Union, as morally bound to take up the formidable task of "saving" it of its gloomy fate. At the same time, specificities of the Western Balkans were handily narrowed down or exaggerated according to the occasion by both local and international policy makers.

The resulting state of affairs created more profound problems than the ones it attempted to solve. On the one hand, it sustained a counterproductive self-image of defeatism and specialness of the Western Balkans and its peoples. On the other hand, it reinforced the EU's habit of promoting inherent defects (lack of leadership and political unity, growing bureaucratization, absence of a common foreign policy and a European demos) as competitive advantages and one-way paths to European integration. Thus, it seriously undermined bottom-up approaches, regional cooperation and the prospect of internally-driven reform efforts.

While these images of the region, reinforced by a particularly troubled transition period continued to prevail, the "Western" orientation of the region was confirmed through the Thessaloniki Declaration signed in 2003. The European Union, a place of political stability and economic growth at that time, effectively pursued the role of the main value exporter in the region. The application of turbo-charged conditionality, characterized by increasing asymmetry in the relations between the EU and the candidate states and uncertainty as to the final outcome of the accession process[1], constituted an effective tool for fostering reform. In that way, the EU managed to promote reform without making any further radical commitments to the countries in the region as regards membership in the EU.

However, five years after the escalation of the European crisis, the stakes for the region and for Europe are rather different. The Union's attractive power is undermined by regression in the integration process, economic crisis and the rise of assertive competitive powers in the region. Technocratic standards appear increasingly simplistic and single-dimensional. The puzzle put forward by the conflict experience and the consequent questions of stateness and actorness seem to exceed the capacities of conditionality and necessitate political solutions and cross cutting approaches.

Finally, the case of the Western Balkans carries significant explanatory power and offers important lessons for the self-conception of the Union as well as for the functionalist viewpoint in general. The necessity to question imposed solutions and ineffective elite politics, and additionally to highlight the inclusion of people and their needs as an integral component of contemporary policy making, appears to be essential for the attainment of long-term solutions and social sustainability.

European Union's agenda for the Western Balkans: A critical appraisal.

A lot of ink has been spilled on the involvement of the EU in the Western Balkans. From the Bosnian regime issue to the Albanian insurgency in F.Y.R. Macedonia and from the accession of Croatia to the Kosovo case, the Union has been harshly criticized; sometimes for being too interventionist, in other instances for being too passive and in some others for interfering in

---

[1] In Heather Grabbe's (2003) typology.

the wrong manner or in bad timing. In any case, inner EU disagreements have so far ensured some kind of relative neutrality in its involvement in the specific region.[2]

Closing up on the second decade past the Dayton Agreement, 15 years after the end of the conflict in Kosovo, more than a decade from the Ohrid Framework Agreement in the FYR Macedonia and the Thessaloniki Summit, Western Balkans' politics and societies are, nowadays, considerably different. The prospect of armed conflict is unlikely, democracy is recognized as "the only game in town"[3] by all major players, and the first phase of the countries' economic transition has been concluded. However, in most cases the achieved progress has not resulted in concrete steps towards integration in "Western" institutions.

This delay highlights the lack of a common plan and unanimous EU agenda for the region. The enlargement fatigue and the widening vs. deepening discourse preponderated in the EU throughout the 2000s until the eruption of the crisis. This seemed to have been an unavoidable part of a generalized introversion process. However, the EU's wavering has at times deprived Western Balkan countries from a clear orientation to the future and has given power to forces of populism and nationalism. Thus, it has obstructed sustainable advancement towards political stability, social cohesion and economic growth.

Opposite to this pattern, in July 2013, Croatia became a fully-fledged member of the European Union while Serbia initiated negotiations for accession in January 2014. Those events seem to have reinvigorated the enlargement process that had been stagnant for some time. They also carry great symbolic importance for the region and for the continent in general. The visible prospect of 'reunification' of the former conflicting countries in the EU promulgates, apart from new and significant prospects for development, the irrevocable end of the imagined region of the "Balkans".

Recent mobility in the enlargement process manifests a renewed readiness of the EU leadership to be more dynamically involved in the region in order to avoid the uncertainty of an increasingly complicated international landscape. On the other hand, it indicates the narrowing

---

[2] This of course does not mean political neutrality since the interventionist approach is a policy choice per se.

[3] The phrase is borrowed by the classic "Problems of Democratic Transition and Consolidation" of H. Linz and Al. Stepan (1996)

distance between the EU and the Western Balkan countries and, thereof, the relative effectiveness of the principle of conditionality in both economic and political terms despite the crisis instance. Successful conception, formulation, implementation, evaluation and duplication of conditionality-driven reform can impact strongly on the enlargement process and the international image of the EU.

Nevertheless, there is still a long way to go. Moving further from the present-day political discourse, the countries' progress towards EU integration is undermined by the legacies of authoritarianism, interethnic conflict and centrally planned economy. As regards political conditionality, these legacies have preserved what North, Weingast and Wallis (2009) referred to as "closed access governance" regimes. Closed access governance regimes are characterized by varying access to state resources based on individuals' closeness to a leader (patrimonialism) or to a fraction, usually a political faction (competitive particularism). In turn, unequal access to state resources perpetuates uneven social equilibria that avert universal agreement on means and ends in the respective societies.

Particularism, in the case of the Western Balkan countries, constitutes an underlying cause of other social symptoms such as corruption and organized crime, low social capital, dysfunctional public administration etc. In turn, these pose impediments to political stability and, therefore, to the candidates' attractiveness for EU accession. Moreover, "closed access governance" order is reinforced by the legacy of conflict. Social mobilization along ethnic lines or formerly conflicting parties, undermines not only the quality of governance but also social cohesion and interethnic relations as it aggravates mutual feelings of victimization and stirs questions of stateness. Clearly, those deep-seated, cross-cutting and self-maintaining realities cannot be confronted through conditionality; a strategy whose nature is largely reactive.

As regards economic criteria, the Western Balkans entered the open market arena rather late. By the time the first phase of economic transition was concluded, the "competitive" economies of Central and Eastern Europe were already full members of the European Union and were presented with all the potentials for foreign investment and mobility that came with it. This delay seriously undermined the functioning of the countries' markets and, therefore, their attractiveness for investments during the 2000s.

However, following the escalation of the economic crisis in Europe and the rise of new players in the region, this competitive disadvantage could be reversed. The region's current socioeconomic condition provides increased investment potentials while political risk is permissible. Importantly, the economic potentials of the region deriving from the "East" come with no strings attached in the form of conditionality. Thus, the application of economic conditionality can boost the countries' economic development only if it is kept free from excessive interventionism and unnecessary antagonisms between major international players. In that way, it can increase the attractiveness of accession while positively contributing to EU's competitiveness.

As previous enlargements have manifested, the accession or non-accession in the Union is, utterly, subject to political decisions[4]. Thus, apart from conditionality-driven policies, the European Union's indirect involvement in the region is equally important. EU accession constitutes a top priority for all Western Balkans' governments. Political discourse is centred on the integration process while, for an important part of the electorate, governmental effectiveness is assessed according to the countries' progress towards accession. All countries in the region are ruled by pro-EU parties while political rhetoric and agenda are being shaped by the necessities set by the membership prospect.

In that context, the level of trust in political institutions is a decisive factor for the progress of the countries towards integration. The European Union is more trusted than national political institutions in all Western Balkan countries. In addition, with the exception of Bosnia, where the long involvement of the EU has gradually eroded its political capital, the Union is among the most trusted institutions, in general (see for instance: PASOS 2014).

---

[4] This was apparent in many of the cases during the 2004 enlargements when a highly diverse group of countries with different levels of effectiveness at transposing EU standards and different capacities of implementing EU norms was integrated simultaneously. Another example is the fast progress of Serbia towards EU integration after the apprehension of war crimes' suspects that is after the fulfillment of a criterion that clearly exceeds the alleged technocratic nature of the pre-accession procedure. A third prominent case would be the stalling of the integration process of FYR Macedonia due to the name-issue dispute with Greece, an issue of symbolic and political nature.

This role does not come without responsibilities and risks. All candidate Western Balkan countries that were surveyed for the latest Eurobarometer feature a dramatic lack of trust in all institutions, be it national or European (European Commission 2014). More importantly, the research highlights that, while higher than national, trust in EU institutions has been significantly contracting in all countries. This is partly related to the damaged international image of the European Union following the escalation of the crisis and partly to its inability or unwillingness to give tangible political rewards to the countries that struggle with the continuously toughening standards set by the EU.

The eruption of the crisis in Europe in 2008 manifested significant structural deficiencies of the EU. Dramatic delays in decision making, overly bureaucratic and phobic confrontation of economic challenges led to unfair and uninspired solutions that failed to take into consideration the conceptual principles of the European Union, to grasp the imagination of the European peoples and to involve them in the decision making process. Yet, while the trust and enthusiasm for EU integration among Western Balkans' peoples seem to have decreased, support for EU accession in quantitative terms is hardly disturbed. The lack of sound alternatives, the large gap between living standards in candidate states and EU member states, as well as the psychological importance of belonging in a traditionally powerful group of countries outshined the negative externalities of the crisis.

Nevertheless, taking into consideration the changing international landscape and the EU's continuous inability to give convincing answers to its own challenges, this pattern is not irreversible. While the application of conditionality is significantly more efficient than in previous enlargements, its dynamics are gradually fading. Political decisions are integral to any sustainable agenda for the Western Balkans. To that end, factoring in regional specificities and peoples' needs appears to be mutually beneficiary for the EU and the countries of the region.

A laborious path to the future

Beyond the attempts to stabilize the region, the EU also acts as a value exporter for candidates, potential candidates and negotiating states. And although the enlargement process progresses according to the Copenhagen criteria and the *acquis communitaire*, due to constant transformation in the

European structure, there are serious impediments in the accession procedure that do not stem from the inability of the states to apply norms but rather from intrinsic EU glitches. Admittedly, the EU is a candid value exporter but at the same time, shows a striking lack of flexibility and adoptability. The same often applies for local governments that attempt to modernize and move away from their unwieldy past.

As Stefan Ćetković, in *The Challenge of Promoting Green Sectors in Serbia* shows, technocratic approaches in many cases fail to see local needs. Of course, one can argue that the decision-makers sometimes know what is good for the people before the people realize it for themselves and that leaders, in many instances, have the charisma to lead through the right path. On the other hand, some may say that the neglect of people's needs by the elites creates social discontent. Lasting denial of needs can generate social inequalities and deep cleavages that may scar societies and foster latent conflict. And while human needs can hardly constitute navigation points for governance (Groom 2007), yet, they have to be kept in mind since Needs Approaches seem to contain some empirical truth; the denial of needs like safety, security, identity, respect and participation is likely to generate popular reactions and in extremis violent responses. In many cases, while some needs are not met, people who are experiencing gratification of some other needs are not willing to engage in radical movements or revolutions for fear of losing what fulfilment they are relatively assured of under an existing order (Sites 1990). As Alma Vardari-Kesler shows in *Statehood without Sovereignty*, there seems to be a need for the peoples of the region to be included in the advancement process; especially when it concerns huge social change like state-building or EU accession.

In the case of F.Y.R. Macedonia, we have the building of a state, based on the Slavic-Macedonian identity hype and the marginalization of the Albanian one. Top-down identity politics based on the creation of an archaic national image along with the opposing foreign policies of Greece and Bulgaria create a scabrous equation for the EU to solve. As Dr Nicholas Rossis argues in *The consequences of the political focus on identity and its effect on Balkan politics and the European integration process: a case study of Macedonia*, sooner or later the EU will have to face the identity politics riddle and face up, irredentist aspirations and ethnocentric voices in the region. This task seems even more challenging given the fact that the Union cannot effectively contain similar phenomena of nationalism and populism within its own range.

Dr Bilge Yabanci in *The EU Democratization and State-building in Kosovo* shows that future member-states have been offered an overdose of top-down, technocratic Europeanization policies. Even if the active involvement of the peoples in such processes seems an overambitious and unreachable plan, local agency needs to be treated as an instrumental part in a convergence process. The neglect of such primary actors in the democratization procedure leads to irreconcilability between the EU agenda and the local priorities and expectations. The Kosovo case shows that the public and the non-state actors perceive the EU focus as irrelevant to their urgent needs and expectations such as employability and security.

In other more complex cases, there is striking lack of will from all the parties involved, to implement change. Dr Miruna Troncota, in *Still "waiting for Godot" in Sarajevo?* analyzes the political situation in Bosnia and Herzegovina and the role of international and local actors in the slow Europeanization process and the non-application of reforms. The "Blame Game" between local and international actors (mainly the EU) supports the preservation of the status quo and the delay of the Europeanization process. Once again, BiH demonstrates the fragmentation of local agency, the EU approach inflexibility and the long-term stalemate imposed solutions produce.

Moreover, the Balkan "troublemaker" image and self-image constitutes in itself an obstacle towards the EU integration. The case of Croatia studied by Jennifer Titanski-Hooper in *(B)ordering in the EU*, shows a gloomy reality; Western Balkan states, for external and internal purposes, need to shake off their Balkan geographic imaginary and shift to a European one. This is because the EU, through a process of (b)ordering, increasingly defines the who, what and where of being 'European'. This procedure is highly linked to geographic imaginaries, which are based in historical, cultural and political experiences and perceptions of place and identity. The geographic imaginary of the Balkans as the underdeveloped, and unstable 'other' in Europe continues to frame, at least in part, the expansion of the European Union into the region. The fervent attempt to throw away the Balkan notoriety raises identity issues. The willingness to disaknowledge the Balkan legacy for the EU prosperity may be a functional choice in the short-run but sooner or later, the chickens will come home to roost. Thus, social sustainability calls for confrontation, introversion and self-criticism of past issues for the establishment of a promising future. The same applies for the EU which is, once more, called to show increased flexibility.

As the Image Theory urges, the human mind can only bear a certain degree of complexity and when complexity becomes unbearable, it retreats into symbolic images (Boulding 1973; Lippmann 1922). These simplified images can be positive or negative and concern both individuals and groups. On the group level these images create a dichotomy between us (in-group) and the "other" (out-group). Negative self-images in some instances entrap peoples into the victim mentality and lead them towards pessimism, passiveness and self-blame. In others, the tough conditions the peer group is experiencing lead to the victimization of a supposedly hostile "other" and make the public opinion vulnerable to populism and nationalistic cries.

The images of the self and the other are shaped by the habitus (Rieber & Kelly 1991) namely the familiar environment in which one moves inside (the family, the school, the peer group and the media etc.). One of the basic factors that form these images is history as transmitted through the oral historical heritage, schooling and the written word. As Dr Tonka Konstadinova analyzes in her, *Reinventing the past: politics of memory in the post-conflict reconstruction of cultural heritage in Bosnia and Herzegovina*, in many occasions, new constructed cultural narratives replace old ones in an attempt to reconstruct the past for the legitimization of power.

Beyond the EU borders, the Western Balkan countries attempt to present a positive international image and to re-brand the region and boost extraversion. A colossal actor like China could not stay outside the process of economic growth of the region. Even if the penetration is of secondary concern for the Chinese side, its economic size cannot be unimportant for the Western Balkan states. Anastas Vangeli in, *On the growing cooperation between China and the Western Balkans*, explains the Chinese presence in the Western Balkans and illustrates why an EU future would further forward economic relations between the Asian economic giant and the region. Vangeli points out that EU and China are not competitive forces in the Western Balkans but rather supplementary economic actors.

As regards the "exportable" image of the Western Balkans to Western Europe, despite the huge effort of the Western Balkan countries to change it, Western perceptions still highly rely on stereotypes and generalizations on the Balkan cultural heritage. Dr Tom Philips lively illustrates the persistence of such stereotypes in the final chapter of the collection (*Western Europe, Western Balkans: Barriers to Cross-Cultural Encounter*).

Conclusions

An Agenda for the Western Balkans emphasizes on three wide and interconnected concepts that are being examined though various disciplines: images, actorness and sustainability. It attempts to show that while both domestic and external solutions applied in the region are potentially effective, there is a need for more cross-cutting and bottom-up approaches. An internally driven, inclusive reform process is essential for creating a promising future for the peoples. A second underlying notion of this volume is that political solutions can never be free of reaction and that there is no such thing as a neutral involvement. Finally, the collection draws attention to the fact that cost-benefit calculations and values systems divergences are not the only frameworks for conceiving decision making. Distorted images of self and other are also important factors for understanding relations of nations and peoples.

Viable living environment presupposes upholding human needs in the process through all available channels. Thus, if there is something to be imposed on the Western Balkans societies is not top-down, remote guidelines, but the active involvement of the citizens in shaping their own lives. Obviously, this is a time and resource-consuming involvement. However, it is rather questionable whether global actors and primarily the EU have real alternatives in an instance of crisis and growing political and economic competitiveness. The current state of affairs seems to be unprecedented for Europe and the EU and it would probably be for the long term stability and prosperity of the region and the continent to be evaluated as such.

In any case, constructive critique and the offering of proposals is the best way to re-involve those interested in the future of the Western Balkans. This is exactly the goal of the contributors; to set the foundations for an innovative debate for the region. This collection of articles is neither a wish list for the Balkan neighborhood, nor a purely theoretical text. It is a grounded set of research and proposals that aims at contributing to the ongoing academic effort of building an alternative conceptual framework for the region and its peoples. At the same time, the volume attempts to give the reader tangible answers to the puzzling questions that stand between the region's past and the aspired goal of social sustainability with the underlying aim of bridging the two in a constructive and fruitful way.

References

Boulding, K. 1959. *The Image, Knowledge in Life and Society*, University of Michigan Press

Grabbe, H. 2003. Europeanization Goes East: Power and Uncertainty in the EU Accession Process. In *The Politics of Europeanization*, eds Featherstone K. and Radaelli, C. M., Oxford University Press, pp. 303–327.

European Commission, Standard Eurobarometer. 2014. Public Opinion in the European Union. (Standard Eurobarometer, No. 80), available at <http://ec.europa.eu/public_opinion/archives/eb_arch_en.htm>.

Groom, A. 2007. *From conflict prevention to conflict resolution: a conceptual tour d'horizon*. In: Teraine, J., Colard, D. and Fontanel, J., eds. La Sécurité Internationale Entre Rupture et Continuité: Mélanges en l'honneur du Professeur Jean- François Guilhaudis. Bruxelles: Bruyant. pp. 219–255 ISBN 9782802722939

Linz, H. & Stepan, Al. 1996. Problems of Democratic Transition and Consolidation. Baltimore, John Hopkins University Press

Lippmann, W. 1922. Public Opinion, New York, Harcourt, Brace and Co.

North, D., Wallis, J. J. & Weingast B. 2009. *Violence and Social Orders: A Conceptual Framework for Interpreting Recorded Human History*, Cambridge University Press

Policy Association for an Open Society (PASOS). 2014. Public opinion survey in six Western Balkan counties. Available at: http://pasos.org/12122/pasos-poll-citizens-of-six-balkan-countries-identify-political-parties-as-the-most-untrustworthy-institution-in-their-respective-countries

Rieber W. Robert and Robert J. Kelly. 1991. *Substance and Shadow, Images of the Enemy*. In Rieber W. Robert (ed.), The Psychology of War and Peace, The Image of the Enemy, New York, Plenum Press

Sites, P. 1990. *Legitimacy and Human Needs*. In: John Burton and Frank Dukes, eds. Conflict: Readings in Management and Resolution. New York: St. Martin's Press, 1990.

BILGE YABANCI

The EU Democratization and State-Building in Kosovo: An Analysis Through the Fragmented Local Agency

Despite the continuously increasing research on conditionality, socialization and compliance dynamics of the local political leaders in the Western Balkans, the fragmented local agency and its complex relations with the EU remains an under-researched topic. This paper aims to fulfil this gap by offering a systematic analysis of 'the local' through the case of Kosovo. It aspires to complement the top-down Europeanization/socialization and rational adaptation perspectives with a critical perspective. The paper argues that a systematic analysis of the local agency and domestic dynamics would improve our understanding of some of the persistent problems of state-building and democratization efforts in the Western Balkans by explaining why some norms and policies are resisted, and some others are supported under certain conditions. The investigation is based on the relevant literature, semi-structured interviews conducted in Kosovo and the analysis of policy documents, civil society reports and local newspaper archives. The findings show that the uneasy relations between the local groups and deeper problems of state weakness, such as lack of legitimacy, constantly pressurize the EU to redefine its state- and democracy building agenda in line with irreconcilable local priorities and expectations.

Key Words: Europeanization, state-building, Kosovo, local agency.

Dr. Bilge Yabanci has recently been awarded a PhD in Politics by the University of Bath.

Introduction

The Western Balkans is a longstanding focus for the EU's state-building and democratization agenda through the export of EU norms. This agenda is closely linked to political conditionality and membership prospect, which provides the Union with leverage to directly influence the local context through offering incentives or disincentives. The EU considers the holistic framework based on promotion of state-building, democratization and membership prospect in the region as 'the ultimate conflict prevention strategy' (European Commission 2006) which gives the Union a 'comparative advantage', over international institutions in terms of facilitating democracy, good governance and state-building (Bechev and Andreev 2005).

The EU's commitment to democratization, state-building and conflict resolution through norm transfer and conditionality (i.e. providing or withdrawing incentives) in the Western Balkans has created an ever growing body of literature supported by theoretical and empirical research. Despite this continuously growing body of literature analysing conditionality and compliance dynamics of the local political leaders in the Western Balkans, the fragmented local agency and its complex relations with the EU remains an under-researched area. This paper aims to fulfil this gap by offering a systematic analysis of the local agency (political elites including the opposition, non-state organizations and public) in the Western Balkans through the case of Kosovo. I argue that the Western Balkans requires a more refined approach than a simple extension of the first and second generation Europeanization literatures which are biased towards the local actors and prioritize (to different extents) the role of the EU incentives and norms. The paper aims to inquire the impact of the fragmented local agency and deep seated problems of stateness in terms not only of lack of capabilities and weak institutions, but also the lack of legitimacy of the state and the ruling elites for the local population.

The first section problematizes a dominant tendency in the Europeanization literature by briefly outlining the main assumptions and findings that underlie the research agenda of Europeanization scholars. The second section discusses the necessity of an alternative analytical perspective focused on local dynamics. It argues that the Europeanization literature focuses on the EU's incentives and norms, while local resources, actors and institutions are treated as passive recipients with limited ability to resist or change the EU agenda. The local agency is analyzed only through political leaderships and as reactionary (acting as spoiler) to the EU norms and policies in the literature. In the third part, the critical analytical perspective is applied to the case of Kosovo. The investigation is based on the relevant literature, semi-structured interviews conducted with the Kosovar political elite, civil society representatives and journalists in Kosovo in May 2011, reports and policy documents of the Kosovo government and local civil society organizations and the local newspaper reports.

Europeanization literature

Research on Europeanization and domestic adaptation in the Western Balkans has boomed after the 2004 enlargement thanks to the success of the Europeanization framework in explaining domestic change in the Central and Eastern Europe (CEE). Although Europeanization was originally used to define policy adaptation in EU member states in line with EU law, the literature progressively developed to analyze the accession candidates in order to explain how the membership perspective and EU criteria affect the domestic political processes in candidate countries (Featherstone and Radaelli 2003; Schimmelfennig 2005; Börzel and Risse 2007). The so-called 'first generation Europeanization literature' demonstrated that the credibility and the size of EU incentives are crucial for explaining the degree of Europeanization (i.e. domestic adaptation) in target countries. According to Schimmelfennig (2008: 921), 'the success of political conditionality' depends on three factors: 'the conditional offer of EU membership to the target government; the normative consistency of the EU's enlargement decisions; and low political compliance costs of the target government'. Usually, incentives less than a credible membership perspective, such as association or financial aid, were found to be too weak to overcome domestic resistance (Kelley 2004; Vachudová 2004). Only if the accession perspective is credible and immediate once the country complies with the EU norms, then the ruling elites are likely to risk 'short-term political losses in return for immediate and long-term gains' (Schimmelfennig 2008).

Various authors have also demonstrated that misfit between domestic institutional structures and EU structures provide the necessary pressure for the local elites to alter the domestic structures in line with EU requirements thanks to the incentives (positive and negative) and socialization in the long term (Börzel and Risse 2003). If the compliance costs are too high for the governments (undermining their grip on power or perceived as a threat to security and integrity of the country) or if there is strong nationalist opposition (veto players), institutional adaptation remains limited and mechanisms of social learning (emulsion, persuasion and imitation) are not sufficient to facilitate democratic reform. In other words, the early Europeanization literature demonstrates that once the membership prospect is strong, successful Europeanization in candidate countries results from three factors: misfit between domestic structures and reforms demanded by the EU, significant EU pressure on local leaderships, weak domestic veto players (Börzel 2011).

After the 2004 enlargement, the Europeanization literature has turned to analyze accession candidates, potential candidates or the neighboring countries (e.g. Coppieters, Emerson et al. 2004; Diez, Albert et al. 2008; Börzel and Risse 2009; Schimmelfennig 2012). Empirical studies within this 'second generation Europeanization literature' showed that political transformation essentially differs from the experience of the CEE countries. The role of indirect mechanisms for institutional change and domestic opportunities and constraints play a crucial role when defining the EU's leverage and impact in institutional and behavioral change.

In this sense, the Western Balkans have been a fertile testing ground to study these indirect mechanisms of Europeanization and the EU's weakened impact on democratization and conflict resolution due to the limited statehood structures and clientelist/corrupt ruling class (Börzel 2011; Noutcheva and Aydin- Düzgit 2011; Börzel and Pamuk 2012). Since then, there is an ever growing body of literature researching on whether the EU conditionality and norm exportation to the Western Balkans would amount to actual power to transform or resolve various conflicts through promotion of democracy, good governance, rule of law, civil society and competitive party politics (Noutcheva and Huysseune 2004; Anastasakis 2005; Tocci 2007; Börzel and Risse 2009; Noutcheva 2009; Renner and Trauner 2009; Freyburg and Richter 2010; Börzel 2011; Noutcheva and Aydin- Düzgit 2011; Elbasani 2013).

Despite a more nuanced look into the domestic dynamics in this second generation Europeanization literature, there is still a great overlap between these two genres of analysis on Europeanization in and beyond Europe in terms of the mechanisms (conditionality vs. normative emulsion/socialization) and logics of Europeanization (logic of appropriateness vs. logic of consequences) (for an overview Schimmelfennig 2005; Bolmer 2007; Schimmelfennig 2012). The changes in the target countries are attributed to direct (coercion, conditionality/capacity-building, persuasion, socialization) or indirect (normative emulsion, lesson drawing and competition) EU impact in facilitating institutional change in the accession countries (Vachudová 2004; Schimmelfennig 2005; Börzel and Risse 2011). The extension of the Europeanization approach to the candidate and potential candidate countries in the Western Balkans did not entirely change the top-down approach that prioritizes EU incentives and norms over local agency. Europeanization students start with a common assumption that EU incentives and "complex learning by which [local] actors redefine their interests and identities" would generate reforms and transform conflict enhancing attitudes, policies and identities (Börzel and Risse 2011). Local resources, actors and institutions intervene as secondary factors in response to the EU agenda with an aim to weaken or divert the intended EU impact.

These studies do not necessarily deny the role of local actors. For instance, the conditionality-socialization model offered by Coppieters et al. (2004) takes complications generated by the federal political systems of the target countries into account when explaining EU conflict resolution policies through incentives and social learning. Similarly, Diez et al. (Diez, Albert et al. 2008) argue that local actors can easily make use of the integration process to securitize or de-securitize the current situation on the ground and thereby, diminish or enhance the conflict. Yet, the EU is considered as the principle agent, and the local context only unfolds to enable or hinder the EU impact by accepting or rejecting the normative EU actorness. According to Coppieters et al. (Coppieters, Emerson et al. 2004) the EU has two instruments: presenting or withdrawing incentives (i.e. conditionality) in the short-term, and the socialising effects of Europeanization in the long-term. During the initial phases of conflict resolution, the EU could secure compliance for demanding conditionality by emphasising the benefits and persuading or subtly coercing the local leadership, whilst over the long term, genuine internalization of EU values by the domestic actors (i.e. socialization) would gain prominence. In cases of persistent rejection to comply with the EU agenda by local politicians, "it is imperative for third parties to improve the benefits of settlement by providing additional resources that would induce the elites to settle" (Coppieters, Emerson et al. 2004). Diez et al. (2006) offer four EU pathways to facilitate conflict transformation that are shaped either by 'the concrete interventions by the EU actors' or 'discursive, legal and institutional framework' of integration/association process. However, local factors remain as medium variables in explaining how the 'EU's perturbation' on the conflict is 'distracted' by local factors (Diez, Stetter et al. 2006).

Different from these authors, Noutcheva (2009; 2012), Tocci (2005) and Christou (2010) aim to move beyond the unidirectional analyses focused only on the EU side in order to understand nuanced local interpretations and constant interaction between local elites and the EU and to explain various degrees of adaptation and compliance. They share a main conclusion that whether or not local actors perceive the EU as a normative power and their ability to resist the EU's agenda preclude the direct impact of conditionality and socialization on conflict resolution. However, these studies have not completely addressed the diversity of 'the local' and 'how' divergent convictions, attitudes, discourses and strategies available to the fragmented local agency can impact on the relevance and authority of the EU in a specific case of conflict resolution.

As a result, the findings of the second generation Europeanization are largely in line with the first generation Europeanization literature. Even when the literature defines some scope conditions (such as state capacity to undertake reforms, democratic or autocratic nature of the target country, domestic incentives and power asymmetries between the EU and target country) to explain the variance in institutional convergence and persistence in local behavior (Börzel and Risse 2011), 'the EU is in the driving seat distributing incentives and re-arranging power relations in conflict territories and local politicians are semi-autonomous respondents to the EU agenda' (Yabanci 2013).

Europeanization and the Western Balkans: a problematic case or a problematic approach?

The dominant Europeanization approach remains insufficient to completely address the diversity of 'the local' and 'how' their independent convictions, attitudes, discourses and strategies can impact the relevance and authority of the EU conditionality and democratization efforts in the Western Balkans for three reasons. First, it is based on an assumption that the EU has the actual control of the whole process. The top-down understanding in explaining the local context and agency assumes that the EU is 'a dominant partner in an unequal relationship' and with the resources available, including normative power, the EU can pursue its own agenda (Pace, Seeberg et al. 2009). The EU sets the framework, decides the main policy tool to intervene in the conflict (integration, association or as a third party mediator) and chooses conditions, incentives and the specific local actors for empowerment. The mainstream Europeanization literature argues that EU conditionality empowers 'liberal reform coalitions' or 'domestic norm entrepreneurs' in target countries. These coalitions would capitalize on the EU demands to pressurize for democratic change in line with the EU norms and facilitate socialization in the long term (Schimmelfennig 2005). In other words, local actors are considered reactionary to the EU agenda without independent attitudes, perceptions and norms. If the local actors perceive the EU as truly normative (Noutcheva 2009) or, in the short term, if the benefits and offers exceeds the costs of compliance for the 'rational' domestic leaders (Tocci 2005), the EU would be able to transform conflicts. In this approach, Europeanization as a conflict resolution tool exerts similar adaptation pressures irrespective of the context of the conflict and local leaderships are expected to comply with the EU requirements thanks to the conditionality and socialization processes (Yabanci 2013). However, as acknowledged by Börzel and Risse (Börzel and Risse 2011), local agents are not "simply passive recipients of EU policies and institutions. Rather, the adoption of and adaptation to EU norms, rules and institutional models into domestic or regional structures mostly involve active processes of interpretation, incorporation of new norms and rules into existing institutions, and also resistance to particular rules and regulations".

Second, the Europeanization literature tends to focus on formal institutional change (or how the local elites, who are responsive to EU incentives or subject to long term socialization with EU norms, adapt domestic institutions to the European/EU standards) over sustainable behavioral change (albeit a few exceptions studying the post-accession trends in the CEE countries). However, the Western Balkans does not fit in the expectations. The (potential) candidates have progressed in terms of legal adaptation; yet, behavioral change or sustained implementation is diverse, and mostly remains very limited in the region (Elbasani 2013). According to Börzel (Börzel 2011), 'decoupling' that results from the difference between legal/formal compliance and behavior needs to be analyzed by "systematically study[ing] the implementation of domestic reforms where factors mediating the domestic impact of Europe become even more important".

Third, the existing accounts tend to treat 'the local' as a uniform body, and mostly evaluate them only through the existing leaderships' point of view without systematically analysing the different perceptions and resources available to micro-level factors or various groups within the local audience. In other words, compliance is an elite-driven process. As Noutcheva (2006) notes "it is the rational calculations and/or normative considerations of political leaders in power that matter most for the compliance pattern with EU pre-accession requirements of candidate countries. Preferences and normative orientations of societies at large are taken into account only to the extent that those are present in the elites' thinking and argumentation". The impact of the diversity of local audience, informal local understandings and norms about appropriate action by the EU, collective and divergent expectations of the fragmented local audience are not assessed in detail. However, especially in the post-conflict setting, the EU has to deal with a fragmented audience in terms of not only ethnicity, but also, ideology, strategy and sources that are available to them (Yabanci 2013).

Therefore, the puzzle of EU state-building and democratization that is linked to conditionality and membership prospect in the Western Balkans suggests that we need a more refined understanding of the local context and fragmented local agency. It is important to take the potential difference between the local understanding of a norm-driven action and the EU norms into account. Pace, Seeberg and Cavatorta (Pace, Seeberg et al. 2009) argue that the recipients of the EU's democracy promotion policy "can signal to the EU what their preferences are, highlighting their position and values in order to influence the ways in which EU policies ... are implemented in practice". Moreover, the irrelevance of 'perceptions of normativeness' for local actors should not be disregarded, although the EU uploads a crucial symbolic meaning to it. It is also to highlight that the locals are not expected to go through a linear and unidirectional process of rational adaptation (cost-benefit calculation) and then, socialization. Local actors are more likely to receive, process and interpret different and often conflicting agendas of multifarious thirds parties and even different EU institutions.

The Western Balkans as a case study of democratization through conditionality and membership prospect also suggests that there is a more deep-seated problem embedded in the weak state structures than foreseen by the second generation Europeanization literature. Recently, Europeanization scholars accepted weak institutions in the region as one of the major obstacles for compliance and socialization (Börzel 2011). However, these scholars focus on the lack of technocratic efficiency of these institutions in implementing EU requirements in order to explain how similar incentives and norms have different impact across the region. However, the weak institutions are related to state and society relations in the Western Balkans. The main problem related to the lack of genuine and broad-based engagement with the EU democratization agenda is the persistence of feeble institutions without capacity to implement EU related reforms in the region as well as the clientelist and corrupt structures. These institutions are perceived by the majority of citizens as monopolized by a dominant ethnic group or the corrupt ruling elites and they lack legitimacy at the societal level (Bechev and Andreev 2005). This legitimacy deficit creates three main problems on the ground:

First, the EU considers the lack of good governance (the fight against organized crime, corruption and clientelism) as one of the main problems of the region and pressurizes the local political elites to tackle with these problems by offering incentives (European Commission 2005–2012). However, the ruling elites in the region generally have embedded interests in the current institutional structure. As a result, the reforms demanded by the European Union are very costly to implement for the local elites since more democratic institutions would mean losing privileges and their grip on power. As acknowledged by the Europeanization literature on the Western Balkans, positive incentives provided to the local elites might only trigger 'fake compliance' (Noutcheva 2009). Therefore, the EU needs to rely on non-state and grassroots actors with a desire to change the current clientelist structures.

Second and related to the first, the EU, as the main international actor strongly committed to the promotion of democracy, the rule of law and development in the region, has generated high local expectation for better governance. However, "'excess' commitment beyond what the EU actually intends to deliver would ignite expectations and mainstream disillusionment in the long-term" (Yabanci 2013). In the case of Kosovo, the EU has committed itself to address the structural deficiencies, and thereby increased local expectations for tangible improvements, especially during the final phases of the Vienna negotiations and in the immediate aftermath of the declaration of independence. This expectation has also generated demands from the EU to take more action, if necessary against the government, to 'correct' Kosovo institutions on their way to democratic and self-sustaining Kosovo. However, the EU is usually unprepared or reluctant to take more responsibility beyond technocratic tasks on the ground (i.e. assisting and mentoring the local authorities according to some pre-defined goals). As a result, what the EU intends to do remains ambivalent for the local actors in Kosovo.

Third, institutional change (prioritized by the Europeanization literature) are not supported by broader societal actors because the citizens do not believe in the reform of the existing institutions since they are alienated from the EU-promoted state-building process and feel disenfranchised by weak state institutions and the elites that control them. So far, the EU efforts of increasing institutional efficiency and state capacity in the Western Balkans has not solved the problem of legitimacy, only worsened it. For instance, there is an increasing perception among the Kosovo citizens that there is a non-transparent and undeclared partnership between the EU and the corrupt political elites. This perception is rather an inadvertent consequence due to the EU's prioritization of political stability over contestation and change in Kosovo. Moreover, the EU criteria of increased capacity of local institutions remain aloof from the expectations and needs of the public. While the EU promotes a decreased role for central state to maintain stability (i.e. absence of inter-ethnic clash), the citizens perceive their government unable to take decisions and implement policies that are demanded by the citizens. These issues are common problems the EU's state-building and Europeanization agenda in the Western Balkans. In the following section, they are discussed in detail with regard to Kosovo.

Democratization, member state building and local actors in Kosovo

Since 1999 Kosovo has occupied a special role, a standardized reference point in identifying and facilitating the EU's role and capabilities as a conflict resolver and a role model for the solution of the ethno-political conflict. The EU has various roles and tasks in Kosovo. Despite the fact that five member states do not recognize Kosovo's independence, Kosovo has a potential candidate status since 2005. EULEX Kosovo is the biggest rule of law mission that the EU has ever undertaken, the EU Special Representative who was until early 2012 served as the head of International Civilian Office, is closely involved in daily political decisions. The European Commission Liaison Office (ECLO) works through local civil society and public authorities to facilitate the future EU integration of Kosovo. Finally, the EU External Action Service (EEAS) assumed the role of a mediator in March 2011 for an ambitious objective of normalizing the relations between Kosovo and Serbia as a crucial step for both countries' membership process.

The parties reached 15 point agreement in April 2013, and the EEAS continues to assist them during the implementation phase.

Rule of law

Despite the consistent EU attempts to improve the rule of law and fight against corruption in Kosovo, the situation on the ground has not showed an impressive improvement over the years (World Bank 2003–2012). According to the 2013 Transparency International Corruption Index, Kosovo ranks 111th of 177 countries (Transparency International 2013).

Since 2008, the EU rule of law mission EULEX is the sole international authority responsible for, together with the Kosovo government, facilitating the development of rule of law and fight against corruption (EULEX 2012). The mission's mandate was initially drawn very broad including some corrective executive responsibilities over the Kosovo government. Overall, the EULEX was tasked to be "responsible for ensuring the maintenance and promotion of the rule of law, public order and security" (Muharremi 2010). However, since the deployment of the EULEX in late 2008, the mission faced multiple challenges on the ground and failed to ensure trust and cooperation from the local groups. The Kosovo public and the majority of the local civil society organizations do not trust the mission and reject or avoid cooperating with it due to a perceived alliance between the EULEX and Kosovo's corrupt political elite. There are two main reasons that resulted in a sharp decrease in the general trust and credibility of the EULEX.

First, the limbo around the actual mandate and the status of the EULEX has created a delay at the deployment stage and practical problems to facilitate rule of law once the mission is deployed. The commitment of the EU to assume UNMIK's responsibilities in terms of the rule of law development was agreed during the Vienna negotiations which resulted in Comprehensive Proposal for settlement (known as Ahtisaari Plan). During the negotiations phase, the EU was actively involved in the design of a future mandate by sending a Planning Team in 2006 with an aim to initiate dialogue with local stakeholders (European Council 10 April 2006). The EU also prepared a package of 42 laws setting up the implementation details of the Ahtisaari Plan in the post-independence period including the role and the working procedures of the EULEX staff which was incorporated into the Kosovo constitution[1]. Finally, in line with the Ahtisaari Plan proposals, the Council issued a joint action outlining the mandate and status of the EULEX that acknowledges a partnership—albeit some executive responsibilities of the mission—with the independent Kosovo institutions (European Council 4 February 2008).

However, with the rejection of the Ahtisaari Plan by the UN Security Council and Serbia, the planned deployment of the mission was not realized; and Kosovo unilaterally declared independence and committed to the implementation of the Ahtisaari Plan on 17 February 2008. In the following months, the UN, EU and Serbia agreed on an alternative plan for the deployment of the EU rule of law mission. According to the new agreement, the EULEX would now "perform an enhanced operational role in the area of rule of law under the framework of Resolution 1244 (1999) and the overall authority of the United Nations" (UNSG 24 November 2008). Known as the Six-point Plan[2], the deal reversed the EULEX's mandate and placed the mission under status-neutral mandate and re-approved UNMIK's authority (stating that UN Security Council failed to reach a new agreement to replace the Resolution 1244). Put simply, the EULEX has become a mission under the UNSCR 1244 which acknowledges the territorial integrity of Serbia. The Six-point Plan also gave extensive rights to Serbia to control policing, customs, justice, infrastructure, border and transport in Kosovo Serb dominated areas (Dzihic and Kramer 2009).

This situation has created two competing constitutional orders in Kosovo to date. In practice, the EULEX has to work under two different systems, i.e. the Kosovo Constitution which incorporates the Ahtisaari Plan in Albanian dominated areas and a mixture of UNMIK and Yugoslav law in Serb dominated areas. After the mission was deployed, the implementation of applicable law has become a daunting task for the EULEX. The existence of two bodies of law in Kosovo has generated various practical challenges such as increasing number of cases pending for a verdict by EULEX judges. In order to bring a practical solution to the confusion, each judge is given discretion to choose the body of applicable law in dealing with cases[3]. In

---

[1] Author's interviews with the EULEX Office, May 2011, Priština/Prishtinë.
[2] Six points refer to six controversial areas—police, justice, customs, borders, Serb orthodox religious heritage, transportation/infrastructure—are considered within the scope of reconfiguration.
[3] Author's interviews with the EULEX office, op. cit.

other words, the mission's role and mandate varies depending on the ethnicity of the person that the EULEX deals with. Kosovars do not know in advance which body of law would be applicable in their situation before opening a case or between their detention and indictment[4]. Usually, whilst Albanians are subject to the Kosovo Constitution and the joint EULEX-Kosovo Assembly legislation in Albanian dominated areas, in Serb regions in the north, the EULEX applies a mixture of Yugoslav codes or UNMIK law adopted between 1999 and 2007 (Grevi 2009). Moreover, the EULEX failed to establish an authority in the Serb dominated northern municipalities.

In relation to the customs component of the EULEX, the applicable rules and regulations are even more complicated. While in the justice component, individual judges can decide the applicable law, as a status-neutral actor in the Serb areas, the EULEX cannot consider customs gates in the north as the legal border dividing Kosovo from Serbia. Therefore, EULEX customs officials are unable to collect customs tax in accordance with the law issued by the Kosovo Assembly[5]. The spokesperson of the EULEX customs declared that the problem 'is not an issue of customs but a political issue, it is not in the scope of the EULEX which is a technical mission'[6]. As a result, the EULEX has so far failed to prevent smuggling and illegal items' trade, the basic objective of the EULEX customs department. Moreover, the spokesperson degraded the mission to merely a technocratic institution which, for the Kosovo public, would equal denying the evident executive responsibilities of the EULEX as the sole customs authority in the northern regions where Kosovo borders Serbia.

Second, the EU prioritizes stability in Kosovo which has hindered the EULEX's progress in fight against high level corruption. The EU's initial

---

[4] Author's interviews with civil society organizations in Kosovo, May 2011, Priština/Prishtinë.

[5] This situation has recently changed when the Kosovo Customs has taken control of two important customs points with the help of KFOR after the June 2011 clashes. Following the turmoil, Kosovo and Serbia have concluded an integrated border management agreement in December 2011. However, the situation on the ground is not totally clear. The Kosovo Serb inhabitants are strongly against the agreement and the Kosovo Customs' control of the crossing points. The implementation of the integrated border management agreement should be closely assessed in order to make a decisive comment.

[6] Koha Ditore, 10.04.2009, 'EULEX without a plan to restore customs authority in the north'.

commitment to establish the rule of law different from the UNMIK initially fed high local expectations. The regular UNDP public surveys reveal that the Kosovo public perceive corruption in public institutions including courts, police, tax administration body, municipalities and customs authorities as one of the biggest problems threatening Kosovo's stability and economic progress(UNDP August 2012; UNDP February 2013; UNDP September 2011). As a result, especially, the civil society and public expected that the EULEX would address the problems that UNMIK and the Kosovo government could not or did not want to tackle, especially in terms of fighting against corruption and clientelism embedded in the Kosovo political system and bureaucracy.

However, the performance of EULEX in dealing with corruption has so far remained below the local expectations in terms of assuming more responsibility in the fight against corruption. The Kosovo public and the civil society organizations were disappointed with the initial investigations and trials concerning the Minister of Transport, Post and Telecommunications Fatmir Limaj and the governor of Kosovo's Central Bank Hashim Rexhepi who were arrested for charges of corruption in April and July 2010, respectively (Visoka 2011; Capussela 2012). The EULEX's dealing with the case of Limaj was perceived by the Kosovo public as an escape from further investigation of high level corruption related to other ministries in order not to destabilize the current political balance in Kosovo[7]. In relation to the case of Central Bank of Kosovo, many people believed that the arrest was unfounded and the government manipulated the EULEX's lack of experience and knowledge of the local context to eliminate Rexhepi as a political rival (Capussela 2012).

The government manipulated the fight against corruption once more in 2011 to gain advantage over the opposition through the EULEX. The mission asked the Kosovo Assembly to adopt a resolution to call the Constitutional Court to clarify the immunities of the members of the Assembly in order to start the corruption trial of the arrested politicians. However, the Assembly rejected the EULEX's request as 'unlawful and unconstitutional' intervention by the EULEX into the Kosovo politics[8]. Despite several warnings from Brussels calling for cooperation, the tension climbed after a number counter statements issued by the EULEX and the

---

[7] Author's interview with KIPRED, May 2011, Priština/Prishtinë.
[8] Zeri, 09.07.2011 and Koha Ditore, 14.07.2011

government officials. Eventually, Prime Minister Thaçi intervened personally to request the relevant clarification from the Constitutional Court by defending his decision that the issue would 'contribute to Kosovo's Euro-Atlantic integration'[9]. The Constitutional Court ruled that the members of the Assembly could be detained and arrested even when they were performing their duties. However, the Court did not extend the ruling to ministers[10]. The decision was interpreted by the opposition as a direct intervention in the judiciary to eliminate Thaçi's rivals (members of the Assembly from the opposition), but not his ministers by manipulating the EULEX's demand to clarify the issue of immunities.

Facing criticism and intervention from the government, the EULEX has recently become over-cautious in taking action against the high-ranking officials. Rather than portraying the EULEX as a part of the solution to the on-going political problems in Kosovo, the mission has a tendency to emphasize its apolitical/technical character and status as a neutral body (Peters 2010). However, the case of fight against corruption has become an incipient case for the public and the civil society organizations to believe that the EULEX is reluctant to take action. Since the mission was deployed in 2008, except a brief period after the EULEX has become operational, the regular public surveys point to a decreasing level of public satisfaction with the mission (as low as 30% by late 2010[11]).Especially compared to high public satisfaction with local security institutions (Kosovo Police and Kosovo Security Force), the Kosovo Albanian public satisfaction with EULEX police sharply decreased to 19% in 2013 (see the graph below for a comparison) (see UNDP 2008, 2009, 2010; UNDP 2011–2013).

---

[9] KohaDitore, 21.07.2011
[10] KohaDitore, 22/23.09.2011
[11] The UNDP Kosovo Early Warning reports between 2008 and 2010 included a section on the overall public satisfaction with the EULEX. After 2010, the UNDP Kosovo changed the methodology of public surveys and replaced 'satisfaction with EULEX' section with EULEX Police.

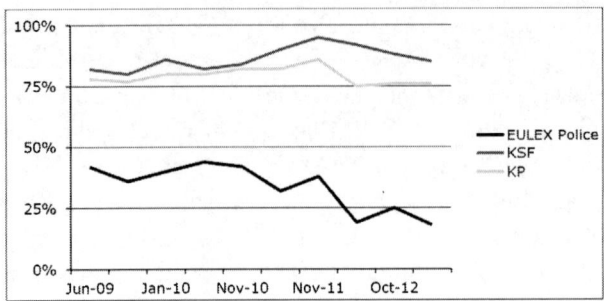

Source: Author's illustration of the latest UNDP Kosovo Public Pulse Report, August 2013

The main reason for low support for the mission is the EULEX's unsuccessful attempts to bring corruption and clientelist structures at the top of Kosovo politics under control. The EULEX's poor performance is not only seen a result of structural deficiencies of the mission (i.e. lack of experience or staff) but of reluctance due to political concerns. For instance, local civil society organizations contend that the EULEX does not keep a low profile and support local ownership for benevolent reasons, but just to evade its main responsibilities. It hesitates to take punitive action to deal with the root causes of the lack of rule of law in Kosovo in order not to disturb the short term stability. Similar convictions are widespread among the Kosovo people as well thanks to widespread criticism of the EULEX in the national media. To give one example, the local newspaper Zeri reported before the 2010 elections that before the general elections, the EULEX 'gave its word' to evade from further investigations of corruption until a new government is consolidated[12] as agreed between the EULEX and the Kosovo leadership[13]. In the view of the Kosovo public, the lack of proper results to fight against organized crime and corruption in Kosovo "is only encouraging local officials to not do anything in this respect"[14].

It is worth mentioning that the government strictly denies such an undeclared relationship in order not to allow the political opposition to monopolize anti-hegemonic discourse. Ambivalent statements from the state officials regarding the future of EULEX make it hard to draw a clear idea about the relations between the government and the mission. On the one hand, the government officially declared that 'there is still a need for

---

[12] Zeri, 27.12.2010, "Politics delays arrests".
[13] Zeri, 02.12.2010, "EULEX in a moratorium".
[14] Zeri, 25.06.2009, "United in Corruption".

EULEX for a number of reasons', despite the disagreements between the government and the EULEX regarding the mission's role and performance (Kabashaj 2013). On the other, during the latest clashes in the north of Kosovo in July 2011 (see Lazarevic 2011a; Lazarevic 2011b), Kosovo President Jahjaga and the current government criticized the way that the EULEX dealt with the Kosovo Serb uprising and stated that the EULEX should consider withdrawing from Kosovo. Moreover, the Kosovo Assembly recently adopted a resolution to take over the responsibilities from the EULEX after July 2014. The resolution calls Kosovo authorities to do necessary preparations to undertake the EULEX's competences (B92 2013).

However, the biggest opposition group the Democratic League of Kosovo (LDK) boycotted the voting claiming that the Kosovo's judiciary is still not capable of dealing with corruption and organized crime. Civil society representatives that are interviewed on the ground mostly concur with the opposition party's position. According to KIPRED, the government pushed this resolution because of the EULEX's action against some officials and members of the Kosovo Assembly on charges of war and organized crime (Kabashaj 2013).

Yet, contrary to what the government claims, the public and some local civil society organizations contend that there is an 'untouchable and unchangeable' partnership between EULEX and the government that is beyond the democratic scrutiny of the Kosovo Parliament or the citizens (Deda and Kursani 2012). Both the EULEX and the government with executive powers often bypasses the Assembly resolutions or treats them as merely "recommendations with no obligatory power" (Deda and Kursani 2012). In this sense, civil society and opposition parties usually criticize the EULEX on the grounds that much of the deliberation is concluded through secretive deliberations before the Kosovo Assembly discusses them[15]. The EU's prioritization of stability over a comprehensive reform of the institutional culture and the ruling elites with embedded interests in the current system has so far perpetuated this ambiguous and non-transparent relationship.

---

[15] Author's interviews with various CSOs, op. cit.

Stabilization and association process and membership conditionality

Kosovo was offered a tangible European integration perspective officially in 2005 in the Communication titled 'A European Future of Kosovo' as part of the EU's broader regional strategy (i.e. the Stabilisation and Association Process (SAP)) (European Commission 2005). The SAP was introduced in 1999 by the Commission as a proactive policy for conflict resolution. It aims to offer a coherent and comprehensive set of instruments for sustainable conflict resolution through the 'added value' of EU membership in the distant future. In order to facilitate conflict resolution and ethnic reconciliation, the EU declared that the SAP would establish bilateral institutional relations with the countries in the region including an eventual membership perspective. However, this perspective is linked to an open prospect or 'a creeping process' during which the EU is committed to encourage local adjustment in certain policy sectors through short-term incentives such as visa liberalization, legal harmonization, financial aid and preferential trade agreements (Renner and Trauner 2009). These incentives are tightly linked to a number of conditions related to democratization, institutional reform, border controls, the fight against organized crime, state-building process and regional cooperation.

Although EU conditionality is demanding, the integration prospect is vague and there is no timetable for accession (Emerson, Aydin et al. 2006). Moreover, the EU emphasizes that the pace and extent of compliance is left to the candidate country. In other words, the capacity of Kosovo institutions becomes a central issue in implementing the reforms requested by the EU. Compared to the other countries in the region, Kosovo's special circumstances (destruction during the war and NATO bombing, the dependency on external aid as an UNMIK protectorate, economic underdevelopment, continuing tensions and clashes between the Albanian and Serb populations and internationally contested statehood) considerably hinder institutional capacity, especially compared to the other countries in the region. According to a widely cited example within the local political circles, Kosovo cannot meet two criteria to progress in its institutional relations with the EU due to the complexities related to statehood. First, meeting regional cooperation criteria is impossible for Kosovo since Serbia refuses to establish neighborly relations with Kosovo[16]. Second, in the

---

[16] Author's interview with the representative of the Kosovo Ministry of European Integration, May 2011, Priština/Prishtinë. However, the relevance of this argument

common view of local actors (political elites, civil society organizations and the public), the failure to provide a coherent European response to Kosovo's independence has generated a chain of related events stumbling Kosovo's EU integration path. Since the EU denies official recognition, Kosovo cannot establish official institutional ties with the EU. As a result, Kosovo has not yet signed the Stabilisation and Association Agreement (SAA). Also, it is the only country in the region that is outside the club of 'no-visa required' countries. It is worth to mention that visa liberalization is especially valued by the Kosovo public. As demonstrated by the UNDP, 90% of the public attribute a lot of importance to a future EU decision to lift the visa requirement for Kosovo citizens (UNDP August 2013). Finally, Kosovo has not been granted a preferential trade agreement yet which, in turn, hinders the development of Kosovo's democracy and economy (Brajshori 2011).

The absence of institutional relations is mainly related to the lack of compliance with the EU criteria on the side of the Kosovo government. However, as the EU Liaison Office in Pristina acknowledges, there is not a common EU position towards Kosovo's independence which "does not prevent the EU to genuinely commit Kosovo's EU integration; but, it raises a serious problem to implement the commitments"[17]. For instance, the issue of name has caused delays in signing the preferential treatment agreement. The Kosovo government rejected to sign an agreement as 'Kosovo under the UNSCR 1244', and the EU member states did not reach a consensus on signing a bilateral trade agreement with 'the Republic of Kosovo' (Palokaj 2013). As a result of these complications, the Kosovo government has called for "a more serious commitment" from the EU to treat Kosovo as an "equal subject with other countries in the region" taking into account the 'unique' case of Kosovo's independence[18]. Public and civil society organizations similarly expect the EU to find an alternative for bilateral relations to solve the conundrum of recognition[19].

---

can now be disputed since the EU mediated Kosovo Serbia talks resulted in a number of agreements foreseeing normalization of relations and regional cooperation between the two countries.

[17] EUCLO, Federica Domanini, May 2011, Priština/Prishtinë.

[18] Author's interview with NGO Celnaja, May 2011, Priština/Prishtinë.

[19] Author's interview with, Kosovar Civil Society Foundation, May 2011, Priština/Prishtinë.

More importantly, the SAP is a complex instrument with an aim to link post-conflict state-building and member state building, which is ultimately controlled by the Commission and the Council. Although the pace of progress in EU integration is left to the country and the each potential candidate is evaluated independently, the SAP is 'an essentially top-down strategy prioritising governance efficiency, rather than building pro-reform constituencies at the grass-roots level' (Bechev and Andreev 2005). As we are assured by the mainstream Europeanization research, bottom-up mobilization and the existence of pro-reform political elite is essential for compliance and domestic adaptation (Schimmelfennig 2005). In relation to the Western Balkans, given the highly polarized political and ethnic situation on the ground, there is no local consensus (reform coalitions) or capable actors (grassroots actors to generate a bottom-up socialization) to successfully implement reforms in Kosovo.

However, the SAP does not aim to facilitate such conditions *per se* due to (i) its sectoral and elite focus (Belloni 2009) and (ii) its prioritization of political stability in the broader region (Elbasani 2008). First, contrary to direct and close link between the Kosovo government and the EU, information-sharing and cooperation activities with non-state actors and the public remain 'largely informal and unstructured' (Palm 2010). The civil society organizations usually find genuine cooperation with the EU over-bureaucratized with too many technical criteria and deadlines. As pointed out by some representatives of local civil society organizations, "the EU [has] an automated tendency to ask civil society opinion and then go its own way"[20]. In other words, civil society empowerment by the EU is not 'a two-way street' which is open to input from non-governmental local actors (Hoogenboom 2011). '[T]he EU engages with the civil society through technical meetings, symbolic consultations to tick the boxes of accountability and transparency, rather than establishing genuine deliberation with all local actors which would allow various groups to express disagreements' (Yabanci 2013). As a result, participation of local civil society organizations in performance evaluations and preliminary meetings of goal setting displays a downward trend.

Second, as mentioned also in the previous section, the EU follows a strategy of not distracting the political balance to maintain Kosovo's political stability. Instead of working towards closing the gap between institutions

---

[20] Author' interview with *Instituti GAP*, May 2011, Priština/Prishtinë.

and citizens, which would mean allowing more tensions in politics and instability in the short term, the EU strategy in Kosovo sustains strong ethnic divides, keeps civic opposition weak and co-opt the political opposition into the institution building and democratization process (Gordon, Sasse et al. 2008). For instance, the EU avoided taking genuine action regarding the report released by the Council of Europe in January 2011 on Kosovo organ trafficking during the war, which involved allegations against the Prime Minister Hasim Thaçi and other high ranking politicians who were once leading members of Kosovo Liberation Army. Only towards the end of 2011, the EULEX established a Special Investigative Task Force (SITF). It works as a part of the EULEX, but conducts a totally anonymous investigation on the allegations (European Council 2011). The earlier EULEX statements triggered international and local criticism that the EU tried to cover up the allegations in the report in order not to risk stability in the country, especially after the widely-condemned December 2010 elections as fraudulent and the following political crisis (Rettman and Krasniqi 2010; The Economist 2010; Marzouk 2011).

Overall, the EU is concerned about improving the technocratic efficiency of Kosovo institutions without tackling with the deeper problems of lack of representation and participation in these institutions while its relations with the non-state actors are driven by 'pedagogic' one-way approach. The indirect EU support for the current political elites keeps political opportunity structures for alternative actors weak. While the requirements of SAP conditionality necessitate pluralist structures that would allow broad based political and civic participation into the decision making, the EU sustains 'a minimalist state' in Kosovo with limited scope of state institutions and weak state functions with dubious legitimacy for Kosovo citizens, which is not able to cope with the EU requirements (Bieber 2011). In the meantime, the political elites exploit the inadvertent support from the EU to sustain their power since engaging with genuine reforms would be too costly and would engender an institutionalized opposition to challenge the clientelist system.

Conclusion

The analysis has shown the importance of the fragmentation of the local agency and the relationship between the political elite and the wider societal actors (non-state organizations and the public) in explaining the complicated relationship between the EU democratization and state-building agenda through conditionality and local compliance and support. Contrary to the elite and institutional focus in the mainstream Europeanization literature, I argued that the literature on the Western Balkans should move beyond an exclusive focus on EU incentives and capabilities of norm exportation towards a more systematic analysis of the complex interaction between the EU agenda and various local dynamics. Local agency is not merely a passive recipient of EU benefits. Nor does it go through a linear process of socialization and natural acceptance of the EU agenda in the long-term. State capacity is a key factor regarding compliance with conditionality; but, it signifies more than technocratic efficiency to comply with the top-down process of institutional reform. As exemplified by Kosovo, state weakness is more related to international recognition and state-society relations (legitimacy). Given the EU's strong support for stability and technocratic efficiency and the contestation of its independence within the EU, state weakness has become a persistent feature of Kosovo's lack of progress in meeting the SAP criteria.

Second, the Kosovo public and non-state actors perceive EU's sectoral and elite focus, irrelevant to their urgent needs and expectations such as dismantling the clientelist system and the promotion of rule of law. Kosovo case shows that the domestic political scene of the Western Balkans is shaped by the uneasy relations between the ruling elites, on the one hand, and the political opposition, the public and non-state actors, on the other. As a result, the fragmented local agency (especially the groups that are disadvantaged under the status quo) constantly pressurizes the EU to redefine its state—and democracy-building agenda in line with local priorities and expectations. This situation has forced the EULEX to over-emphasize the local ownership and technocratic nature of its mandate and reject its executive responsibilities on the ground. However, as the findings show, it has become hardly sustainable for the EULEX to remain sterile from the highly securitized and politicized issues without risking foundational local criticism.

Moreover, in Kosovo, the existing institutions are distrusted by the public (both Albanian and Serbian communities) since they are perceived as exploited for the particularistic interests of the political elites. The situation has generated high public expectation from the EULEX for better governance, and thereby, better economic conditions. These expectations have been partially engendered by the EU's strong commitment to democratization in Kosovo. However, the EULEX and the SAP are not sufficiently linked to reconcile democratization efforts and state-building. In the absence of wide scale changes and visible EU action in accordance with the local expectations and priorities, the direct executive responsibilities of EULEX and the slow and unclear approach of the SAP creates confusion and symbolizes the EU's inconsistency or the local groups. It is not clearly comprehensible for the public why Kosovo is constantly criticized by the Commission and the member states in terms of its lack of progress in the rule of law, fight against corruption and organized crime, while EULEX, as an equally responsible actor besides the Kosovo government with its executive tasks in police, justice and customs areas, evades taking genuine responsibility.

The findings also allow us to focus on the importance of contextual factors behind the persistence of strong and unified support for EU membership, yet the limited progress in meeting the EU criteria for further integration (especially behavioral change) in Kosovo. Despite the complications surrounding the democratization process and EULEX performance, the overall support for EU integration in Kosovo remains intact. Across the Western Balkans, the Kosovo Albanian public is the most supportive of EU accession (EUPK 2010). European integration is seen as a national goal that should supersede narrow policies of the incumbent government[21].The public and the local civil society organizations perceive the Kosovo government as the main actor that has failed to achieve concrete progress in meeting the EU criteria for visa liberalization, trade agreement and the SAA (UNDP March 2011). The April 2013 Kosovo-Serbia Agreement which was a result of the mediation efforts of EEAS is supported by the majority of Kosovo citizens (UNDP August 2013) (except Kosovo Serbs in the north) and the opposition parties (except the nationalist and anti-EU party *Vetëvendosje*) because normalization of relations with Serbia is perceived as the only way for Kosovo to achieve progress in terms of EU integration (Bassuener and Weber 2013; Deda and Qosaj-Mustafa 2013). Despite the lack of consultations with the opposition and the public during the negotiations and the challenges surrounding the implementation, the majority of local actors agree that if the EU offers tangible incentives within the SAP framework, it can further strengthen Kosovo's institutions and democracy. Put simply, the diffuse support for EU membership is resilient among all local actors, while the current engagement of the EU in Kosovo is

---

[21] Author's interview with KIPRED, op. cit.

seen as an important factor perpetuating the lack of democracy and rule of law and strengthening the strong clientelist political system.

Overall, the analysis has demonstrated that paying attention to the local agency through a more nuanced approach and the relationship between various local actors and the EU would explain the reasons for local support or lack thereof for externally-driven state-building and democratization efforts. In this sense, comparative studies on local expectations, strategies and ideologies would further reveal the limits of the EU's normative and allegedly universal actorness and material incentives as the ultimate guideline for democratization and state-building. Such studies would also increase policy-relevant academic discussions beyond purely technical Europeanization process by offering an alternative insight about how the EU could confront the real challenges of democratization and state-building agenda and reform or tailor its conflict resolution practice in line with the demands from local actors in the Western Balkans. In this sense, this article can be only a beginning for more empirical and comparative research in the field.

References

Anastasakis, O. 2005. *Europeanization of the Balkans*. Brown J. World Aff. 7(1), pp. 77–88.

B92 2013. *EU, Kosovo to decide on EULEX mandate*.

Bassuener, K. and Weber, B. 2013. *Not Yet a Done Deal: Kosovo and the Prishtina-Belgrade Agreement*. Democratisation Policy Council Policy Paper.

Bechev, D. and Andreev, S. 2005. *Top-Down vs Bottom-Up Aspects of the EU Institution: Building Strategies in the Western Balkans*. Occasional Paper No. 3/05.

Belloni, R. 2009. *European integration and the Western Balkans: lessons, prospects and obstacles*. Journal of Balkan and Near Eastern Studies11(3), pp. 313–331.

Bieber, F. 2011. *Building Impossible States? State-Building Strategies and EU Membership in the Western Balkans*. Europe Asia Studies63(10), pp. 1783–1802.

Börzel, T. A. 2011. *When Europeanization Hits Limited Statehood: the Western Balkans as a Test case for the Transformative Power of Europe*. KFG Working Paper Series No. 30.

Börzel, T. A. and Pamuk, Y. 2012. *Pathologies of Europeanization: Fighting Corruption in the Southern Caucasus*. West European Politics35(1), pp. 79–97.

Börzel, T. A. and Risse, T. 2003. *Conceptualising the Domestic Impact of Europe*. The politics of Europeanization. K. Featherstone and C. M. Radaelli. Oxford, Oxford University Press, pp. 57–83.

Börzel, T. A. and Risse T. 2007. *Europeanization: The Domestic Impact of EU Politics*. Handbook of European Union Politics. Knud Eric Jorgensen, M. A. Pollack and B. R. (eds.). London, Sage, pp. 483–504.

Börzel, T. A. and Risse, T. 2009. *The Transformative Power of Europe*. KFG The Transformtive Power of Europe, KFG Working Paper Series N.1.

Börzel, T. A. and T. Risse 2011. *From Europeanization to Diffusion: Introduction*. West European Politics 35(1), pp. 1–19.

Brajshori, M. 2011. *Lack of preferential trade measures with EU hits Kosovo exporters*. SETimes. Pristina, 22 December 2011.

Bulmer, S., P. 2007. *Theorizing Europeanization. Europeanization: New Research Agendas*. P. Graziano and M. Vink. New York, Palgrave Macmillan, Basingstoke, pp. 46–58.

Capussela, A. 2012. *EU Fiasco: the case of Kosovo's Central Bank*. Osservatorio Balcani e Caucaso 24 January 2012.

Coppieters, B., M. Emerson, et al., Eds. (2004). Europeanization and Conflict Resolution: Case Studies from the European Periphery, Academia Press.

Deda, I. and Kursani S. 2012. *The Unsupervised State: Internally Divided, Internationally Half-Legitimate*. KIPRED Policy BriefNo.1/12 August 2012.

Deda, I. and Qosaj-Mustafa A. 2013. *The Implementation of Agreements of Kosovo-Serbia Political Dialogue*. KIPRED PaperNo. 4/13.

Diez, T., M. Albert, et al. 2008. The European Union and border conflicts: the power of integration and association Cambridge, Cambridge University Press (Kindle Edition).

Diez, T., S. Stetter, et al. 2006. *The European Union and Border Conflicts: The Transformative Power of Integration*. International Organization60(3): 563–593.

Dzihic, V. and Kramer H. 2009. *Kosovo After Indepedence*. Friedrich Ebert StiftungJuly 2009.

Elbasani, A. 2008. *Just what is this 'absorption capacity' of the European Union?* EUI Working Paper SPS No 2008/03.

Elbasani, A. 2013. European Integration and Transformation in the Western Balkans: Europeanization or Business as Usual. London, Routledge.

Emerson, M., Aydin, S. et al. 2006. *Just what is this 'absorption capacity' of the European Union?* CEPS Policy Brief No. 113.

EULEX 2012. EULEX Programme Report 2012: Rule of Law Beyond Headlines.

EUPK 2010. Survey of Awareness of the EU and European Integration in Kosovo. EU Perspective in Kosovo. Pristina, EU Liaison Office. July–August 2010.

European Commission 2005. Communication from the European Commission, A European Future for Kosovo. European Commission, COM 156, 2005.

European Commission 2005–2012. Enlargement Strategy. http://europa.eu/legislation_summaries/enlargement/western_balkans/index_en.htm.

European Commission 2006. Western Balkans: Prospect of EU Membership Incites Peace in the Western Balkans. http://ec.europa.eu/world/peace/geographical_themes/west_balk/index_en.htm.

European Council 4 February 2008. Council Joint Action of 4 February 2008 on the European Union Rule of Law Mission in Kosovo European Council, 2008/124/CFSP O.J. (L 42)(16 Feb. 2008).

European Council 10 April 2006. Council Joint Action on the establishment of an EU Planning Team (EUPT Kosovo) regarding a possible EU crisis management operation in the field of rule of law and possible other areas in Kosovo. 2006/304/CFSP. E. Council. OJ L 112/19.

European Council 2011. Kosovo Progress Report. accessible at: http://ec.europa.eu/enlargement/countries/strategy-and-progress-report/.

Featherstone, K. and Radaelli, C. M. 2003. The politics of Europeanization. Oxford, Oxford University Press.

Freyburg, T. and Richter, S. 2010. *National identity matters: the limited impact of EU political conditionality in the Western Balkans*. Journal of European Public Policy17(2), pp. 263–281.

Gordon, C., G. Sasse, et al. 2008. *Specific report on the EU policies in the Stabilisation and Association process*. Report for Project *Human and Minority Rights in the Life Cycle of Ethnic Conflicts*.

Grevi, G. 2009. EULEX Kosovo. European Security and Defence Policy The First 10 Years (1999–2009). G. Grevi, D. Helly and D. Keohane. Condé-sur-Noireau Corlet Imprimeur

Hoogenboom, J. 2011. *The EU as a Peacebuilder in Kosovo*. Civil Society Dialogue Network (CSDN) August 2011.

Kabashaj, S. 2013. *Kosovo unprepared for EULEX to withdraw*. Southeast European Times.

Kelley, J. G. 2004. Ethnic politics in Europe: the power of norms and incentives. Princeton, NJ ; Oxford, Princeton University Press.

Lazarevic, T. 2011a. *The Northern Kosovo Crisis*. Osservatorio Balcani e Caucaso 29 July 2011.

Lazarevic, T. 2011b. *The Northern Kosovo Barricades*. Osservatorio Balcani e Caucaso 2 August 2011.

Marzouk, L. 2011. Kosovo Opposition to Appeal Presidential Election. Balkan Insight, accessible at: http://www.balkaninsight.com/en/article/kosovo-presidential-vote-was-unconstitutional.

Muharremi, R. (2010). *The European Union Rule of Law Mission in Kosovo (EULEX) from the Perspective of Kosovo Constitutional Law*. ZaöRV70: 357–379.

Noutcheva, G. 2006. EU Conditionality, State Sovereignty and the Compliance Patterns of Balkan States. 3rd Pan-European Conference on EU Politics European Consortium for Political Research. Istanbul, Bilgi University, 21–23 September 2006.

Noutcheva, G. 2009. *Fake, Partial and Imposed Compliance: The Limits of the EU's Normative Power in the Western Balkans.* Journal of European Public Policy16(7), pp. 1065–1084.

Noutcheva, G. 2012. European Foreign Policy and the Challenges of Balkan Accession: Conditionality, Legitimacy and Compliance. Oxon, Roudledge/UACES.

Noutcheva, G. and Aydin-Düzgit, S. 2011. *Lost in Europeanization: The Western Balkans and Turkey.* West European Politics 35(1), pp. 59–78.

Noutcheva, G. and M. Huysseune (2004). Serbia and Montenegro. Europeanization and Conflict Resolution: Case Studies from the European Periphery. B. Coppieters, M. Emerson, Michel Huysseune et al, Academia Press.

Pace, M., P. Seeberg, et al. 2009. *The EU's democratization agenda in the Mediterranean: a critical inside-out approach.* Democratization16(1), pp. 3–19.

Palm, M. 2010. Accountability and Effectiveness of CSDP Missions: The Role of Civil Society. Brussels, European Peacebuilding Liaison Office.

Palokaj, A. 2013. Kosovo-EU Relations The History of Unfulfilled Aspirations? Kosovo Foundation for Open Society. Pristina.

Renner, S. and Trauner, F. 2009. *Creeping EU Membership in South-east Europe: The Dynamics of EU Rule Transfer to the Western Balkans.* Journal of European Integration31(4), pp. 449–465.

Rettman, A. and E. Krasniqi (2010). Thaci camp hits back at organ trafficking allegations. EU Observer, accessible at: http://euobserver.com/foreign/31557.

Schimmelfennig, F. 2008. *EU political accession conditionality after the 2004 enlargement: consistency and effectiveness.* Journal of European Public Policy15(6), pp. 918–937.

Schimmelfennig, F. 2012. *Europeanzation beyond Europe.* Living Reviews in European Governance7(1).

Schimmelfennig, F., and Ulrich Sedelmeier, eds 2005. The Europeanization of Central and Eastern Europe. Ithaca, NY, Cornell University Press.

The Economist 2010. Calm now, a storm to come?, accessible at: http://www.economist.com/blogs/easternapproaches/2010/12/kosovos_election.

Tocci, N. 2005. *Conflict Resolution in the Neighbourhood Comparing the Role of the EU in the Turkish-Kurdish and Israeli-Palestinian Conflicts*.CEPS Working Document No.221/March 2005.

Tocci, N. 2007. The EU and conflict resolution: promoting peace in the backyard. London, Routledge.

Transparency International 2013. Corruption Perceptions Index. accessible at: www.transparency.org/cpi2013/results.

UNDP 2008, 2009, 2010. Early Warning Reports. accessible at: http://www.ks.undp.org/kosovo/en/home.html. (accessed om January 2012)

UNDP 2011–2013. Public Pulse Report. a. a. http://www.ks.undp.org/kosovo/en/home.html, (accessed in January 2012).

UNDP August 2012. Public Pulse Report 4, http://www.kosovo.undp.org/repository/docs/PULSE_ENG_409069.pdf.

UNDP August 2013. Public Pulse Report 6. Pristina.

UNDP February 2013. Public Pulse Report 5, http://www.kosovo.undp.org/repository/docs/PPR5_anglisht_412612.pdf.

UNDP March 2011. Public Pulse Report 1, http://www.kosovo.undp.org/repository/docs/public-pulsenglish-web.pdf.

UNDP September 2011. Public Pulse Report 2, http://www.kosovo.undp.org/repository/docs/Public-Pulse-web-eng.pdf.

UNSG 24 November 2008. Report of the Secretary General on the United Nations Interim Administration Mission in Kosovo. S/2008/692.

Vachudová, M. A. 2004. Europe undivided: democracy, leverage, and integration after communism. Oxford, Oxford University Press.

Visoka, G. 2011. *International governance and local resistance in Kosovo: The thin line between ethical, emancipatory and exclusionary politics*. Irish Studies in International Affairs22(1), pp. 99–125.

World Bank 2003–2012. Governance Indicators. accessiable at: http://info.worldbank.org/governance/wgi/index.aspx#reports.

Yabanci, B. 2013. Legitimation of EU Conflict Resolution through Local Actors: Cases of Kosovo and Northern Cyprus. Politics, Languages and International Studies. Bath, University of Bath. Doctor of Philosophy.

JENNIFER L. TITANSKI-HOOPER

(B)ordering in the EU: Croatia's Path Toward Becoming 'European'

Croatia's entrance to the European Union (EU) on July 1st, 2013, signaled, for many, a change in Europe's relationship to the former Yugoslavia and the Balkans more broadly. But, beyond the positive rhetoric of Croatia's EU accession lies a decade of negotiations in which the Croatian state had to address its Balkan and post-Yugoslav geographies to demonstrate its preparedness for EU membership. Drawing on a study completed in 2010 and ethnographic research conducted in 2012–2013, this paper employs a qualitative analysis of texts from the Croatian state and the European Union to examine the persistence of Balkan and post-Yugoslav discourses throughout Croatia's EU negotiation process. This paper demonstrates how the Croatian state strategically shifted its geographic imaginary from the 'Balkans' to 'Europe' and considers the potential futures that Balkan and post-Yugoslav imaginaries will play as other former Yugoslav republics seek EU membership.

Key Words: Croatia, EU, post-Yugoslavia, (B)ordering, othering.

Jennifer Titanski-Hooper is a PhD Candidate in the Department of Geography at Pennsylvania State University.

Introduction

On July 1st, 2013, Croatia became the 28th member of the European Union (EU). Aside from Slovenia, Croatia is the only former-Yugoslav republic thus far to earn membership in the EU, and its accession was met with praise from the international community that the Croatian state had finally proved itself as stable, modern, democratic, and ultimately, 'European'. The European Commission congratulated the Croatian state on overcoming the effects of war, nationalism and ethnic division, for demonstrating an effective political and economic system, and has further highlighted that these accomplishments are a model for other former-Yugoslav states to strive for on their own paths to EU integration. It seems then, that the Croatian state has finally earned its place in the 'European' club. But, beyond the positive rhetoric of Croatia's EU accession lies a decade of negotiations in which the Croatian state had to address its Balkan and post-

Yugoslav geographies in order to demonstrate its preparedness for EU membership. This paper examines the role that geographic imaginaries of the Balkans and the dissolution of Yugoslavia played throughout Croatia's EU negotiation process, and analyzes the discursive strategies employed by the Croatian state to reposition itself as less 'Balkan' and more 'European'.

The Balkans have occupied a persistent and often negative place in the historic and geographic imaginaries of Europe; a place where religions, ethnicities and cultures from the East and the West meet and are contested, sometimes violently. This experience between violence and ethnic nationalism features heavily in the European imaginary of the Balkans, as evidenced by discourses like that of the "Balkan powder-keg," and the creation of a verb to describe the region, "Balkanization."[1] The dissolution of Yugoslavia in the 1990's only furthered the stereotypes of the Balkans as a region that is perpetually war-torn and unstable. This image conflicts with that of Western Europe as modern, developed and progressive. This relationship between a stable, modern greater Europe and an underdeveloped conflict-ridden Balkan Peninsula now plays a very interesting role in the function and expansion of the EU in the region.

While being 'Balkan' occupies a persistent historical imaginary, the geographies and meanings of being 'European' are increasingly defined by the EU. While continuing to emphasize its dedication to 'unity in diversity', the EU promotes certain practices and characteristics as ideally 'European'. Using the critical geography framework of (b)ordering, this paper demonstrates how the EU engages in a process of geographic bordering and cultural, political and economic ordering, where states must continuously defend their 'European-ness' by (1) implementing the rules, standards and expectations set forth by the EU, and (2) addressing the geographic imaginaries that promote some places and regions as more 'European' than others.

Throughout its EU negotiation process, the Croatian state experienced this (b)ordering firsthand. The state not only had to demonstrate material changes to its economic, political and judicial systems, but also had to address the underlying memories, discourses and imaginaries of socialism, nationalism, being part of the former-Yugoslavia, and being 'Balkan' in

---

[1] Merriam-Webster's English Dictionary still lists Balkanization as a term meaning to break-up, sometimes violently, into smaller units. This term has geopolitical origins in Europe during and after WWI.

order to prove its 'European-ness'. Drawing on a study completed in 2010 and ethnographic research conducted in 2012 and 2013, this paper employs a qualitative analysis of texts from both the Croatian state and the European Commission in order to examine the persistence of negative Balkan and post-Yugoslav discourses in the EU's process of (b)ordering; to analyze how the Croatian state strategically shifted its geographic imaginary from the 'Balkans' to 'Europe'; and to consider the potential future that Balkan and post-Yugoslav imaginaries will play as other former-Yugoslav republics seek EU membership.

(B)ordering Europe

The critical turn in geography led to a (re)questioning of the definitions, meanings and experiences of borders, particularly in relation to an increasingly globalized world. Traditional geopolitical perspectives viewed borders as fixed entities in time and space that were generally associated with natural landscapes or the boundaries of nation-states (i.e. Hartshorne 1933; Mackinder 1904; Ratzel 1901). These perspectives fell into the territorial trap warned against by Agnew (1994), which is the assumption that all of society can be contained within discreet political borders. Post-structural geographic perspectives sought to move beyond these traditional views to reconceptualize borders as fluid, discursive and ongoing processes. The concept of geographic bordering and cultural, political and economic ordering, or (b)ordering came out of this critical turn in geographic thought.

(B)ordering is a framework for understanding borders as processes and practices influenced by human activity and difference in spaces, or as Van Houtum (2005) put it, "the border is now understood as a verb, in the sense of bordering" (672). The processes of (b)ordering no longer occur at physical political borders, but instead "marks some bodies as legitimate and others as out of place...through document procurement...data monitoring...and exclusionary narratives in media and popular culture," (Johnson et al. 2011: 61) to name a few.

Parallel to the rise of globalization studies in the 1990's, which argued that an increased movement of people, capital and ideas was leading to a borderless world, studies like those mentioned above demonstrate how the processes of globalization are leading to a reinscription of borders across space, place and scale (see also: Newman 2006). This reinscription of borders is heavily visible in Europe where, "this liberalization and cross-border integration that characterizes the process of globalization, and which is deliberately sought for by the EU, coincides with a seemingly relentless reproduction of mythically imagined borders of the past and scalar fixations of borders of solidarity" (van Houtum & van Naerssen 2002).

One on hand, the EU seeks to embody its motto, 'unity in diversity', welcoming diverse languages, ethnicities and nationalities into the fold. On the other, the EU promotes specific practices and characteristics as ideally 'European'. States must continuously defend their 'European-ness' by implementing the rules, standards and expectations set forth by the EU. More specifically, the EU economically and politically orders members and potential members by demanding the support of democratic institutions, the maintenance of a free-market, capitalist economy and the promotion of human rights and justice. Simultaneously, cultural ordering occurs, where a system of power relations that is based in historical, cultural and geographic imaginaries contributes to determining who belongs in 'Europe' and who doesn't. Through (b)ordering, the EU is engaged in a process of 'European' nation-building, whereby EU members are thought to hold the same goals and ideals, and those who are unable or unwilling to assimilate are not given full access to the rights and benefits of 'European' citizenship. Throughout Croatia's EU negotiation process, the EU has reproduced the geographic imaginaries and borders of the Balkans to discipline the Croatian state and the broader region to a more ideal 'European' way of life.

Being 'Balkan' in Europe

The Balkans have been historically characterized as a borderland between East and West (Banac 1984; Glenny 1999; Tanner 1997). In some ways, this is true. The meeting place of the former Ottoman and Austro-Hungarian empires, the Balkans are the home of many religions, ethnicities and cultures, and have long played a strategic geopolitical role in Europe. However, the perception of the Balkans as a borderland has also led the region to become a dumping ground for negative stereotypes, which the rest of Europe is measured against. If Europe is civilized and developed, then the Balkans are barbaric and war-torn. These stereotypes have engaged the Balkans in a process of othering that persists today, particularly as the EU expands into the region.

One of the most well-known works dealing with the process of othering and the creation of geographic imaginaries from a post-colonial/post-imperial perspective is Edward Said's, *Orientalism* (1979). Said sought to examine the "political vision of reality whose structure promoted the difference between the familiar (Europe, the West, 'us') and the strange (the Orient, the East, 'them')" (Said 1979: 43). He analyzed how the West constructed an imaginative geography to represent the social, political, cultural and economic boundaries that separates 'us' from 'them' in a process of othering (Said, 1979).

Famously, Maria Todorova built on Said's work in, *Imagining the Balkans* (1997). Todorova set out to understand the historical and political narrative constructed by the West to identify those peoples residing in the Balkan Peninsula. She argues that:

> "By being geographically inextricable from Europe, yet culturally constructed as 'the other' within, the Balkans have been able to absorb conveniently a number of externalized political, ideological, and cultural frustrations stemming from tensions and contradictions inherent to the regions and societies outside the Balkans. Balkanism became, in time, a convenient substitute…exempting the West from charges of racism, colonialism, eurocentrism, and Christian intolerance against Islam. After all, the Balkans are in Europe; they are white; they are predominantly Christian…the Balkans have served as a repository of negative characteristics against which a positive and self-congratulatory image of the 'European' and the 'West' has been constructed" (Todorova 1997: 188).

The geographic imaginary of the Balkans is part of a larger process of cultural and geographic (b)ordering where the perceived negative characteristics of the Balkans are measured against a Western ideal. Todorova demonstrates that the process of othering the Balkans is rooted in discourses begun prior to WWI. However, more than any other geopolitical event, the ethnic violence and nationalism associated with the dissolution of Yugoslavia continue to frame Europe's relationship to the Balkans today. An examination of key texts from Croatia's EU negotiation and accession demonstrates how the EU (b)orders Europe by emphasizing the importance of particular 'European' values, and how the geographic imaginary of the Balkans and former-Yugoslav republics as violent, unstable and nationalistic are held up in relation to the positive images of the EU as peaceful, democratic and developed.

In 2003, leaders from Croatia, Albania, Bosnia-Herzegovina, the Former Yugoslav Republic of Macedonia and Serbia and Montenegro signed the "EU-Western Balkans Summit—Declaration." [2] The Declaration was signed at the Thessaloniki Summit on June 21, and is a ten point commitment to pursue membership in the European Union and to implement the democratic, social and economic reforms required to achieve this aim. The Declaration reveals the image that the EU has for itself and the greater 'European' project, but it also reveals the perception that Balkan states do not yet represent the economic and political (b)orders that the EU strives to promote. The points of the Declaration affirm that Western Balkan states value democracy, human rights and a market economy, and that they pledge their condemnation of extremism:

> "1. We all share the values of democracy, the rule of law, respect for human and minority rights, solidarity and a market economy, fully aware that they constitute the very foundations of the European Union. Respect of international law, inviolability of international borders, peaceful resolution of conflicts and regional co-operation are principles of the highest importance, to which we are all committed. We vigorously condemn extremism, terrorism and violence, be it ethnically, politically or criminally motivated" (European Commission for Enlargement 2003).

While emphasizing those characteristics that are desirable to a 'European' way of life, the Declaration also acknowledges certain characteristics and behaviors that are un-European:

> "5...Fragmentation and divisions along ethnic lines are incompatible with the European perspective, which should act as a catalyst for addressing problems in the region..." (European Commission for Enlargement 2003).

And, ultimately, although the EU supports the "European perspective of the Balkans", EU membership is dependent on the ability of Balkan states to

---

[2] Here, the term 'Western Balkans' is used to denote the Balkan states to the west of Bulgaria and Romania, both of which have been EU members since 2007. Throughout EU documentation, 'Western Balkans' is generally interchangeable with the former-Yugoslav republics, excluding Slovenia, and often indicates a larger connection to fighting and war during the dissolution of Yugoslavia. The strategic use of this term once again demonstrates the complicated imaginative geographies of the region.

implement European standards. In other words, EU membership will not be given to the Balkans; it will be earned:

> "2. The EU reiterates its unequivocal support to the European perspective of the Western Balkan countries. The future of the Balkans is within the European Union. The ongoing enlargement and the signing of the Treaty of Athens in April 2003 inspire and encourage the countries of the Western Balkans to follow the same successful path. Preparation for integration into European structures and ultimate membership into the European Union, through adoption of European standards, is now the big challenge ahead...The speed of movement ahead lies in the hands of the countries of the region" (European Commission for Enlargement 2003).

The "EU-Western Balkans Summit—Declaration" is not just a statement of commitment by Balkan states to join the EU. It is a statement acknowledging specific negative Balkan experiences, in particular violence, nationalism and ethnic strife, which are incompatible with the geographic imaginary of Europe supported by the EU. The Declaration is an acceptance by Balkan states of the process of economic, political and social (b)ordering that awaits them during their respective EU negotiation processes.

During its own negotiation process, the Croatian state is celebrated for leaving the negative experiences of the Balkans to join a modern, developed and peaceful European community; or, for shifting its geographic imaginary from that of the Balkans to that of Europe. For example, the "Opinion on Croatia's Application for Membership of the European Union" (2004), which was published shortly after the submission of Croatia's EU application in 2003, lays out the reforms and concessions Croatia will have to make in order to gain full membership to the European community, and highlights the value that EU membership has for the Croatian state.

> "The Croatian application for membership is part of an historic process, in which the Western Balkan countries are overcoming the political crisis of their region and orienting themselves to join the area of peace, stability and prosperity created by the Union...'the pace of further movement of the Western Balkans countries towards the EU lies in their own hands and will depend on each country's performance in implementing reforms..." (Commission of the European Communities 2004: 4)

Again, two very distinct geographic imaginaries are visible in the language used in the Opinion. The negative imaginary of the Balkans as fraught with crisis and instability is once again highlighted in reference to a stable, peaceful and prosperous imaginary of European Union ('us' vs. 'them'). Even more interesting is the not-so-subtle assertion that Croatia is not just choosing to work toward European integration, but is also choosing to overcome its Balkan-ness. Croatia's annual EU progress reports and negotiation press releases are fraught with this kind of language. This is not to say that the Croatian state does not have real structural issues that need improvement, but rather demonstrates that 'Europe' or the 'West' views the Balkans, and specifically the former-Yugoslavia, through a lens colored by the perceptions, experiences and imaginaries of nationalism, war and regional instability. It's no surprise then that being 'Balkan' has become a complicated and somewhat undesirable identity for those in the region who wish to be more 'European'.

Being 'Balkan' in Croatia

In addition to (b)ordering the Balkans through discourses of underdevelopment and violence, Western Europe has also (b)ordered the physical geographic limits of the Balkans throughout history. The prescribed geographic boundaries of the Balkans have swollen and shrunk to include states as north as Austria and Hungary, as east as Romania, Bulgaria and Turkey, and as South as Albania and Greece. Maria Todorova also engages in this geographic (b)ordering by defining Albanians, Bulgarians, Greeks, Romanians and most of the former-Yugoslavia (excluding Slovenia) as Balkan. She also includes the Turks, due to their central role in the Ottoman experience (Todorova 1997: 30–31). This changing geographic imaginary has led to conflicting ideas of territoriality and identity in the region.

Particularly in Croatia, being 'Balkan' is highly contested. While Todorova includes Croatia in her own geographic (b)ordering of the Balkans, the Croatian imperial experience lies much more with the Austro-Hungarian Empire than with the Ottoman. This has led to a greater historical, cultural and geographic association with the 'West' than with the 'East' or the 'Balkan' that the Ottoman experience usually denotes. Further, within the region, there is an awareness of the negative connotations associated with being Balkan, and this affects the degree to which individual Croats, as well as the Croatian state are willing to accept this cultural, political and geographic distinction.

In 2010, I conducted open-ended online surveys with 20 young Croat adults as part of a larger research project examining discourses of national identity in relation to Croatia's EU negotiation process. Part of the survey sought to gauge how young Croats perceived their country's geography both domestically and regionally. The answers were complicated, and demonstrated that Croats are very conscious of the negative connotations associated with being Balkan. When asked where Croatia was located (the Balkans, Eastern Europe, Central Europe, or other) and why, respondents often admitted to their Balkan identity, but justified it in cultural, historical, economic, or political terms:

> "...we have much in common with other countries in Balkan(s)—similar language, tradition, culture. But in some way I see Croatia more advanced than other (Balkan) countries—so because of that I classify Croatia also in Eastern Europe, which I see more prosperous than Balkan(s)" (Respondent 10).

> "the Balkans isn't a geographic region but rather the term was manufactured to separate this part of Europe, because of its recent violent past and so on. I could go on forever on why this is so...from a west/center/east point of view Croatia is in the center part" (Respondent 14).

> "CE (Central Europe)—historical reasons + our desire to be part of it + influence Austro-Hungarian Empire on architecture and tradition (and) BALKANS—recent history + social repercussions (pessimism, corruption, faulty legal system) of war (sic)" (Respondent 15).

> "...even though being a Balkan should not be considered as something bad, it mostly is... the word Balkan just represents our culture, specific as it is, and our tradition" (Respondent 19).

The survey respondents accepted that, as a term, Balkan is a discursive invention that carries negative historical, cultural and political connotations. Further, even if they conceived of Croatia as geographically outside of the Balkans, they acknowledged that Croatia's recent historical, cultural and political experiences make it a part of the Balkans. This conflicting relationship between Croatia and being Balkan has also been acknowledged by the Croatian state. Former Croatian President, Stjepan Mesić, discussed the meaning of being Balkan in Croatia at the "Europe's Balkan Partners" conference in 2006:

"I cannot deny that in Croatia too there still exist individuals and minor groups wishing to convince first themselves and then the whole world that Croatia does not belong to the region (the Balkans) and that we have really nothing in common with the countries in the region. Both views are false and stupid. And neither reflects Croatian political positions. Geographically and partly historically we belong to Southeast Europe, the Balkans, the Western Balkans, regardless which term we use. We are there to stay and so are our neighbours. These are simply facts" (Ured Predsjednika Republike Hrvatske 2009).

Despite Mesić's acceptance of Croatia's Balkan geography, the Croatian state has had to address the geographic imaginaries of the Balkans when framing its own value to the European community. The rest of this paper briefly examines how the Croatian state has discursively shifted Croatia's geography away from being 'Balkan' to being more 'European'.

Becoming more 'European'

As this paper has shown so far, discourses of the Balkans as underdeveloped and unstable have been used by the EU to justify the process of (b)ordering Croatia to a specific 'European' way of life. The Croatian state is aware of the negative geographic imaginaries of the Balkans, and throughout its EU negotiation process, has found ways to strategically use these perceptions to both demonstrate its value to the EU and to prove that it is less 'Balkan' and more 'European'. A brief examination of how the Croatian state frames its geography on embassy websites indicates how this strategic geographic shift was accomplished.

Prior to gaining EU membership, the Croatian state used its embassy websites to promote a specific geographic imaginary to the global community. This exert from the Croatian embassy to the United States is one example:

> "Republic of Croatia, as a democratic and stable modern European country...plays an important role in... a world of globalisation, regional, political and economic integrations, democratisation of international relations, but also a world of international terrorism and violence. Croatia is located at the heart of Europe as a Mediterranean, Central European and Danube region country, and its geographical location is one of its key strategic advantages. The current European integration processes add a special value to its location, turning it into a potentially key impetus for the country's overall economic development.

Croatia's role in establishing permanent peace, stability and development in South East Europe is irreplaceable, but the establishing of a permanent security and stability system in this part of Europe is possible only on the principles of justice, equality and law, with the respect for the interests of all nations and countries in the region, and the agreement of the international community. In conducting its foreign policy, Croatia will adhere to these principles, thus giving its contribution to turning what once was a region of fierce and direct confrontation into a place of renewed co-operation and partnership" [emphasis added] (Ministry of Foreign Affairs and European Integrations of the RC 2006).

Here, the Croatian state is drawing attention to the strategic importance of Croatia's geographic location in the 'heart of Europe'. The text goes on to describe Croatia's location as Southeastern European, Mediterranean, Central European and Danube country. The term 'Balkan' is never used to situate Croatia's location. Instead, images of Croatia as Western and wholly European are evoked, perhaps in an attempt to carefully avoid the negative connotations associated with being a part of the Balkan Peninsula.

Beyond carefully situating Croatia's geographic location, the text highlights Croatia's economic and political importance. Whereas EU documentation repeatedly mentions the restructuring and development that Croatia must achieve in order to earn EU membership, this text allows the Croatian state a forum in which to represent itself as already democratic, stable and modern. Further the text is an opportunity for the Croatian state to emphasize its commitment to justice, equality and regional stability. Croatia, therefore, becomes strategically necessary in promoting regional development, cooperation, peace and even the fight against terrorism.

Since gaining EU membership, the content of embassy websites has become more standardized, particularly within the European community. Embassy sites for Germany, Austria and the UK all reveal similar aesthetics (with EU colors prominently displayed) and aims to present Croatia as an official and historical member of Europe.[3] Users who are interested in learning more about Croatia are redirected to Croatia.eu, *Land and People*, which offers a detailed look at Croatia's history, geography, politics and culture. Once again, Croatia uses this opportunity to present an image of

---

[3] Croatian embassy websites for Germany, Austria and the UK can be found at http://de.mfa.hr/hr/, http://at.mfa.hr/, and http://uk.mvep.hr/hr/; respectively.

itself as eternally European, Westward oriented and political and culturally significant to the greater European community:

> "Croatia has been present on the contemporary international political stage since its independence from the Yugoslav Federation...but in terms of history and culture, it is one of the oldest European countries...The geopolitical situation of Croatia is determined, therefore, by the convergence and influence of different ethnic, religious, economic and political factors. With respect to the complex position of the country, Croatian authors usually define it as Central European and Mediterranean.
> According to the predominant historical orientation of most of the present-day territory, which gravitated towards Vienna and Budapest, and according to the geographical characteristics of its continental interior, Croatia is a Central European country. On the other hand, its exceptionally long sea front which, with the immediate inland region, fell under the historical influence of the powers of Venice, make it a Mediterranean country...The location of the country has brought it into contact with different cultures, traces of which can be found in various kinds of tangible and spiritual heritage, which today, alongside the original Croatian tradition, have been incorporated into the national identity and recognised in the European community of nations...Croatia's sovereignty and western orientation have been affirmed by entry into the European Union, and, once again, the country is in the position of being a border, which places it in a unique position to participate in the process of extending the European Union to non-member countries, by showing its special interest in them, and also its understanding of them" [emphasis added] (The Miroslav Krleža Institute of Lexicography 2014).

The same language regarding Croatia's geographic location as Mediterranean and Central European indicate that Croatia is implicitly not Balkan. As previously mentioned, Croatia's long history with the Austro-Hungarian Empire has complicated the acceptance of a Balkan identity in Croatia, and this text reveals how the Croatian state continues to perpetuate a geography that is historically, culturally and politically linked to that of Western Europe. Still, this text alludes to Croatia's position as a borderland, and emphasizes its ability to influence and understand non-EU countries in the region, which, like the US embassy website, highlights Croatia's strategic importance to European stability and development. In these ways, Croatia is able to shift its geographic imaginary away from the discourses of war, ethnic nationalism and Balkanism, to that of a stable, modern and developed European nation.

This discursive reframing of Croatia as less 'Balkan' and more 'European' has been successful in promoting Croatia as an important European ally in regional politics and future EU expansion into other Balkan states. The European Commission's Opinion on Croatia's application for accession says as much:

> "(14) The enlargement of the European Union, through the accession of Croatia, will contribute to strengthening stability, freedom and prosperity in Europe. Croatia is expected to continue to play an active role in regional cooperation in the Western Balkans. The Commission welcomes Croatia's declaration on promoting European values in South-East Europe and in particular Croatia's commitment that bilateral issues should not obstruct the accession process of candidate countries. Croatia's accession confirms the EU's commitment to the European perspective of all the Western Balkan countries" [emphasis added] (European Commission 2011: 4).

And, further, at Croatia's accession celebration in Zagreb on June 30th, 2013, the President of the European Council, Herman Van Rompuy, and the President of the European Commission, José Manuel Durão Barroso, both acknowledge Croatia's place in Europe, and its role and responsibility to the rest of the region.

> "As midnight struck, your country crossed an important threshold. It will change the life of this nation for good. You have always been Europeans—and you are now members of the Union...Your country has worked hard for it—with success...As new challenges arise, you will discover that membership is not just about respecting and shaping rules, but as much about sharing the responsibility for our common endeavour...we must remain united as a Union. The European Union is one of peace, built on the spirit of reconciliation. In the recent history of the Western Balkans, your country's entry marks a milestone towards a shared future: living together, in peace and prosperity. Over the past months, jointly with Slovenia, you have courageously overcome hurdles; also with Bosnia Herzegovina. Following the same path, Belgrade and Priština have also reached a historic agreement...As a trailblazer for the region, your country, now as a member state, has a vitally important role to play," [emphasis added] (European Council of the President 2013).

"We are here on a historic night. And that is thanks to you, the Croatian people. It was your desire to join the European Union and your hard work which have made this possible. You have returned Croatia to its rightful place in the heart of Europe...Croatia has changed enormously over the last decades. It is a fully democratic nation, with respect for freedom, for fundamental rights and the rule of law. Croatia is thus well-placed to benefit fully from all that the EU has to offer...Croatia is also an example to others in the region. You have undergone difficult reforms and held out the hand of reconciliation. As an EU Member State you have made clear that you will help others follow your path. I welcome this commitment as our Union is open to those who share our European values," [emphasis added] (European Commission 2013).

Reconciliation, peace, prosperity and European values are now a part of Croatia's geographic imaginary. "A trailblazer for the region," Croatia has "returned to the heart of Europe," and now has a responsibility to assist other Balkan states on the path toward European integration. But, this praise of Croatia does not signal a change in the broader view of Balkan politics and society. Rather, it shows that Croatia has managed to earn its place in the EU through reform, and as shown here, through a strategic rebranding of itself as a less 'Balkan' and more 'European' ally.

Conclusion: Balkan futures in Europe

Through a process of (b)ordering, the EU increasingly defines the who, what and where of being 'European'. This (b)ordering is inextricably linked to geographic imaginaries, which are based in historical, cultural and political experiences and perceptions of place and identity. The geographic imaginary of the Balkans as the underdeveloped, violent and unstable 'other' in Europe continues to frame, at least in part, the expansion of the European Union into the region. In particular, the recent experience of war, ethnic conflict and nationalism during the dissolution of Yugoslavia has been used to distinguish the Balkans from a modern, stable and developed 'Europe'. Potential member-states must earn their place in the European community by addressing these geographic imaginaries and demonstrating the effective implementation of 'European' values, standards and practices.

As this paper has shown, the Croatian state earned its place in Europe, not only by adopting a decade's worth of reforms and standards, but also by addressing its position in the Balkans, and strategically shifting its geographic imaginary away from the Balkans and towards Europe. When Croatia became an EU member on July 1st, 2013, the European Commission praised the Croatian state for overcoming political crisis and committing itself to European values and standards. It seems that the Croatian state has proven itself as democratic, stable and modern; those characteristics that the Balkans has been historically and geographically constructed as lacking.

In addition to earning its place in Europe's in-crowd, the Croatian state has also demonstrated its strategic economic and political value to the European community. The EU continues to highlight its commitment to expansion in the Balkans, and Croatia's path toward EU integration now stands as a positive model for other Balkan states to aspire to. According to the EU, Croatia now has a responsibility to assist and lead other former-Yugoslav republics and the greater Balkan Peninsula toward inclusion in the European community.

The question remains then, what does this all mean for the future of the Balkans in the EU? Croatia's admittance to the European Union does not necessarily indicate a more positive view of Balkan politics, culture, or geography. Rather, it demonstrates an attempt by the EU to discipline or (b)order the Balkans to a more 'European' way of life. Other former-Yugoslav republics will more than likely have to address their Balkan-ness in their own EU negotiation processes. What Croatia's entrance to the EU has done is reinforce existing power dynamics within the Balkans. Historically, Croatia has been positioned as more 'West' than 'East' or more 'European' than 'Balkan'. Now, EU membership has secured a discourse of Croatia as the 'more developed', 'more peaceful' and 'more desirable' economic, political and cultural model for other non-EU Balkan states to strive to imitate. The challenge for other Balkan states pursuing EU membership is not to erase their Balkan-ness, but to negotiate the processes of (b)ordering, which seek to perpetuate old geographic imaginaries of the region, by reclaiming Balkan identities as culturally and historically valuable members of the European community.

Acknowledgements

The research conducted in 2010 was funded by the Department of Geology and Geography at West Virginia University. The research conducted in 2012 and 2013 was funded by the Department of Geography at Penn State University, the Fulbright Commission, the American Association of Geographers Cultural Geography Specialty Group and the Penn State College of Earth and Mineral Sciences Centennial Travel Award.

References

Agnew, J. 1994. *The Territorial Trap: the Geographical Assumptions of International Relations Theory*. Review of International Political Economy, 1, pp. 53–80.

Banac, Iv. 1984. The National Question in Yugoslavia: Origins, History, Politics. Ithaca & London: Cornell University Press.

Commission of the European Communities. 2004. *Communication from the Commission: Opinion on Croatia's Application for Membership of the European Union, Brussels, April 20, 2004*, http://eur-lex.europa.eu/LexUriServ/LexUriServ.do?uri=COM:2004:0257:FIN:EN:PDF [Accessed October 2009]

Glenny, M. 1999. The Balkans: Nationalism, War, and the Great Powers, 1804–1999. New York: Viking Penguin.

European Commission. 2013. *Speech by President Barroso at the ceremony to mark the accession of the Republic of Croatia to the European Union*, Ceremony to Mark the Accession of the Republic of Croatia to the European Union/Zagreb 1 July 2013, Speech 13/589.

European Commission. 2011. *COMMISSION OPINION on the application for accession to the European Union by the Republic of Croatia*, COM(2011) 667 final.

European Commission for Enlargement. 2003. *EU-Western Balkans Summit — Declaration, Thessaloniki, June 21, 2003*, http://ec.europa.eu/enlargement/enlargement_process/accession_process/how_does_a_country_join_the_eu/sap/thessaloniki_summit_en.htm [Accessed July 2009].

European Council of the President. 2013. *Speech by President of the European Council Herman Van Rompuy on the occasion of the entry of Croatia into the European Union*, EUCO 155/13, PRESSE 309, PR PCE 137.

Hartshorne, R. 1933. *Geographic and Political Boundaries in Upper Silesia*, in Annals of the Association of American Geographers, Vol. 23, No. 4 (Dec.), pp. 195–228.

Houtum, H. Van. 2005. *The Geopolitics of Borders and Boundaries*, Geopolitics, Vol. 10, No. 04 (October), pp. 672–679.

Houtum and Naerssen. 2002. *Bordering, Ordering, and Othering*, Tijdschrift voor Economische en Sociale Geografie, Vol. 93, No. 2, pp. 125–136.

Johnson, J. et al.. 2011. *Interventions on rethinking 'the border' in border studies*, Political Geography, 30, pp. 61–69.

Mackinder, H. J. 1904. The Geographical Pivot of History, in The Geographical Journal, Vol. 23, No. 4 (Apr.), pp. 421–437.

Mesić, S. 2009. *President Mesić's Speech at the Conference "Europe's Balkan Partners*, Ured Predsjednika Republike Hrvatske, December 5th, 2006, http://www.predsjednik.hr/Default.aspx?art=13366&sec=917. [Accessed January 2010].

Ministry of Foreign Affairs and European Integrations of the RC. 2006. *Embassy of the Republic of Croatia in the United States of America*, http://www.croatiaemb.org/ [Accessed December 2013].

The Miroslav Krleža Institute of Lexicography. 2014. *Croatia in Brief: Position*, http://croatia.eu/article.php?lang=2&id=6 [Accessed January 2014].

Newman, D. 2006. *Borders and Bordering: Towards and Interdisciplinary Dialogue*, European Journal of Social Theory, Vol. 9, No. 2, pp. 171–186.

Ratzel, F. 1901. Der lebensraum: Eine biogeographische studie.

Said, Ed. 1979. Orientalism. New York: Random House.

Tanner, M. Croatia: A Nation Forged in War. London: Yale University Press, 1997.

Todorova, M. 1997. Imagining the Balkans. New York: Oxford University Press.

STEFAN ĆETKOVIĆ

The Challenge of Promoting Green Sectors in Serbia: Between International Demands, National Controversies and Sectoral Struggles

The paper investigates the promotion of two green economy sectors in Serbia: renewable electricity and organic farming. It argues that participatory governance is essential for sustainably advancing green sectors and seeks to offer a theoretical framework for studying the factors and mechanisms that affect the emergence and effectiveness of participatory governance in the context of green sectors. It is argued that only by looking at sectoral policy network structures and their dynamic interplay with the broader context and actors' behavior it is possible to provide a nuanced explanation of the emergence and effectiveness of participatory governance arrangements. The paper demonstrates how the more affirmative policy network structure in conjunction with policy entrepreneurs have led to somewhat stronger governing capacity in the organic farming sector. Furthermore, the technocratic approach of the EU, fragmented political system and mounting socio-economic problems, have been the key impediments to effective participatory governance in both sectors.

Key words: Renewable energy, organic farming, green economy, policy networks, Serbia.

Stefan Ćetković is a Research Associate at the Environmental Policy Research Centre, Free University of Berlin. He holds a PhD in political science from the Free University of Berlin.

Introduction

The conditions for long-term economic growth have never been more challenging in the post-war Europe than they are today. The global financial and economic crisis which unfolded in 2008 has caused pervasive economic stagnation coupled with the widespread surge in unemployment and public indebtedness. This has hit hard the economic prospects in the EU periphery, including the countries of the Western Balkans (WB) (Burgess and Körner 2012). In parallel to the deteriorating socio-economic situation, the world has witnessed the aggravation of the major global environmental problems, such as the decline in basic ecosystems

(Millennium Ecosystem Assessment, 2005: 6) and the increase in greenhouse gas emissions causing climate change (WMO 2011: 1). As a result, the old model of economic development based on excessive resource exploitation and unrestrained material consumption fuelled by highly polluting fossil-based energy sources has increasingly been questioned. This has prompted a renewed global interest in ways of achieving environmentally sustainable and socially equitable economic development. As Barbier (2009, 5) put it: "reviving growth, ensuring financial stability and creating jobs should be essential objectives. But unless new policy initiatives also address other global challenges, such as reducing carbon dependency, protecting ecosystems and water resources and alleviating poverty, their impact on averting future crises will be short-lived." Recently, influenced by the advances in green technologies and the growing global market for environmental goods and services, the concepts of green growth and green economy have been launched as a solution to the economic and ecological crisis. Although there are different approaches to green economy varying in their scope and objectives, they all share the basic notion that by promoting environmentally friendly technologies and sectors (e.g. sustainable agriculture, renewable energy, energy efficiency) it is possible to reverse negative environmental trends while generating new jobs and incomes (UNEP 2011).

However, the question of whether and how the green economy vision can be successfully implemented, particularly in less developed and transition economies, is yet to be answered. There is a growing consensus among scholars that a close state-societal relationship and the involvement of a variety of actors and resources in the policy process are essential, if not the key components of successful governance for green economy (Daugbjerg and Halpin 2010; Najam and Selin 2011). The participatory policy-making in the context of green sectors is important for two main reasons. First, it should secure a policy dialogue and exchange of relevant and timely information necessary for formulating inclusive, equitable and context-tailored policies for green sectors. As Culpepper (2003, 188) pointed out, "States need to develop access to social information that they are poorly equipped to find out on their own." Second, given that the promotion of green sectors is a multifaceted task which cuts across different jurisdictions and levels of government, participatory policy-making should secure effective policy implementation by ensuring collaboration and concerted actions from multiple state and non-state actors. This style of participatory policy-making in which state actors act autonomously but relying on local information and networks of societal interactions is also called "embedded policy-making" (Culpepper 2003; Evans 1995).

Yet, there is little understanding of the multiple factors and mechanisms that shape the conditions for governance arrangements based on embedded policy-making to emerge and be effective. In this paper I argue that only by focusing on the institutional structure at the level of a sector and examining its dynamic interplay with the broader context and network actors' interests, resources and behavior can we gain a nuanced understanding of the drivers and obstacles to developing and sustaining governing capacity for promoting green sectors. To demonstrate this point, I explore the development of two green sectors in Serbia: organic farming and renewable electricity. The main objective of the study is to offer an analytical framework for understanding and explaining the factors behind the commonalities and differences in policy responses and achieved results in the two green sectors.

The paper is structured as follows. It begins by providing a brief overview of the governing capacity and achieved progress in the organic farming and renewable electricity sectors. Subsequently, the analytical framework is introduced. The paper then applies the outlined framework and demonstrates its value for explaining the successes and failures in building governing capacity and ensuring stable and inclusive growth in the two green sectors. The paper concludes with a discussion of the findings and their theoretical and empirical implications. The study is based on secondary materials and semi-structured interviews and covers the period through the end of 2012.

Governing capacity in organic farming and renewable electricity in Serbia

This section provides a brief assessment of the level of governing capacity and achieved policy progress in the organic farming and renewable electricity sectors in Serbia.[1] It will be shown that the organic farming sector has produced somewhat better policy performance measured against the three dimensions of green economy (social, environmental and economic), compared to the renewable electricity sector. The better performance of

---

[1] For a more comprehensive discussion of the policy development and governing capacity in the two sectors, see Ćetković (2014).

organic farming, as will be argued, has been associated with higher governing capacity, characterized particularly by close state-society interactions. Nonetheless, both sectors continue to face serious obstacles in developing and maintaining their governing capacities and delivering tangible policy results.

Organic farming policy

The beginnings of organic farming in Serbia date back to the activities of grassroots groups in the early 1990s, but it is only in recent years that the regulatory framework and the government support for the sector have started to mature. Something of a turning point occurred in 2008 when the new Minister of Agriculture placed the development of organic farming on the top of the policy agenda. As a result, a number of policy initiatives and regulatory changes were put forward. In 2009, the first action plan on organic farming was drafted at the initiative of the ministry supported by the key domestic stakeholders and the German Society for International Cooperation (GIZ) (MAFWM 2009). In 2011, the revision of the action plan was launched aimed at assessing and renewing overall goals and activities (Rural 21 2012). In 2010, the ministry adopted the new Law on Organic Production (Parliament of Serbia 2010), which harmonized national legislation with the EU framework and established for the first time the separate national Department for Organic Production (DOP). The law strengthened the control over the organic production system by requiring all active organic farming certification companies to be authorized by the national authority and disclose their data on certified organic land to the DOP. In terms of the direct financial support, the subsidies for organic farming have marked a substantial increase since 2009, both in terms of the amount of the allocated budget and the scope of actors eligible for support (MATFWM 2011). The ministry, GIZ and domestic organic farming associations also invested efforts in raising public awareness and providing a variety of targeted education and training programs on organic production (Serbia Organica, n.d.). Nonetheless, after the personnel changes in the Agriculture Ministry in mid-2011 and the entry of the new government in mid-2012, many ongoing activities were postponed and the planned subsidies for organic farmers for 2012 were completely abolished.

The organic farming sector have also produced some tangible policy results in terms of the increase in the overall area under organic production and the number of organic producers, although no firm conclusions can be made given the lack of reliable data. The available figures show that the size of the registered land area under organic farming expanded from 596 ha in 2009 (MAFWM 2009: 4) to around 7500 ha, according to the latest estimates from September 2013 (Kalentić et al. 2014: 9).

The achieved progress in policy outputs and outcomes has correlated with improvements in the governing capacity of the organic farming sector, reflected particularly in the enhanced policy dialogue between the state and stakeholder groups. The groundwork for this was laid in 2009 when the National Association for Organic Production Development, Serbia Organica, was formed at the initiative of the Agriculture Ministry with an aim to unify the fragmented sector, foster mutual collaboration and strengthen its position in relation to policy-makers. Serbia Organica soon grew into a representative umbrella association comprising of around 800 members (März, et al. 2012: 6). The ministry granted Serbia Organica access to the policy process and utilized its expertise and organizational structure to formulate and implement policy actions. Thus, virtually all introduced regulatory changes and support measures during that period were initiated by, or developed in cooperation with, Serbia Organica. The originally informal state-society policy dialogue evolved into an institutionalized form of policy deliberation embodied in the Expert Council on Organic Production established under the new law in 2010.

Despite the notable improvements recently, the organic farming sector and the established policy-making structures continue to face formidable challenges in securing sustainable sectoral growth. These challenges are exemplified in insufficient inspection capacities, lacking inputs for organic production, underdeveloped domestic market and overall policy uncertainty.

Renewable electricity policy

Similar to organic farming, the issue of promoting the deployment of renewable energy sources (RES) came into the focus of policy makers in 2009. The major step was made with the enactment of the feed-in tariff (FIT) scheme which provides secured preferential tariffs for the period of 12 years for electricity produced from RES (Government of Serbia 2009a). Subsequent bylaws and the new Law on Energy adopted in 2011 (Parliament of Serbia 2011) specified further the regulatory framework for RES and harmonized it largely with the EU's requirements. While the conditions for investing in RES were improved with the adopted documents, the overall framework entailed important deficits, reflected particularly in its narrow scope, lack of transparency and built-in uncertainty.

The major concern of policy makers in the energy field was to minimize the potential increase in the electricity prices resulting from the deployment of RES and to avoid what were considered to be technologically and organizationally demanding steps for integrating new RES, especially wind and solar energy. Consequently, the regulatory and policy framework targets particularly hydropower as economically most affordable and proven technology, while imposing a rather restrictive long-term cap on wind and solar energy which together comprise around 19% of the country's RES potential, compared to 14% in hydropower (Government of Serbia 2009c).[2] Somewhat contrary to the good international practice (Mendonça, Jacobs and Sovacool 2010: 15), the framework discourages individuals and households from benefiting from FIT by securing the right to it only to legal entities and energy entrepreneurs (Government of Serbia 2009b). Finally, the environmental issues have received only scant attention in formulating policy measures.[3] With regard to the built-in uncertainty, the RES framework has been criticized for regulating the field mainly through bylaws (European Commission 2011: 84), which are often subject to changes or not adopted within the legally specified time period, as it was the case in practice.[4] Furthermore, little has been done to ensure more transparent and streamlined administrative procedures for implementing RES projects.

In terms of the delivered results, the data from the state-owned Electric Power Industry of Serbia (EPS) from December 2012 shows that the renewable electricity capacity of 18.5 MW was connected to the grid (EPS, personal communication, 7 December 2012). This stands in stark contrast

---

[2] The decree on FIT from 2009 (Government of Serbia, 2009a) introduced the cap on wind and solar energy to 450 MW and 5 MW, respectively. The new decree from 2013 (Government of Serbia, 2013) lowered the cap on wind energy to 350 MW by 2015 while establishing a long-term limit on wind and solar power by 2020 to 500 MW and 10 MW, respectively.

[3] For a discussion of the lack of environmental and sustainability assessments on biomass in Serbia, see Stojadinović (2010, 16).

[4] The necessary bylaws envisaged by the Law on Energy from 2011 (Parliament of Serbia, 2011) were adopted only in late 2012 while some bylaws were still pending at the time of writing, see Turković (2012).

with the proclaimed government objective of reaching 102 MW in new renewable electricity sources by 2012 (Government of Serbia 2009c).

An important part of the explanation for the modest policy outputs and outcomes in the renewable electricity field lies in the restrictive and hands-off policy approach. Rather than promoting a policy dialogue and opening up the policy process to a variety of relevant actors, the policy-makers have confined their role to performing basic regulatory and administrative functions while granting policy access only to a few most powerful actors and interests, such as the state-owned company EPS and some individual private investors. This has negatively affected the ability of policy-makers to explore new policy options, secure sectoral consensus and effectively manage the implementation process.

Analytical framework

This section outlines the analytical framework for explaining why the organic farming sector adopted a more embedded governance approach than the renewable electricity sector and why both sectors continue to face considerable challenges in developing and making use of their governing capacities. In doing so, the paper draws on theoretical insights from the governance literature and the concept of policy networks. The key observation concerns the changed nature of contemporary public policy-making, characterized by several important trends including the increasing scope and complexity of public problems, the blurring of boundaries between state and private sector and the internationalization of domestic policy realms (Kjær 2004). The increasing complexity and fragmentation of government affairs has resulted in "the emergence of policy subsystems in which state (principally bureaucratic officials) and non-state actors were implicated in both policy formulation and implementation" (Skogstad 2008: 205). The concept of policy networks came into use in an attempt to conceptualize this complex pattern of relationships between state and non-state actors across different policy domains and provide a more accurate explanation of policy processes and their outcomes. Policy networks are thus understood as "crucial political structures through which we are governed or ruled" (Daugbjerg and Marsh 1998: 55).

The most prominent categorization of policy networks, proposed by Rhodes and Marsh (1992), places various forms of policy networks on the continuum between two ideal policy network types: policy community and issue network. These two ideal types of policy network structures differ from each other along four main criteria: membership, integration, resources and power relation (Rhodes and Marsh 1992: 187). Whereas policy communities are considered closed, well integrated networks with a few actors who share the same policy paradigm and have a balanced power relationship, issue networks are open and fragmented with a large and unstable membership and lack of policy consensus. The key contribution of this and other policy network typologies is that they assert that different policy network structures produce different policy contents (Daugbjerg 1998: 38). Smith (1993: 71) argues that policy communities are generally associated with policy stability and continuity, while in the case of issue networks "the potential policy outcomes are likely to be more varied and that it is much easier for groups to get alternative policy options onto the agenda. However, the downside is that it is much more difficult for these policy options to be implemented because government actors have less control over the policy process."

There is obvious relevance of the policy network approach for understanding the development of governing capacity for green sectors. More concretely, it is reasonable to assume that the interest in promoting green industries and building necessary governing capacity is less likely to occur within closed sectoral policy communities. This is due to the fact that integrated policy communities have an established policy agenda and institutionalized ways of dealing with policy issues which are generally resistant towards new actors and ideas. Often the expansion of green sectors can directly conflict with the interests of some key actors within the old policy community. On the other side, less integrated issue networks without strong veto points provide a more favorable environment for green sectors to come on the policy agenda and attract government support. Still, to institutionalize the embedded policy-making style, next to the affirmative network structure, it is necessary to have policy entrepreneurs who are able to seize the network conditions and engage in capacity-building. This leads to another important insight that it is not only the structure of policy networks that matters for the policy process, but also actors' behavior and, equally important, the broader context. As it has been recognized in the latest contributions in the policy network literature, it is the interplay among these three factors that influences the policy process and determines policy outcomes (Marsh and Smith 2000). For the purpose of this study, the key elements of the broader context which are part of the analysis include: national political system, socio-economic setting and EU policy. The analytical framework thus entails an investigation of the character of these three contextual factors and how their influences affected, and were mediated by, distinctive sectoral network structures and actors' interests, resources and behavior to shape the emergence and effectiveness of the governing capacity in the two green sectors (see Figure 1).

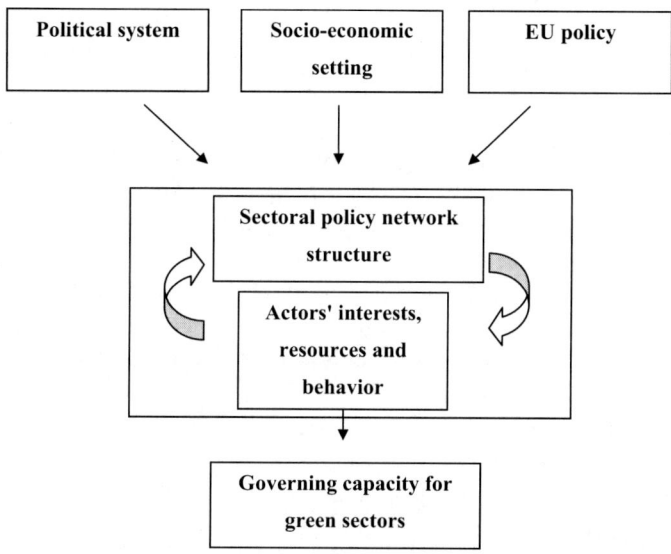

Figure 1. A 'dialectical' policy network approach to analyzing the emergence of governing capacity for green sectors. Adapted from Marsh and Smith (2000: 10).

Empirical analysis

This section applies the outlined analytical framework to explain policy developments in the organic farming and renewable electricity sectors in Serbia. It begins with a brief discussion of the three main factors that form the broader context within which the policy networks operate. In the next step the characteristics of the policy network structures at the sectoral level are introduced. Finally, the interplay of these factors together with actors' interest, resources and behavior is presented and its impact on the governing capacity in both sectors is examined.

Broader context

Political system

Serbian political system is characterized by the dominance of narrow political parties' interests on the one side, and the hegemony of the executive power, the government and the president, over the legislative and judiciary branches of government, on the other side (Milenković 2011: 32). The fragmented and unstable party system gives rise to frequent personnel and organizational changes in the government and polarization of the government cabinet along party lines. As an illustration, in the period from 2000 to 2012, five parliamentary elections were held in Serbia and as many different cabinets held power. The changes of the heads of ministries were even more frequent. During the same period, the ministers in charge of agricultural policy changed eight times and ministers of energy, seven times. The strict division of the government departments along party lines, a phenomenon termed as "feudalization" (Milenković 2011: 32) gives ministerial departments significant independence in making policy decisions while at the same time undermining necessary cooperation on cross-sectional policy issues.

The role and capacity of the public administration are also negatively affected by the high politicization of the government's work and regular political and organizational restructurings. Cohen (2010: 15) observes that "below the top tier of political ministers, among non-elected officials in the public administration, such changes, divisions and uncertainty tend to feed bureaucratic inertia and non-accountability." Furthermore, the adverse effect of partitocracy on the performance of the public administration is related to the widespread practice of political patronage, which involves the recruitment of civil servants on the basis of their loyalty to the party and their personal relationship to the leaders of the party. Cohen (2010: 15) quotes one Serbian deputy minister who stated that "some ministries do not even function at all. The employees are neither interested nor involved in their work. They were employed because they once had the right connection, not because they might have been professionally qualified." As a result, the public administration in Serbia suffers from the lack of expertise, considerable organizational inertia and overstuffed personnel.

Socio-economic setting

The Republic of Serbia is a country in transition that has gone through a fundamental socio-economic transformation over the last two decades from the socialist system of a planned economy to the market-oriented economic system. The change in the ownership over the means of production through the process of privatization of formerly socially owned firms marked the central element of the Serbian economic transition. However, the state has continued to play an important role in economic activities given that many public enterprises, including EPS, have remained non-privatized (Orlović 2011: 270). Even though not every policy sector has been equally exposed to, and reshaped by, the market reforms, the process of integration into the global market and the EU structure has affected virtually every segment of the socio-economic system.

The overall economic situation has seen improvements over the last decade in comparison to the period of the political and economic crisis in the 1990s. However, the structural flaws in the political and economic system and their inability to cope with the internal and external challenges resulted in a slow and uneven progress marked by high unemployment and rising public indebtedness. The economic situation has been additionally aggravated by the global financial crisis of 2008. The level of public debt in 2012 exceeded the legally established limit of 45% of GDP and accounted for 55% of GDP while unemployment was at a historic high of 25.5% (Vukojčić 2012). Due to the political and economic reforms aimed at opening up the economy, in the period between 2000 and 2010 Serbia attracted direct foreign investments to the amount of €15 billion. However, since the largest part of investments was directed to non-tradable sectors, such as banking or the real estate sector, the positive impact on export capacity was limited (European Commission 2011: 52). As a result, policy-makers have been faced with the pressing need of fostering economic growth and export-oriented sectors without aggravating further the fragile socio-economic situation of a large part of population.

EU policy

European integration and the profound impact that this process has had on the politics, polity and policy in Serbia is difficult to overestimate. Following the democratic political changes in 2000, EU membership was eventually adopted by all key political actors as their main political vision and an overarching political objective. The realization of this objective is tied to comprehensive reforms reflected in the transposition of EU norms, standards and practices in all domestic fields of government. Emphasizing the influence of the EU legal system on the law-making process in Serbia, Crnobrnja and Trbović (2008: 61) observe that in Serbia "every piece of legislation is drafted with the *acquis* in mind." On March 1, 2012 Serbia obtained EU membership candidate status.

In the area of RES, EU policy has had direct and strong implications on Serbia. In October 2005, Serbia, together with other countries of Southeast Europe, signed the Treaty Establishing Energy Community with a primary goal to harmonize the energy market and energy policy of the region with EU laws and standards. An important element of the EU's energy policy, which the contracting parties to the Energy Community are obliged to implement, is the EU regulation on the promotion of RES. At the Ministerial Council of the Energy Community in 2012, the official decision was made to transpose the EU Renewable Energy Directive 2009/28/EC into national legislations. In accordance with the directive, Serbia was required to adopt the binding targets for increasing the share of energy from RES in the final energy consumption from 21.2% in 2009 to 27% by 2020 (Ministerial Council of the Energy Community 2012). The existence of clear and obligatory national targets suggests a strong conditionality of the EU's renewable energy policy. Still, it is important to note that the environmental dimension of the EU energy strategy, including the issue of renewable energy, has not been given the equal importance as the central energy goals of market integration and liberalization (Buchan, 2009). The dominant focus on market liberalization, which is also reflected in the work of the Energy Community (Lindstrom 2011), downplays to some extent the stringency of the EU renewable energy conditionality.

Similarly to the policy on renewable electricity, the EU's organic farming policy represents a type of a positive policy model providing guidelines and defining minimum standards which must be adopted and implemented in member states. Nonetheless, unlike the case with the renewable energy policy, the EU neither legally obliges member states and candidate countries to promote organic farming, nor does it impose any binding organic farming national targets on the national states. The EU thus only provides a regulatory framework for organic farming and encourages member states to support organic production through economic incentives and strategic documents such as the national action plans for organic farming. Being an EU candidate country, Serbia is required to fully transpose all valid organic farming standards and requirements defined under the EU's organic farming framework. It is also expected from Serbia to harmonize its institutional structure and strategic policy documents related to organic farming with those in the EU in order to prepare the country's accession to the EU system and enable the organic farming sector has to benefit from the available support mechanisms. As a country which is still not a member of the EU, Serbia provides economic support to its agriculture sector, including direct payments to organic farming, almost entirely from the state budget. However, the organic farming sector considerably benefited from various programs made available by international donors and different state development agencies, the most active been those from the EU countries.

Sectoral context: Policy network structures

For analytical purposes, it is useful to make a distinction between three dimensions of a policy field which vary in their scope: policy area, policy sector and policy sub-sector (Wilks and Wright 1987: 300). Thus, organic production denotes a sub-sector, agricultural production is a sector and agriculture is a policy area. Likewise, renewable electricity is a sub-sector, electricity production and distribution is a sector and energy is a policy area. It is the impact of sectoral on sub-sectoral policy networks that it is of main concerns in this analysis.

The agriculture production sector in Serbia is characterized by a strong state actor, the ministry, and weak and fragmented societal actors. There exist several farmer associations which are in competitive relations and none of them succeeded in securing a privileged position in the policy-making process over the longer period of time. Different farmer associations attempt to advance their interests and express their views in relation to the ministry but they have only a consultative role in the policy process. Frequent policy changes in the area of agriculture, which have coincided with the personal changes on the top of the ministry (World Bank 2011: 30), indicate that the agricultural policy goals and priorities are mainly decided at the level of high ministry officials. The changes in policy priorities also show the lack of a policy consensus. Therefore, the agriculture production policy network can be described as a state-led issue network.

The electricity sector incorporates one strong state actor, the ministry, and one dominant non-state actor, EPS. Due to its important economic and political role, EPS has enjoyed a privileged status and has been an integral part of the sectoral policy-making. The representatives of EPS take part in all relevant working groups and are additionally consulted on all important policy decisions. In addition, despite personnel changes in the ministry, there has been a notable continuity in terms of the key goals and priorities in the energy field. This policy continuity is based on the established policy framed which rests on two main principles: (1) the provision of sufficient electricity supply at affordable subsidized price and (2) the privileged position of EPS as a strategic company which manages an essential natural resource. It can thus be concluded that the electricity policy network in Serbia resembles a closed and integrated policy community.

Dynamic interplay of macro, sectoral and micro-level factors and its impact on governing capacity

Drivers and challenges to governing capacity for organic farming

Consistent with the broader institutional context, the Ministry of Agriculture has undergone frequent personnel and organizational changes. In 2008, the person who previously served as the Minister of Environment was appointed the Minister of Agriculture. He identified organic farming development as one of the policy priorities and tasked one of the state secretaries to coordinate and monitor policy measures for promoting organic farming. From the policy network perspective it can be argued that the fragmented and pluralist agriculture production network without a firm policy agenda and strong veto players enabled the new minister to place organic farming issue high on the policy agenda. The decisive moment, however, was the decision or a 'strategic action' (Jessop 2000) of the ministry to create the national organic farming association, Serbia Organica, and so connect and mobilize the fragmented sub-sectoral network. The active entrepreneurial role of the leadership of Serbia Organica contributed to uniting the sector and establishing a policy dialogue between organic farming stakeholders and the ministry. Another essential role was performed by multiple foreign donors and development agencies that not only financially supported organic farming producers and associations, but also provided organizational support and expertise to both the government and business and civil society actors. The German development agency, GIZ, was particularly active in assisting policy-makers and societal actors and enhancing state-society relations in the organic farming policy field. At the same time, the dominant focus of organic farming development in Serbia on supplying foreign markets can partly be attributed to the activities of GIZ and its policy agenda. The role of GIZ was also criticized by some actors for placing an emphasis on *ad-hoc* and short-term projects, rather than on strategic goals and genuine local needs (Haas, personal communication, 5 March 2013). It is also worthwhile noting that during 2011 and 2012 one German organic farming expert worked for the Serbian ministry as advisor to the newly established DOP.

Once the new network structure was established and organic farming development set into motion, organic farming advocates among state and non-state actors exploited several affirmative broader factors in convincing policy-makers about the need for continuing and expanding the government support. The necessity to transpose EU organic farming standards and the increasing demand for organic products on the EU market were among the key forces from the broader context that strengthened the position of organic farming interests in Serbia. The economic benefits of promoting organic farming, coming mainly from exporting organic products to foreign markets, have often been stressed by organic farming stakeholders and politicians in publicly justifying government policy for fostering organic farming.

Despite the positive developments and considerable improvements of the organic farming governing capacity caused by the interplay of the EU conditionality, the EU market demand, affirmative sectoral network constellation and presence of policy entrepreneurs, a number of broader and sector-related factors undermined the capacity of the organic farming network and constrained the policy performance. With regard to the socio-economic setting, the unfavorable economic conditions and increasing global and domestic pressure on reducing country's trade deficit impeded the emergence of the domestic organic market directing almost exclusive attention towards the export of organic products. This has had both important negative environmental and socio-economic consequences, particularly for organic farmers who due to their small size or the type of cultivated organic products were dependent on the domestic local markets. In terms of the political system and state structure, the instability of the government, the politicized public administration and the lack of interdepartmental cooperation hampered the policy continuity and long-term planning and inhibited effective policy implementation. Next to the already mentioned decision of the ministry to scrap organic farming subsidies in 2012, the policy and organizational uncertainty was marked by the fact that state secretaries responsible for organic farming together with some mid-level civil servants were changed on both occasions, after the reshuffling of the government in mid-2011 and with the entry of the new government in mid-2012. It is important to note here that the negative effects of the volatility in the broader politico-economic context on the organic farming network were further augmented by the fragmented sectoral issue network. This confirms the already stated proposition from the policy network literature that issue networks are conducive to new policy issues but can be detrimental to long-term policy-making and policy implementation. Finally, the inherent lack of the cross-departmental collaboration in the state apparatus caused the insufficient institutional cooperation between the organic farming department and other important state authorities such as agricultural inspection, the customs administration responsible for controlling exports of organic products and the directorate for plant protection in charge of regulating inputs for organic production.

It is thus the interplay of the discussed factors from the broader context and sectoral network structure that have prevented the embedded policy-making arrangements in the organic farming domain to advance and deliver better policy results.

Drivers and challenges to governing capacity for renewable electricity

Owing to the existence of the integrated sectoral policy community and firm policy agenda, the frequent changes in the government have not had a strong impact on energy and electricity policy in Serbia. Still, the increasing pressure by the EU towards liberalization and stronger environmental protection in the electricity sector posed a considerable challenge to the existing policy community and the established policy consensus. The EU's demands in the field of renewable electricity were more prominent than in organic farming due to the obligatory character of the EU renewable energy policy and the binding targets for increasing the domestic share of renewable energy use. The external EU pressure combined with the activity of some domestic actors, such as the Serbian Wind Energy Association

(SEWEA), contributed to the increased organizational capacity of the ministry and the improved policy and regulatory framework for renewable electricity projects. It is no coincidence that the creation of the separate ministerial unit for renewable energy sources in 2008 and the adoption of FIT in 2009 occurred in parallel to the process of drafting and officially adopting the renewable energy directive at the EU level, which took place during 2008 and 2009. This demonstrates the critical role of the EU's policy in placing the issue of renewable energy on the policy agenda in Serbia. However, whereas the EU's role was prominent in affecting the domestic energy policy agenda, it was far less effective in exerting the influence over the direction and pace in which the new policy objectives will be addressed. Different agencies from the EU and member states, such as the European Bank for Reconstruction and Development (EBRD) and the Dutch NL Agency, provided financial assistance and expertise to the Serbian Energy Ministry in designing policy instruments and formulating strategic documents, including the national action plans for RES and biomass development. Nonetheless, these support initiatives not only did little to promote more inclusive policy deliberation given that they were implemented as government to government projects, but they also often had limited effects in practice as final policy decisions and policy implementation rested with the domestic state authorities.

Faced with the pressure for incorporating renewable energy goals into the policy agenda, which could not be easily disregarded, the reaction of the main policy actors within the electricity policy community was mainly directed towards accommodating new policy demands in accordance with the existing policy frame. The position of the Energy Ministry was that rapid deployment of RES for power production was generally expensive and not affordable for the country. On a more affirmative note, the Energy Ministry partly conceived renewable energy policy as an opportunity for attracting foreign investments and reviving economic activity of domestic energy-related industries. However, the goal of maintaining the low electricity prices coupled with the domestic pressure from the entrenched interests for preserving the existing structure of the electricity system dominantly influenced the position of the ministry. Hence, the strategy for attracting foreign investment projects was mainly directed at the established hydropower sector with the primary aim of exporting green electricity. This was materialized, for instance, in the signed energy agreement between the Serbian government and Italian company, Seci

Energia, ratified by the Serbian parliament (Parliament of Serbia 2012). This agreement envisages investments of the Italian partner in small hydropower plants in Serbia under the condition that the entire generated electricity is exported back to the country of investors. Although such projects do not contribute to increasing the domestic use of RES, they are seen by the government and EPS as important instruments for generating much needed revenues and promoting exports. The second major actor, EPS, had an interest in securing the dominant position in the market and avoiding the costs and technical challenges imposed on the company from connecting and balancing the power from new renewable electricity facilities.

Hence, the closed sectoral policy community in conjunction with the lack of leadership and entrepreneurial actors was able to keep the issue of promoting renewable electricity off the policy priority list and to shape the policy process according to the core interests and the dominant policy frame within the policy community. This implied a restricted access to the policy deliberation process for new actors and thus little room for embedded policy-making to take place.

The unfavorable external politico-institutional and socio-economic factors further reinforced the deep-seated views within the electricity policy community and additionally constrained the occurrence of embedded policy-making structures. For instance, the impact of the deployment of RES on the increase in the electricity prices posed a serious obstacle for renewable electricity advocators by making the arguments in favor of promoting renewable electricity sound less convincing to the decision-makers and broader public. Furthermore, the fragmented ministerial departments and the relative independence of the Ministry of Energy in formulating the policy and regulatory framework reduced the chances of renewable electricity issue to come on the policy agenda through other venue points in the state apparatus.

From the above said it does not come as a surprise that participatory and embedded policy-making structures could not gain ground in the renewable electricity policy field given the restrictive sectoral network constellations fortified by the troublesome politico-economic conditions and the technocratic approach taken by foreign agencies.

Conclusions

The conducted analysis has shown the existence of multiple and interdependent factors which shape the ability of emerging green sectors to develop and sustain governing capacity based on the inclusive and embedded policy-making approach. The constellations of sectoral policy networks have been found to be the key nexus points of decision-making and capacity-building, conditioned by the broader politico-economic setting and continuously contested and reinforced by the impulses from the international system and actors' interests, skills and actions. Theoretically, the study has demonstrated the value of the recent insights from the policy network literature which suggest that the impact of policy network structures on policy processes and outcomes can be best understood in the dialectical relationship with the macro and micro accounts. Such approach seems particularly suitable for studying governance processes in the WB countries given their high exposure to macro-level influences, particularly those from the international system. In terms of policy lessons, the findings from the study indicate that efforts for sustainable advancement of green sectors should inevitably involve concerted actions at different levels of government. Considering the exceptional role of EU actors and policies, the change in their approach appears particularly important, away from top-down and goal-driven strategies toward a stronger emphasis on the empowerment of stakeholders and the inclusiveness of the policy process. Furthermore, without resolving the controversies in the national and international political and economic system which generate short-term and inconsistent policy choices, any green economy initiative in Serbia is bound to be ineffective and short-lived.

References

Barbier, B. E. 2009. *Rethinking the economic recovery: a global green new deal*. Cambridge, New York: Cambridge University Press.

Buchan, D. 2009. *Energy and climate change: Europe at the crossroads*. Oxford: Oxford University Press.

Burgess, R., and Körner, K. 2012. *Western Balkans: Bumps on the road to EU accession*. DB Research, Current Issues: Emerging Markets. Available at: http://www.dbresearch.com/PROD/DBR_INTERNET_EN-PROD/PROD0000000000293226.pdf.

Ćetković, S. 2014. *Policy capacity for promoting green sectors reconsidered: Lessons from the renewable electricity and organic farming sectors in Serbia*. Journal of Environmental Policy & Planning. DOI: 10.1080/1523908X.2014.886505.

Cohen, L. J. 2010. *Administrative development in 'low-intensity' democracies: governance, rule-of-law and corruption in the western balkans*. Simon Fraser Papers in Security and Development No. 5. Vancouver: School for International Studies, Simon Fraser University.

Crnobrnja, M., and Trbović, A. 2008. *Relations between Serbia and the EU: history and prospects*. Research Papers No. 2. Belgrade: Singidunum University.

Culpepper, P. D. 2003. *Creating cooperation: how states develop human capital in Europe*. Ithaca [u.a.]: Cornell Univ. Press.

Daugbjerg, C, and Halpin, D. 2010. *Generating policy capacity in emerging green industries: the development of organic farming in Denmark and Australia*. Journal of Environmental Policy & Planning, 12 (2), pp.141–157.

Daugbjerg, C. 1998. Policy networks under pressure: pollution control, policy reform and the power of farmers. Aldershot: Ashgate Publishing.

Daugbjerg, C., and Marsh, D. 1998. *Explaining policy outcomes: integrating the policy network approach with macro-level and micro-level analysis*. In: D. Marsh, ed. Comparing policy networks. Buckingham: Open University Press, pp. 52–71.

European Commission. 2011. *Analytical Report*. Available at: http://ec.europa.eu/enlargement/pdf/key_documents/2011/package/sr_analytical_rapport_2011_en.pdf.

Evans, P. 1995. Embedded autonomy. Princeton: Princeton University.

Government of Serbia. 2009a. *Decree on incentive measures for electricity generation using renewable energy sources and for combined heat and power (CHP) generation*. Official Gazette of RS, 99/09.

Government of Serbia. 2009b. *Decree on the requirements for obtaining the status of the privileged electric power producer and the criteria for assessing fulfillment of these requirements*. Official Gazette of RS, 72/09.

Government of Serbia. 2009c. *Energy sector development strategy implementation programme 2007–2012 — Amendments*. Official Gazette of RS, 99/09.

Government of Serbia. 2013. *Decree on the procedure and requirements for obtaining the status of the privileged electric power producer*. Official Gazette of RS, 8/13.

Jessop, B. 2000. *Institutional (re)turns and the strategic-relational approach*. Lancaster University, On-line papers. Available at: http://www.lancaster.ac.uk/fass/sociology/research/publications/papers/jessop-institutional-%28re%29turns.pdf.

Kalentić, M., Stefanović, E., Simić, I., and März, U. 2014. *Organic agriculture in Serbia 2014: At a glance*. Belgrade: Serbia Organica.

Kjær, A. M. 2004. *Governance*. Cambridge [u.a.]: Polity Press.

Lindstrom, N. 2011. *Power trips: Europeanization, market-governance, and energy policy in the Western Balkans*. Policy and Society, 30, pp. 197–207.

MAFWM (Ministry of Agriculture Forestry and Water Management of Serbia). 2009. *National action plan for the development of organic farming in Serbia*.

Marsh, D. and Smith, M. 2000. *Understanding policy networks: towards a dialectical approach*. Political Studies, 49, pp. 4–21.

März, U., Stolz, T., Kalentić, M., and Mišković, N. 2012. *Organic agriculture in Serbia 2012: At a glance*. Belgrade: Serbia Organica.

MATFWM (Ministry of Agriculture Trade Forestry and Water Management of Serbia). 2011. *Organska proizvodnja u Srbiji*. Presented at "Organska proizvodnja—Šansa za razvoj", Leskovac, Serbia.

Mendonça, M., Jacobs, D., and Sovacool, B. 2010. *Powering the green economy: the feed-in tariff handbook*. London [u.a.]: Earthscan.

Milenković, D. 2011. *Stanje političkih institucija u Srbiji i njihov uticaj na kreiranje i vođenje javnih politika*. In: M. Podunavac, ed. Javne politike Srbije. Beograd: Heinrich Böll Stiftung, pp.21–41.

Millennium Ecosystem Assessment. 2005. *Ecosystems and human well-being: synthesis*. Washington, DC: Island Press.

Ministerial Council of the Energy Community. 2012. *Decision on the implementation of Directive 2009/28/EC and amending Article 20 of the Energy Community.* Available at: http://www.energy-community.org/pls/portal/docs/1766219.PDF.

Najam, A. and Selin, H. 2011. *Co-conveners' synthesis making sustainable development real: institutional architectures for a green economy.* In: A. Najam and H. Selin, eds. Beyond Rio+20: governance for a green economy. Boston, MA.: Boston University, pp.1–11

Orlović, S. 2011. *Political transformation and socio-economic changes in Serbia.* In: M. Stambolieva, and S. Dehnert, eds. Welfare states in transition: 20 years after the Yugoslav welfare model. Sofia: Friedrich Ebert Stiftung, pp. 262–288.

Parliament of Serbia. 2010. *Law on organic production.* Official Gazette of RS, 30/10.

Parliament of Serbia. 2011. *Law on Energy.* Official Gazette of RS, 57/13.

Parliament of Serbia., 2012. *Law on ratification of the agreement between the Government of the Serbia and Government of Italy in the field of energy.* Official Gazette of RS- MU, 7/12.

Rhodes, R. A. W., and Marsh, D. 1992. *New directions in the study of policy networks.* European Journal of Political Research, 21, pp. 181–205.

Rural 21. 2012. *Paving the way for Serbia's organic agriculture towards the EU.* Rural 21 International Journal for Rural Development (News). Available at: http://www.rural21.com/english/current-issue/detail/article/paving-the-way-for-serbias-organic-agriculture-towards-the-eu-0000442/.

Serbia Organica (n.d.). *Aktivnosti.* Available at: http://www.serbiaorganica.info/o-nama/aktivnosti/.

Skogstad, G. 2008. *Policy networks and policy communities: conceptualizing state societal relationships in the policy process.* In: L. A. White, R. Simeon, R. Vipond, R. & J. Wallner, eds. The comparative turn in Canadian political science. Vancouver: UBC Press, pp. 205–220.

Smith, M. J. 1993. *Pressure, power and policy: state autonomy and policy networks in Britain and the United States.* Hemel Hempstead: Harvester.

Stojadinović, D. 2010. *Serbia: The institutional aspects of wood energy issues in energy sector.* Available at: http://www.woodybiomass.org/PagesRS/www.woodybiomass.org/userfiles/files/ Final%20report_dejan_stojadinovic-TCPYUG3201%20(D)%20-%20Annex%2011_1_1.pdf.

Turković, M. 2012. *Large scale wind projects in Serbia: regulatory challenges and future prospects.*

Vukojčić, S. 2012. *New Serbian government ensnared in economic problems.* EurActiv. Available at: http://www.euractiv.com/enlargement/new-serbian-government-gets-enta-news-514304.

UNEP (United Nations Environment Programme). 2011. *Towards a green economy: pathways to sustainable development and poverty eradication.*

Wilks, S., and Wright, M. 1987. Comparative government industry relations: Western Europe, the United States and Japan. Oxford: Clarendon Press.

WMO (World Meteorological Organization). 2011. *WMO greenhouse gas bulletin: the state of greenhouse gasses in the atmosphere based on global observations through 2010.* Available at: http://www.wmo.int/pages/prog/arep/gaw/ghg/documents/GHGbulletin_7_en.pdf.

World Bank. 2011. *The road to prosperity: productivity and exports.* Republic of Serbia country economy memorandum. Vol. 1.

MIRUNA TRONCOTA

Still "Waiting for Godot" in Sarajevo?
Europeanization of Bosnia and Herzegovina—Between the
Contradictions of EU Conditionality and Local Ownership[1]

The article uses a case study analysis on Bosnia and Herzegovina (BiH), which represents "a test case" for Europeanization in the WB. The question of who should solve the deadlock in BiH still preoccupies both scholars and practitioners in search of a viable solution. The present article rephrases this concern by asking—Are we still waiting for Godot in Sarajevo? The aim of the article is to explore several causes of 'the never ending' governance crisis that took place in the last decade in BiH. It focuses on the following explanatory factors—the role of the international community (with the EU as a leading actor) and the dynamics of local ownership as depicted in the debate about constitutional reform. The main focus of the analysis is local ownership of reform as the underlying principle of the Europeanization process in BiH. The purpose is to analyze the way the ownership principle developed in relation to (1) the SAA negotiations, (2) the changed role of the international community in BiH and (3) to the competing versions of the constitutional change in the country between 2005–2011. In the conclusion the research shows that the politicization of EU conditionality was a determinant factor for the governance crisis (a part of the problem, and the solution at the same time). The argument is illustrated with empirical evidence focused on the debate on constitutional reform (2005–2011). By exploring the various perceptions of both policy makers and external observers over the constitutional reform, the article concludes by showing why 'the blame game' that marked the constitutional reform debate (understood as the strategy of 'Waiting for Godot') had detrimental effects for inducing reforms in BiH.

---

[1] This paper was possible with the financial support of the Sectoral Operational Programme for Human Resources Development 2007-2013, co-financed by the European Social Fund, through the project POSDRU/159/1.5/S/134650 with the title "Doctoral and Postdoctoral Fellowships for young researchers in the fields of Political, Administrative Sciences, Communication Sciences and Sociology".

Key words: Bosnia and Herzegovina, constitutional reform, EU Enlargement, Europeanization, local ownership.

Dr Miruna Troncota is a Postdoctoral Researcher at the Department for International Relations and European Integration, National University of Political Science and Public Administration, (Bucharest, Romania).

Introduction

'Who should solve the deadlock in Bosnia and Herzegovina (BiH)?' is still a question that preoccupies both scholars and practitioners in search of a viable solution. The present article rephrases this concern by asking—Are we still waiting for Godot in Sarajevo?[2] The aim of the article is to explore several causes of 'the never ending' governance crisis that took place in the last decade in Bosnia and Herzegovina (BiH) and its impact on the process of EU accession. The analysis points to the 'blame game' that takes place between local authorities and international community in BiH as a factor of destabilization in itself which impedes the implementation of EU conditionality. The analysis concentrates on the evolution of the 'local ownership of reform' as the underlying principle of the Europeanization process in BiH and incumbent contradictions when applied to the special case of BiH. The purpose is to analyze the way the ownership principle developed in relation to (1) the SAA negotiations, (2) the changed role of the international community and (3) the competing versions of the constitutional change in the country between 2005–2011.

The article is structured as follows: in the first part the article focuses on the context of Europeanization in the EU enlargement policy in the Western Balkans, and the 'special' role of the EU in Bosnia and Herzegovina, the case study. This part of the analysis will present the main assumptions on which the empirical study was conducted and the main methods employed.

The second part aims to analyze the main sequences and the main policy ideas that have defined EU conditionality in BiH between 2005 and 2011 stressing the importance of constitutional reform for BiH and the principle of local ownership. It also discusses the results of the qualitative data

---

[2] "Nothing to be done." ("*Nista ne moze da se uradi.*")—the opening line of the play *Waiting for Godot* by Samuel Beckett could be depicted as a motto that still characterizes the political deadlock in BiH. The American writer Susan Sontag staged this play at the National Theater during the siege of Sarajevo (during the period 1992–1993).

gathered on the ground by identifying the actors' interpretations of EU conditionality and the main arguments that actors have used in order to justify the policy outcomes.

The conclusions reflect on the politicization of EU conditionality in the particular case of BiH and the contradictions encountered by the principle of local ownership of reform. It shows that the way the EU effectively governs Bosnia entrenches partitions: it deals with nationalist elites as their privileged partners, mediating between them.

The challenges of europeanizing an "outlier"

As a starting point, this section discusses the concept of Europeanization applied to the Western Balkans region, the relevance of a case study on Bosnia's delayed Europeanization, and finally presents the main assumptions on which the empirical study was conducted and the main methods employed.

To date, we find a wealth of academic literature using the 'catch-all' term Europeanization, generally referring to all the transformations that occurred in Europe after the end of the Cold War and mostly focused on the process of EU integration with its subsequent enlargement. Going beyond its post-colonial connotations, from a neo-institutionalist perspective, Europeanization studies focus on the institutional mechanisms that a range of actors use to project, or 'upload', their policy preferences and approaches onto the European level, concentrating mainly on the impact of Europeanization on domestic structures (Schimmelfennig 2009). In this article, the term Europeanization refers to the mechanisms and processes through which the EU disseminates its institutions and rules of governance in the wider international system through the tools of EU conditionality[3].

In particular, the Europeanization of the Western Balkans (WB hereafter)[4] is one of the most challenging subjects in recent EU studies. The topic provided a handful of analyses that highlighted the new obstacles the EU

---

[3] More precisely, since the launch of the Copenhagen criteria in 1993 the purpose of EU conditionality as a mechanism of Europeanization was to set a common system of norms and rules perceived as legitimate by the future candidate countries in order to obtain EU membership.

[4] The WB denominates the following countries that aim at EU membership—Albania, Bosnia and Herzegovina, Kosovo, Former Yugoslav Republic of Macedonia, Serbia and Montenegro.

has encountered in the WB inside its norm transfer process, after its experience with the 10 countries from the Central and East Europe (CEE). The EU was thus confronted with a region with very specific problems, marked by the violent dissolution of Yugoslavia, and the aftermath of the other conflicts in Kosovo (1999) and FYR Macedonia (2001). The region was most commonly regarded as an 'outlier' inside EU's conditionality-led enlargement policy initially designed for the CEE countries. Therefore the EU policymakers had to experiment various formulas for inducing policy change in this new context, by adapting their instruments and their incentives to the peculiarities of the WB.

In a period marked by the very positive performance of several countries from the region (such as Croatia's membership of the EU on the 1st of July 2013 and the official start of EU accession negotiations for Serbia in January 2014) there is a need to reflect more on the situation in the other countries that do not follow this trend. Contrary to this evolution, in the case of Bosnia and Herzegovina (BiH hereafter) the situation has actually worsened in recent years, against the intense efforts of the international community to move the country forward from post-conflict stabilization to integration and democratization. In its externally driven struggle for stabilization and democratization and finally for future EU membership, Bosnia is worth being more closely analyzed as it comprises a complex set of factors that account for this 'outlier' position in the EU's enlargement policy, or as some call in more negative terms 'the periphery of the periphery'.

There is a widely accepted opinion that the current stalemate in BiH has a detrimental effect on the region that questions the EU's tool of conditionality in the enlargement process. As such, the following study tries to tackle the main challenges of Europeanization in BiH through the eyes of the most active actors engaged in the process focusing on the period between 2005–2011 connected to the Stabilization and Association Agreement (SAA) negotiations[5]. Focusing on the case of BiH can be fruitful in order to show that there are numerous lessons which were already learnt

---

[5] The analysis stops at the year 2011 because it marked an important shift in EU's approach towards BiH—EU reshaped its position in BiH, by placing the EUSR as the Head of the Delegation of the European Union in BiH, creating therefore a strengthened position that reports both to the European Commission and to the newly founded institution European External Action Service (EEAS).

in recent years. But one can also point to the lessons not yet learnt from EU's 'test case', valuable for further application on the entire Balkan region. There are multiple ways of approaching the concept of Europeanization in contemporary European integration studies, but I have chosen a neo-institutionalist perspective for exploring the topic. I also assumed a more constructivist understanding of political negotiations in the EU enlargement framework, based on qualitative research techniques because I believe that this particular case study requires a more contextualized and nuanced analytic perspective.

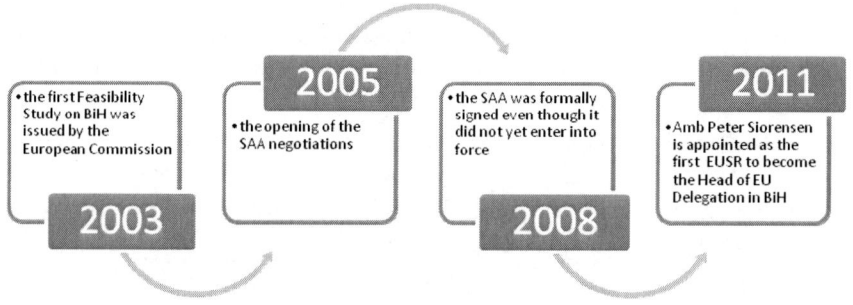

Picture 1. Focal Points in BiH's timeline to the EU, edited by the author

BiH has been a potential candidate for EU membership since 2003. Negotiations on a SAA were opened in 2005, but due to rather slow progress in implementing reforms it was only signed in 2008 and since then no other change has occurred (BiH did not fully implement the SAA and could not send its application for membership as it was expected to in 2011) (as depicted in Picture 1). Analyzed in the EU conditionality context, BiH is placed at the end of the 'enlargement queue' (blocked in the 'EU's waiting room' under the status of 'potential candidate countries') together with the other problematic state in the region which declared independence in 2008, Kosovo. Studies so far show that Europeanization in the case of BiH has been for a long time dependent on external incentives, not on local initiatives and this became a major obstacle for development (Soberg 2009; Chandler 2006; Bieber 2010). Literature on the topic concludes that despite EU conditionality, most reform processes are "stuck" because of the deeply divided society and the prevalent conflicts between the ethnic groups. On one hand, this type of approach puts the whole responsibility for the failure on local politicians. But on the other hand, it also points to the fact that the EU has not performed impressively in persuading local authorities in BiH to engage with radical reforms (regarding, for instance, the constitutional area). This type of "blame shifting" from one side to the other motivated me to conduct a series of interviews with relevant policy makers but also with external observers of the process in order to find out who is exactly the Godot that all actors have been waiting for and who is able to solve this political deadlock that has existed in BiH for the last 5 years. The basic assumption of the research is that the interplay between internal and external factors is one of the main challenges for Europeanization in BiH. As a consequence, the main focus of the analysis is the concept of "local ownership of reform" as the underlying principle of the Europeanization process in BiH.

As such, it is also necessary to provide a few details about the qualitative methodology employed in the research project. Firstly, I mapped the main political events that have influenced the evolution of EU conditionality in BiH (2005–2011) by identifying constitutional reform as one of the core policy issues in BiH and "the local ownership of reforms" as the guiding principle in that debate. Secondly, I conducted a series of interviews with relevant policy makers but also with experts from Brussels, Banja Luka, Brcko, Mostar and Sarajevo in order to explore their perceptions over this period and the impact of the constitutional reform debate on BiH's road map towards EU accession. The analysis presents the main results and an interpretation of the data gathered during the field study.

Based on the neo-institutional perspective assumed here, Europeanization is understood as an essentially elite driven process, being a process of high-level negotiations that involves both bureaucrats and politicians. In the EU Enlargement process (described as rule transfer process aimed at EU integration) both bureaucrats (policy makers) and politicians interact in specific institutional settings which both restrict and enable their decisions with the result of compliant or non-compliant behavior. Such an understanding of the term requires an in-depth focus on the way elites, in a strategic manner (either in their own interest or constrained by the main institutional structures as explored using semi-structured interviewing as the main method) master the 'rules of the game'. The aim was to confront the main literature driven observations with the perceptions of several policy makers both from EU and BiH which were directly involved in the implementation of EU conditionality in BiH.

Why is Bosnia "special"? The narratives of exceptionality

Studies in the field point to various reasons why Bosnia is considered an "exception" inside the Thessaloniki enlargement package. The legitimate question to be asked is thus "what are the implications of this status of 'exception to the rule' for the implementation of EU conditionality in BiH?" I have grouped the various answers that both scholars and practitioners try to offer to this question as "narratives of BiH's exceptionality" and this constituted the starting point that guided the empirical part.

Firstly, the "exceptionality" of the BiH case study lies in the fact that Bosnia is often perceived as an epicentre of the entire Balkan region, within the privileged position of so-called "little Yugoslavia".[6] Most of its domestic issues (such as internal security and police, safe borders, functional institutions, a centralized type of managing EU affairs and so on) have direct connection with either its neighbors, or by the direct intervention of foreign powers and the international community. This complicated interdependence of factors makes the process of conflict transformation in BiH a priority for both the international community and the other ex-Yugoslav countries, placing BiH as the key to regional cooperation and effective Europeanization in the WB.

Secondly, BiH is often described as an exceptional case challenging the strategy of EU conditionality because of its Post-Dayton institutional structure. In scholarly discourses, as well as in the accounts of practitioners, the root of all the problems that BiH faces in its road to the EU is to be found in the Dayton Peace Agreement (DPA). This type of narrative concentrates on the fact that BiH has an institutional structure which is unique in the world. The country's population of 3.8 million is governed by no fewer than 14 governments—1 at the state level, 2 at the entity level (Republika Srspska and Federation of Bosnia and Herzegovina), 10 at the cantonal level (in FBiH municipalities) and 1 for the autonomous District of Brcko. With 14 constitutions and governments with legislative powers, the political system of Bosnia is both inherently complex and dysfunctional,

---

[6] There is also a saying in the local language that confirms this observation—"Bosna je srce Balkana". In translation from Bosnian Croat Serbian (BCS) language—" Bosnia is the heart of the Balkans".

with levels of governance with overlapping authorities. This constitutional structure, which evidently accords primacy to ethno-national rights and demands, is outlined in Annex 4 of the Dayton agreement. Due to the war legacies and the multiethnic nature of the population, BiH became a 'multiethnic consociational experiment'—a unitary state without a clear majority but with three main ethnic-religious groups (Bosniak-Muslims, Serb-Orthodox and Croat-Catholics) alongside various other smaller groups of different ethnicities. "The state administratively weak at the centre and politically polarized by ethno territorial governance" (Bieber 2006: 7) is also governed by the Office of the High Representative (OHR hereafter), an ad hoc international institution responsible for overseeing implementation of civilian aspects of the DPA. OHR has become an integral institution to the Dayton order in Bosnia, which under the so-called "Bonn Powers" given in 1997 has made nearly 900 decisions over thirteen years, e.g. enacting laws and removing elected officials (Szewczyk 2010). As such, the political system of BiH exhibits an essential feature of a "hybrid regime" where democratic (power sharing principles) and non-democratic (international supervision and Bonn powers) institutions and mechanisms have co-existed for more than a decade. Consequently, another factor frequently used in the narrative pointing to BiH's exceptionality is the overlapping authority of the various actors of Europeanization (actors in charge with policy formulation at both national and EU level). Both the EU and BiH provide a myriad of actors involved in the process of Europeanization, resulting from multi-layered structures of governance in both cases, each with its own specificity and complexity (for BiH the DPA institutional structure, for the EU 'the pillarization' of competences between inter-governmental and communitarian policies before the Lisbon Treaty entered into force in 2009). Related to the issue of representation, this set of narratives claim that BiH is different than other countries as it does not "speak with one voice" and it lacks coordination between the main institutions especially with regards to the EU affairs (where state, entity and even cantonal competencies overlap).

Moreover, BiH's exceptionality is based also on the EU's complex involvement in the country. In the aftermath of the war, BiH provided conditions for the EU to "test" its operational capabilities and as such it has "experimented" its foreign policy potential in neighboring areas, especially when it deployed EUFOR Mission Althea as its first ever peace-building project. The EU deployed all means at its disposal to support BiH reform, ranging from technical and financial support to meet *acquis* standards long before the SAA negotiations had started. Ever since, the EU also continues to be present in BiH within the framework of the Common Foreign and Security Policy (CFSP previously called European Security and Defence Policy) with three instruments—EUFOR a military mission which maintains stability in the country, EUSR a Special Representative that supports reform processes on a daily basis and coordinates EU actors on the ground and EUPM—EU Police Mission in Bosnia-Herzegovina, that became the EU's first civil crisis management operation in January 2003 and was closed in 2012. These three bodies, which reported to the inter-governmental arm of the EU (the Council of the EU and after 2010 to the EEAS) have complemented the policy making and technical aid given by the European Commission (EC) Delegation in BiH. Even though the Delegation of the European Commission in Bosnia was the main actor responsible for identifying issues, setting the agenda and framing the EU's policy in BiH, all CFSP actors cooperated though in different degrees for the implementation of EU conditionality and the closure of the OHR.

Thirdly, inside this narrative of BiH's exceptionality from a multi-layered institutional perspective, a special highlight is put on the 'double hatted' position of EUSR and High Representative (HR) which lasted until late 2011. Back in February 2002, the European Union's General Affairs Council (GAC) appointed the HR as the EUSR in BiH which was added to the Office of HR (instituted by Annex 10 of the DPA)—international envoy responsible for the supervision of the implementation of civilian aspects of the DPA. Thus, Lord Paddy Ashdown (2002–2006) became the first to hold the double-hats of EUSR and HR simultaneously.

And finally, the type of domestic power elites in charge with EU affairs in BiH also features in the narrative of BiH's exceptionality. As a consequence of the power sharing mechanisms of the DPA, the consensus between the main party leaders in BiH is decisive in any type of policy debate and decision making mechanism in BiH. Opposite to other countries, in BiH the domestic actors hold "special" powers to block the reforms based on the DPA institutional arrangement (and the system of ethnic vetoes that are at their disposal in the national Parliament). In order for any policy change to take place they all need to agree over the course of action and the decision needs to be taken by consensus. These veto rights enable them to act strategically through what can be called "ethnic entrepreneurship" by invoking the "vital national interest" of their ethnic community in order to block the adoption of laws (more in Bieber, 2006). As such, structurally local party leaders in BiH use ethnic-based discourses to win their electorates and maintain power, which means they have no incentives for reaching consensus.

From "Bonn powers" to "Brussels powers"? Constitutional reform and the politicization of EU conditionality

This section focuses on the perceptions of various actors on the formalized interactions between the EU and BiH inside the enlargement framework depicted in the main policy narratives that I analyzed, classified and put together in an explanatory framework.

All actors who have been interviewed have pointed to the inadequacy of the Dayton constitutional system for the EU integration process. They have also identified as the core obstacle for any further EU driven reform in the country the internal conflict between the central state and the entities (a specific feature of BiH's Dayton institutional order). This issue is mainly tackled by one of the most contentious aspects for the proper implementation of the EU conditionality—the constitutional reform debate. As such, the structures of Dayton itself are seen as a real obstacle to stabilization, efficiency and prosperity. Therefore, I have identified constitutional reform as a policy issue which was intensely debated in connection with EU conditionality between 2005 and 2011 and which is still on the agenda at the moment.

Another important element is the fact that the EU's overall perception of the importance of constitutional reform in BiH has fluctuated over time. Several respondents have indicated the year 2006 as an important one for the EU's shift of policy towards a more active role in BiH with implications also on its position in the constitutional reform debate. In early 2006 the Peace Implementation Council (PIC)[7] made a decision on the conditional OHR closure (what later became the 5 plus 2 conditionality), inside which

---

[7] The Peace Implementation Council (PIC) was established on December 8–9 1995 in London, after the Dayton Peace Agreement. It comprises 55 countries and agencies that support the peace process in many different ways—by assisting financially, providing troops for EUFOR, or directly running operations in Bosnia and Herzegovina. More details on http://www.ohr.int/pic/default.asp?content_id=38563 (accessed on 10.09. 2013)

the prevailing idea was that the EUSR should become the primary representative of the international community in BiH. Indeed, soon after that, the EU opened the SAA negotiations for BiH. Inside the constitutional reform debate, the exit-strategy of the OHR from BiH also had an important place. The main policy prescription that pervaded this debate accentuated the need for the transformation of the role of the HR from a decision-maker into that of a mediator. In this context, the EU's role in general was expected to be more visible, and to deal efficiently with its ongoing challenges (one of them being the revision of the DPA). Therefore, a strengthening of the EUSR's mandate was required in order to replace the HR but without any Bonn powers (the decoupling of HR and EUSR occurred in September 2011, when Peter Sorensen was named the head of the Delegation of the EU in BiH and the first EUSR to be separated from the OHR). Interviewed policy makers have pointed to the fact that the constitutional reform debate opened the 'Pandora's box' of the international community in BiH.

Since early 2006 the constitutional reform process was associated with the EU's view that the process should be internally driven, in a democratic way and placed under the leadership of local leaders[8]. However, this was visible more at the level of policy statements than in practice. Many interviewees have argued that the DPA was not the top priority for the EU in BiH in that phase. Actually, constitutional reform has never been "per se" a condition

---

[8] Commissioner Olli Rehn, responsible for Enlargement at that time, has synthesized EU's perspective on the issue in a speech in front of the European Parliament in Strasbourg in 2006 entitled "Perspectives for Bosnia and Herzegovina"—" *The reform of the "Dayton Constitution" is another important task Bosnian political leaders need to undertake. The country needs a constitution that:—ensures full compatibility with the European Convention for Human Rights;—allows smooth decision-making and proper governance;—streamlines the various level of government and makes it less costly. It is necessary for the country to develop a democratic, functional and affordable multi-ethnic state able to serve better all its citizens and to support the reforms that EU integration entails. I welcome the recent efforts by the leading political parties in Bosnia and Herzegovina to find practical and workable solutions to constitutional challenges. I encourage political leaders to continue their dialogue so as to achieve more ambitious results. I do not expect a constitutional revolution to take place, rather an evolution. Indeed, I consider that constitutional reform has to be a consensus-driven process with Bosnia and Herzegovina clearly in the lead. The international community can act as facilitator, but Bosnian politicians must be in the driving seat".* http://europa.eu/rapid/press-release_SPEECH-07-147_en.htm [accessed on 10.09.2013]

for concluding the negotiations of the SAA[9]. But for the country to make sure that constitutional provisions guarantee the proper implementation of the Agreement, a consensus over the DPA was acknowledged as a sensitive political and technical issue that would "make Bosnia work"[10]. Commission's Progress Reports have noted each year that constitutional reform is necessary "to improve functionality and to ensure the protection of human rights" (EC Enlargement Strategy 2006–2007: 6). These two main reasons have become the key justifications whenever the EU tackled the need for constitutional reform (relying in this perspective on the technical and very precise recommendations made by the Venice Commission in 2005 and the ECHR in 2009 on the Sejdic and Finci ruling). Just as police reform was the main priority for signing the SAA, in the new version of EU conditionality for BiH the main priority is to change the constitution to comply with a ruling that the European Court for Human Rights (ECHR) made in 2009[11]. Nevertheless, the more engaged involvement of the EU since 2009 in the constitutional reform (starting with "the Butmir process") did not help the process.

When interacting with these elites, the position of the EU tried to 'technify' and 'depoliticize' both the police and the constitutional reform debates. As such, my observation was that EU policymakers did not acknowledge the fact that the attempt to "shake" Dayton risks reopening unsettled issues and it is perceived by the local elites as a threat to the interests of the main ethnic groups of BiH, which still maintain a low level

---

[9] The key elements that for BiH to fulfil in order to give a credible membership request to the EU as defined in 2010
-the amendment of the Constitution of BiH in accordance with the Sejdić-Finci ruling;
-the consistent implementation of the Interim Agreement on Trade and Trade related Issues;
-the implementation of the Stabilisation and Association Agreement and
-the establishment of effective coordination of EU affairs

[10] The HR/EUS Miroslav Lajčák concluded in a statement from 2008, which is indicative of the cautious EU approach to constitutional reform "Constitutional reform is neither a requirement for OHR closure nor for BiH's further journey towards the EU. Nevertheless, "the constitutional framework must evolve to ensure effective state structures capable of delivering on EU integration, including the requirement to speak with one voice." (quoted in Venneri, 2010:126).

[11] The so-called "Sejdic and Finci ruling" says that Bosnia must find a way to ensure that all its citizens, whatever their ethnic identification, be allowed to stand for the state-level presidency.

of intra-communal trust. As I could conclude during my interactions with the members of the ethnic communities I could draw the following picture—the Bosniak community, for example, saw the institutional and procedural changes outlined in the April Package, Prud or Butmir processes as a good starting point to promote further centralization, from the Entities to the national government and as such it used the EU requirement for better coordination as a way to legitimize centralization and more Sarajevo-based power. In contrast with this approach, Bosnian Serb leaders have been for the maintenance of a highly decentralized system based on the recognition of strong prerogatives to the Entities. The Serbs saw the parameters proposed by the international community as an attempt to set the scene for a change of the system established by the Dayton Agreement and consequently as a direct attack on the very existence of the Republika Srpska in the long run. For both the Serbian and Croatian populations these efforts for constitutional reform are perceived as an attempt to somehow 'revise the results of the war' as one of the respondent argued, and transform the currently confederal structure into 'a unified state in which the Bosniaks, (as the largest ethnic group), "are elevated to the position of titular nation" (interview nr 40, min 8). Based on these perceptions, obstruction has become their main aim.

I would therefore propose that for EU representatives the constitutional reform process is first of all filtered through the instrumental logic of cost and benefit calculations. As such their overall perception of the issue was that constitutional reform aimed to establish a new consensus over the Bosnian state in more efficient terms (reducing the overlapping and dysfunctional administrative layers and finding better procedures for inter-institutional coordination). In their eyes, efficiency and functionality were the dominating principles that should have guided the process. Seen as a matter of technicality, the reform process would not require any "special need" from the part of the EU (especially not in the context of SAA negotiations, as it was assumed that all the enlargement countries in general had had to make such demanding administrative changes). With this "neutral" approach towards the DPA reform, EU policy makers would have expected to avoid any further politicization of the process and to wither away the ethnic rhetoric. Conversely, in the view of the local actors interviewed, this policy had other implications because changing the DPA is associated with a more complex and profound array of arguments translated in the end in fuzzy policy prescriptions and the "traditional" zero sum game of non-cooperation. These observations point to certain specific features that lead to the politicization/instrumentalization of the EU integration perspective in BiH, which has weakened the instrument of conditionality, deepening the divisions rather than uniting forces for a common project. This rapid shift from "the Bonn powers" to "the Brussels powers" has contributed to the continuous politicization of EU conditionality in BiH.

In this context, the analysis argues that changing the DPA is perceived at the same time as a 'carrot' and 'a stick' by the diverse group of domestic elites. This ambivalence is misleading and does not make the cost and benefit calculation of the EU conditionality effective. Divergence of meanings attached to EU conditionality is therefore one of the causes of the institutional paralysis and the failure of EU driven reforms in BiH (what one party sees as a stick, the other perceives as carrot). This observation questions the strategy of using the EU membership "carrot" as an incentive to induce significant policy changes in a divided society, as well as a tool to face nationality-sensitive matters and unresolved post-conflict issues (a similar argument applied on the case of Croatia, see Freyburg, Richter 2010).

Who should take the lead in BiH? The narrative of local ownership

As it can be observed in the failed attempts to reach a general view about changing Annex 4 of the DPA (April package, Prud Agreement and Butmir process) the main policy prescription put forward by EU policy makers (and which is mostly visible in EC Progress reports starting with 2007) is the principle of" local ownership of reforms" which implies the empowerment of local elites in BiH in a shared project towards the implementation of EU conditionality. An important observation is that various meanings have been attached to this leading concept of "local ownership. Based on these various understandings, there are multiple policy-making initiatives either to strengthen or to soften the EU's intervention in Bosnian politics.

The 'local ownership narrative' started to manifest among policy makers from the beginning of the SAA negotiations in 2005. In very general terms, this principle states that only a greater involvement by the local elites inside an internally driven approach might help BiH overcome the current phase of stagnation. In June 2006 the PIC-SB Political Directors adopted a communiqué titled: *'Towards Ownership: From Peace Implementation to Euro-Atlantic Integration'*, which clarified that the process for the closure of the OHR had to start immediately, in order to be completed within at most one year and therefore allow BiH 'to take full responsibility for its own affairs" (PIC-SB, 2006). This was the first meeting of the PIC-SB after initialling the SAA", in which the five objectives and two conditions were identified as a final mandatory test for Bosnian political elites prior to giving the green light for the OHR closure which was planned for 2008. What I would like to underline at this point is that the debate about the closure of the OHR started around the same date as the failure of police reform, which occurred after the first failed rounds of negotiations of the constitutional reform (the April package in 2006). This is the main argument in favor of the observation made by that several policy makers that I have interviewed — that the plan for closing the OHR motivated EU's shift of policy toward an accentuated locally driven approach to policy making in BiH.

The first root of the problem as identified in this narrative is the long dependency of BiH authorities on international aid (whether in moral or material support). A policy prescription based on this observation is that foreign aid should be reduced in BiH in order for the country to move forward from a semi-protectorate to a full sovereign country with a realistic prospect of a future EU membership. This perspective stresses the fact that a strengthened local ownership of BiH reformist project should be based on the democratic principles of transparency, responsibility and accountability of local leaders in front of their constituencies (BiH citizens). Another policy implication of this is that the use of Bonn powers to impose certain reforms is not compatible with the status of EU candidacy, as it is undemocratic. As such, democratization should be the first pre-requisite of Europeanization and this is incompatible with the presence of the HR in BiH. The OHR closure touched upon the 'double-hatting' of HR and EUSR, which was envisaged as a provisional arrangement during which the political focus in BiH would shift from Dayton implementation to the EU integration process. The EUSR aimed to coordinate and ensure the coherence of the EU presence in BiH, and its responsibilities were clearly separated from the ones of the HR, especially during police reform (2004–2008) proved not to have succeeded in this attempt (Batt 2009; Tolksdorf 2011). Its role extended for over 9 years (2002–2011).

The main ideas promoted in this context were that the policy of "top-down international imposition" (in which the Bonn powers of the OHR were dominating the reforms, over riding any local initiative and 'punishing 'nationalist rhetoric that opposed any compromise as it was the case with the partially failed police reform) had detrimental effects on the political life of BiH and it directly influenced its policy making capacity on the road to the EU. Moreover, this "policy of strong hand", which created domestic dependency on inducing reforms and taking the decisions, showed its limits and needed to be changed. In turn, according to this narrative, the EU had to assume the position of a "soft" external pressure in order to induce local ownership and the implementation of EU conditionality, so that BiH could apply for membership by 2011. Since 2006, the EU took the leading role in the international community for the democratization of BiH but at the same it preserved a "moderated" involvement in any discussions over the constitutional reform ('a hands off' approach as Venneri (2010) calls it). This "hands off" approach was correlated with the "local ownership narrative. This perspective was interestingly illustrated by one EU senior advisers during interviews, who clearly stressed the main points in EU's definition of local ownership in BiH—"What we mean by ownership of reform? It's simple. Responsibility of the Bosnian elites in front of all citizens of BiH. Someone needs to counter act to the present policy of ethnic mobilization practiced by political elites, in their "divisive rhetoric" and behavior that further polarizes the political atmosphere in BiH in an artificial way. There is no sign of responsibility in their attitude and this is what Bosnia needs most." (interview nr 47, min 10–12). Another diplomat from an EU country also stressed this point—. "Local elites in Bosnia lack the exercise of engaging in common, inclusive projects. Therefore they need to practice coordination on their own. In Europe we have learned to do this after World War Two, and it was worthy in the end." (interview nr 16, min 7).

Therefore, as a solution for the institutional deadlock this narrative underlined the need for the principle of local ownership to guide the reforms in order to enforce changes within a bottom up approach (unlike the DPA which was an externally driven constitutional order adapted to the rough conditions of the war). Another correlated policy prescription of this perspective is the need to rethink the structure of the international presence in BiH and promote a transfer of responsibilities from the OHR to domestic authorities which is an essential element which also implies constitutional reform (the OHR being part of the DPA order). "Europe's philosophy is a philosophy of partnership, while strengthening the OHR is a continuation of the protectorate" as one of the journalists in Sarajevo stated (interview nr 45, min 7). Therefore, the closure of the OHR should be backed by the policy of local ownership mediated by the soft powers of the EU. To put this in the terms of one of the scholars I interviewed: "The presence of an institution equipped with the Bonn Powers represents a serious limitation on the country's 'ownership for decision-making and reform'; the EU prospect of membership cannot substantially stimulate a domestic constitutional debate if it is not backed up by a constant and active mediation, without any "outside" intervention in the decision making processes". (interview nr 23, min 67). In opposition to the past OHR's strategies of 'Europeanization by decree', this approach pleads for a" locally owned process" based on shared meanings that would facilitate the smooth implementation of EU driven reforms. In order to fully implement EU requirements, local elites need to share a common vision of the country's future and this internally driven vision would be the basis for any potential constitutional reform. "The EU cannot impose a solution. What we can do is use our policies to encourage and facilitate progress, and we will continue to do that" as one independent expert working with the Delegation of EU in Sarajevo stated (interview nr 1, min 7). The main policy prescription of this narrative is that EU will not impose any of its conditionality provisions in BiH as this goes against the basic principles of EU enlargement comprised in the Copenhagen criteria, which are constructed on the premises of "shared values" between the aspiring country and the EU. In contrast to the previous set of narratives in the local ownership narrative the EU should avoid using any of the executive powers used by the HR. An EU policy maker phrased that idea in the following way: "a EUSR with any form of executive powers, as this would be in contrast to European values". (Interview nr 56, min 8). The subsequent policy prescription which follows from this perspective is that EU's role in BiH should be the one of mediator, not enforcer.

Nevertheless, I would argue that one of the main flaws in this policy prescription was that it was unrealistic for the assumed correlation between closure of the OHR and an increase in local ownership to take place in such a short period of time. In order for Bosnia to continue to function, the OHR has frequently been forced to impose, amend or strike down laws as well as remove recalcitrant politicians and police officials. The idea that the closure of the OHR would automatically result in local ownership and a more responsible political attitude on the part of domestic elites was not based on solid grounds[12].

These characteristics relating to the 'special type of elites in BiH' need to be correlated also with another significant factor which also occurred during these three rounds of failed negotiations—namely that EU conditionality was used by domestic leaders as an opportunity for political gains along with the use of divisive rhetoric. Local actors therefore have systemic incentives to "over-politicize" the SAA negotiations, far beyond the EU's policy prescriptions in relation with its political conditionality. The strategic element of bargaining various versions of the DPA in the last 5 years has empowered local politicians to "ethnicize" EU conditionality and delay the progress on requested reforms. It gave them "room for political maneuver". As such I would like to draw attention to the fact that the local ownership narrative posits the danger of bringing into BiH's political life an incentive for deepening 'ethnicization' of all major reform debates in the EU conditionality framework. The EU's strategy for strengthening local ownership in BiH might end by creating the premises for the failure of EU conditionality itself because instead of using the EU driven policy ideas as integrative and consensus building "spaces", the so-called "Ethnocrats" have instrumentalized them as rather divisive factors in order to increase their "exclusivist" bargain power deeply rooted in the DPA system. The results were not encouraging—the OHR was not closed, local ownership was not achieved and no substantial change in the political agenda has occurred since 2008.

Several respondents have mentioned during interviews a sort of 'Bosnia fatigue' at the level of EU representatives, correlated with an 'EU fatigue' at

---

[12] I would illustrate this argument with the point of the renown political anthropologist specialized on BiH Robert Hayden who stated that "the idea of, for example, Arend Lijphart that one can just walk in there and implement a 'consociational democracy' is one of the biggest political myths of all times. (..)Consociational models, in the end, depend on the elite's ability to ignore the population. In Bosnia, for example, there is no consociational democracy simply because there isn't a 'Bosnian' elite; there's a Serb elite, a Croatian elite, and so on, who respond not so much to each other's action, but to the action of those they claim to represent. Robert Hayden, online interview 2010 http://www.theory-talks.org/2008/08/theory-talk-16.html [accessed on 10.07.2013]

the level of BiH representatives. Both parties were thus perpetuating a sort of "policy of postponing concrete reforms and "waiting for an abstract Godot" that would make Bosnia work. Lack of success in the process of democratic consolidation and reforms resulted in frustration from both sides of the population and the international community in BiH, and this gave space for a rising ethnicization of the debate by the local elites. As such, I would argue that the principle of local ownership as contextualized in the case of BiH cannot be successful in implementing EU conditionality and this policy could be more effective if implemented gradually, just as EU policy makers started to do after the year 2011. The change of policy that occurred in 2012[13] confirms that policy makers acknowledged the shortcomings of their previous strategy towards the WB and towards BiH in particular.

Conclusions: Europeanization in Bosnia and Herzegovina—the "policy of waiting for Godot" ?

The article concludes by providing an overview of the role of the EU in BiH, reviewing the main instruments and practices used by the EU to make a shift from post-war stabilization to an agenda of enlargement.

The main argument on this issue is that the two groups of elites that managed BiH's Europeanization have continually reproduced divergent interpretations of EU conditionality in BiH ('the Blame Game' between locals and internationals) which ended up with maintaining the status quo and further delaying the process of Europeanization. In the negotiation process the political representatives of the three constituent peoples are being 'reinforced' in their authority as exclusive representatives of their ethnic communities in detriment to other "different" voices which are not even heard (as the 2009 ECHR Sejdic and Finci ruling on the discrimination of minorities in BiH confirmed). As such, there is almost no space for "alternative" voices that would change the overall dynamics of this "ethnicized" policy making process, as the main leaders (some of them being directly involved in the Bosnian war and continuing its legacy in their political rhetoric) are being re-elected and given the centre-stage position by the citizens (as it happened in the 2006 and 2010 elections).

---

[13] In June 2012 The European Commission launched the High Level Accession Dialogue with Bosnia and Herzegovina and the Road Map for BiH's EU membership application.

Similarly to the play written by Samuel Beckett—where the lead characters are waiting for someone who never appears—the analysis argued that the Europeanization of BiH is characterized by various policy narratives of legitimizing failure, pointing as the root of all negative facts to the "Other" side (the Blame game) and waiting for a solution to come from elsewhere. The local ownership narrative promoted by the EU ended up in an institutional paralysis. After 2008, in place of 'the strong arm' of the OHR, the international community relied more consistently on the EU's soft power and therefore the local ownership narrative became predominant. The context in which these reform attempts took place in BiH was rapidly moving from the resolute and more interventionist use of special powers (for example Bonn Powers) to a more proactive reform-pushing approach, and from conditionality-compliance relationship to partnership (what the article called "Brussels powers"). As such, I conclude that the meanings attached to EU conditionality by the main actors could not provide a basis for a common narrative for the accession of BiH to the EU. The EU focused its strategy (in the SAA negotiations) on this type of consensus building activities which were meant to be achieved with the help of the "technical" benchmarks of strict EU conditionality (especially the European partnerships were designed as such). What I would like to add in this perspective is that all actors had their share of contribution in this process.

In such a context, Europeanization became a process marked by asymmetry and uncertainty between power elites, which in fact empowered local authorities to act with a non-compliant behavior and to contribute even further to the "politicization" of EU conditionality. The move from the strong 'Bonn powers' (external intervention narrative) to the soft "Brussels powers" (local ownership narrative) proved to be a very fast and unsustainable shift from one extreme to the other.

The analysis showed that, despite the revival of EU's emphasis on partnership between the two parties and a call for domestic ownership of the process, the process of European integration in BiH exemplified some of the limits of earlier *top-down policies* conducted under the external intervention of Bonn powers. As long as Europeanization is structured around the idea of the increasing involvement of the EU in BiH with the intent of including BiH into European institutions and socializing it by means of European norms, its results were distorted by the 'legacy' of the previous external imposition strategy practiced by the OHR which characterized international intervention in BiH for the most part of the last decade. This policy left BiH in a perpetual crisis of governance at the intersection of these top down and bottom up conflicting pressures.

In conclusion, the article argues that the local ownership principle as depicted in the constitutional reform debates was not beneficial for the fulfilment of EU conditionality as it risked to deepen "the ethnicization" of the accession agenda and to empower domestic veto players. Local ownership, in order to produce the desired policy change, needs to be gradually achieved through trust-building activities between all actors involved. The shift from one policy to the other was too rapid, so the local elites, after being socialized with Bonn powers "sticks" than the EU "carrots" could not cope with change to their political non-cooperative practices. The shift between the two policies needs to take longer, to be gradual and more focused on 'small steps' and this seems to be the position EU has adopted since 2011 after Ambassador Sorensen became the new enforced EUSR. The OHR is still formally present in BiH (even though it now has a rather symbolic role, without any concrete interference in the decision making system) but the EU is now more coherently engaged pleading again for more responsibility in the process and lowering the benchmarks. Nevertheless, it is hard to evaluate whether this moderated strategy (that combines elements from both external imposition and local ownership narratives) will be efficient in inducing reform in BiH.

This type of explanation touches upon the intrinsic political nature of EU conditionality that implies profound changes not only in the field of policy, but also in the more intricate fields of polity and politics. In order to address this problem of fragmented elites and divergent policymaking in BiH I focused on the discursive interactions between the 'technifying' approach with the equally influential 'politicizing' approach to EU conditionality in the broad debates about how to change the DPA. The study concludes by observing that subsequent policy shifts and un-coordinated institutional practices targeted at advancing reform have produced quite the opposite—stagnation and institutional paralysis. As such, the study opts for the term 'delayed' and not for the term 'failed' Europeanization as it sees it as an open-ended process in continuous evolution, not as a frozen set of factors able to be standardized as a "failure". This analytic perspective is therefore based on a dynamic view on Europeanization as a matter of reciprocity between EU and domestic institutional practices which mutually adapt to each other. The continuous "blame game" between local authorities and the international community (mainly the EU) for this situation has rather deepened the problem, instead of offering a solution. Thus the research identified this as one of the main reasons for the delayed Europeanization of BiH and its deep institutional crisis inside what I tried to comprise with the metaphor of "the policy of waiting for Godot" in search of a miraculous and abstract solution to the Bosnian constitutional deadlock.

References

Communiqué of the Steering Board of the Peace Implementation Council, Towards Ownership: From Peace Implementation to Euro-Atlantic Integration, November 2006 Available at: http://www.ohr.int/pic/default.asp?content_id=37503. [accessed at 10.09.2012]

Communique by Olli Rehn in the European Parliament, 2006. Strasbourg *Europe's next frontiers*. Available at: http://stajano.deis.unibo.it/UP2006/3.Enlargement/OlliRehn-SPEECH-06-626_EN-Europe%92sNextFrontiers.pdf [accessed at 10.09.2012]

Batt, J. 2009. *Bosnia and Herzegovina: The International Mission at a Turning Point*, Fride Policy Brief, No. 5, February, available at http://www.fride.org/download/PB5_Bosnia_Herzegovina_ENG_feb09.pdf [accessed at 10.09.2012]

Bahtić-Kunrath, B. 2011. *Of Veto Players and Entity Voting: Institutional Gridlock in the Bosnian Reform Process*, Nationalities Papers: The Journal of Nationalism and Ethnicity, 39(6), pp. 899–923;

Bieber, F. 2006. Post-War Bosnia: Ethnicity, Inequality and Public Sector Governance, London: Palgrave, pp 6–7.

Bieber, F. 2006, "*After Dayton, Dayton? The Evolution of an Unpopular Peace.*" Ethnopolitics, 1, pp. 28–30.

Bieber, F. 2010. *Constitutional reform in Bosnia and Herzegovina: preparing for EU accession*, European Policy Centre Brussels Policy Brief, available online at www.mercury.ethz.ch/serviceengine/Files/ISN/.../PB_04_10_Bosnia.pdf [access date 10.09.2013]

Chandler, D. (ed). 2006. Peace without Politics? Ten Years of State-building in Bosnia, London:Routledge.

Dzihic, V. 2009. *Europeanization and new constitutional solutions—a way out of the vicious crisis cycle of crises in Bosnia and Herzegovina*, in The Political Science Research Center, available at http://www.cpi.hr/en-10665_bosnia_and_herzegovina_how_to_come_to_a_sustainable_solution.htm [accessed at 10.09.2012]

Dzihic, V. and Wieser, An. 2011. *Incentives for Democratisation? Effects of EU Conditionality on Democracy in Bosnia & Hercegovina*, 63(10) Europe-Asia Studies, pp. 1803–1825.

Dizdarević, S. 2005, *The Need to Change the Constitution of Bosnia and Herzegovina*. Südosteuropa Mitteilungen. 04–05 , pp. 90–93.

Interview with Prof Dr Robert Hayden, 2010 http://www.theory-talks.org/2008/08/theory-talk-16.html [accessed on 10.07.2013]

European Commission Enlargement Strategy 2006–2007, available at http://ec.europa.eu/enlargement/pdf/key_documents/2006/nov/com_649_strategy_paper_en.pdf [accessed at 10.10.2013]

Freyburg, T. and Richter S. 2010. *National Identity Matters*, 17(2) Journal of European Public Policy, pp. 263–281.

Kulundžic, Z. et al. eds., .2005. *Arithmetic of Irresponsibility: When and how to make a functional transition of responsibilities from the international community to the local authorities,* Sarajevo: Friedrich Ebert Foundation. Available at: http://www.vpi.ba/eng/content/documents/Arithmetic_of_Irresponsiblity.pdf [accessed at 10.09.2012]

International Crisis Group. 2012. Bosnia's Gordian Knot: Constitutional Reform, Europe brief nr 68, available at http://www.crisisgroup.org/en/regions/europe/balkans/bosnia-herzegovina/b068-bosnias-gordian-knot-constitutional-reform.aspx[accessed at 10.09.2012]

Juncos, An. 2011. *Europeanization by decree? The Case of Police Reform in Bosnia*. Journal of Common Market Studies, vol 49 (2), pp. 367–389.

Juncos, An. 2012. *Member state-building vs . peacebuilding. The contradictions of EU state-building in Bosnia and Herzegovina*. East European Politics, vol 29(1), pp. 58–75.

Marko, J. 2007. *Constitutional Reform in Bosnia and Herzegovina 2005–2006*, 5 European Yearbook of Minority Issues, Brill, Leiden, pp 207–218.

Noutcheva, G. 2009. *Fake, Partial and Imposed Compliance: The Limits of the EUs Normative Power in the Western Balkans*, Journal of European Public Policy 16 (7), 1065–1084.

Schimmelfennig, F. 2009. Europeanization Beyond Europe, in: Living Reviews in European Governance, 4/3, available at http://www.livingreviews.org/lreg-2009-3 [accessed at 10.09.2012]

Sebastian, S. 2009. *The Role of the EU in the Reform of Dayton in Bosnia-Herzegovina*, Ethnopolitics, 8, pp. 3–4.

Szewczyk, B. 2010. *The EU in Bosnia and Herzegovina: powers, decisions and legitimacy*, The Institute for Security Studies (EUISS), Occasional Paper March available at http://www.iss.europa.eu/publications/detail/article/the-eu-in-bosnia-and-herzegovina-powers-decisions-and-legitimacy/ [accessed at 10.09.2012]

Tolksdorf, D. 2011. *Stuck between State- and Member State-Building Processes: The difficulties of the European Union in supporting the Europeanization of Bosnia and Herzegovina*, EU Frontiers—Policy Paper No. 7, Center for EU Enlargement Studies, Central European University. Available at http://cens.ceu.hu/publications/tolksdorf/2011/24226 [accessed at 10.09.2013]

Venneri, G. 2010. *'Conquered' vs. 'Octroyée' Ownership: Police Reform, Conditionality and the EU's Member-Statebuilding in Bosnia-Herzegovina*, article available at http://www.westminster.ac.uk/__data/assets/pdf_file/0011/81596/Venneri.pdf [accessed at 10.09.2013]

Vettori, Em. 2013. *EU Conditionality on Nationality Sensitive Matters in Bosnia and Herzegovina: Promoting Democracy or Maintaining the Status Quo?*, European Diversity and Autonomy Papers, (EDAP):05 Available at http://www.eurac.edu/en/research/institutes/imr/activities/bookseries/edap/Documents/2013edap_05.pdf [accessed at 10.09.2012]

NICHOLAS ROSSIS

Macedonia: The Consequences of the Political Focus on Identity and How This Affects Balkan Politics and the European Integration Process.

Macedonia emerged and detached itself from a federal past with the call for the re-establishment and the reinvention of its cultural, political and social backbone. The political elites demonstrated a predilection towards identity politics as the post-federal environment was ideal for the encouragement of a clear nationalistic sentiment or for the brewing of national consciousness. Internal antagonism and intolerance coupled with the regional antipathies legitimatize the resurgence of identity politics as the means to achieve the broader political agenda and serve the interests of the political elites. Identity politics in the long run may be pernicious for Macedonia as it convinces the public to fixate on and augment the logic of domestic or regional discrimination and prejudice despite the remarkable yet overlooked societal, political and economic homogeneity amongst all the Balkan countries. Therefore, regardless of the counterproductive dispute over the constitutional name with Greece, will the scope of identity based politics pave the way for the Macedonian re-integration in regional and international entities or will it intercept the democratic development in Macedonia and as a result challenge the European perspective? The current precarious path of identity based politics may be acting to defeat its own purposes.

Key Words: Identity politics, Macedonia, European integration, regional cooperation.

Dr. Nicholas Rossis holds a PhD in Middle Eastern & Islamic studies from the University of Durham. He is currently a research associate at Inter Alia.

Introduction

A walk around the city centre of Skopje in Macedonia reveals the perpendicular burden of what appears to be a medley of individuality and distinctiveness upon the citizenry. Yet the interactions within the local community signify a remarkable yet overlooked societal, political and economic homogeneity with Macedonia's neighbors. Whether the Macedonians are descendants of Samuil or Alexander the Great may be scientifically interesting, regardless of this however is the internal and regional divisions that have been consistently catered to by the negative consequences of identity politics. Perhaps identity politics is an artificial contraption to pursue patriotic, chauvinistic or even racial uniformity very much yearned in the emerging nationalistic fermentations of the 19th and 20th century.

Nevertheless, even though not obsolete in the contemporary context of an emerging regional political entity like the European Union, identity politics may be a double edged sword. Regardless of the dispute over the constitutional name with Greece (Macedonia Vs FYROM) and its counterproductive implications for both sides, identity politics may be catastrophic for Macedonia when it convinces the public to fixate on and augment the logic of domestic or regional discrimination and intolerance. Towards the broader realization of a European integration, sense of identity may be a basic conceptualization of any individual but it may easily reach a point that could neutralize the process of constructive regional stabilization and cooperation. Given that Macedonia stems from a federal past heading towards another regional political entity like the European Union the current precarious path of identity based politics may be acting to defeat its own purposes.

This research investigates through inductive empirical and situational analysis the consequences of the current Macedonian political focus on identity, and how this situation affects the relationship between identity and regionalism in the Balkan politics in light of a potential Macedonian accession into the European Union. More specifically, the paper will shed light on the modus operandi of identity politics through a historical prism. It will then follow to interpret the reasoning and the rationality of the political elites. Lastly it will scrutinize the impact of this tendency on the domestic level and on the prospects of the Macedonian re-integration in regional and international entities. The fundamental aim of this paper is to transition the theoretical background of identity politics, which is apparent in Macedonian society, to a contemporary post-paroxysmal setting.

Identity politics in the Macedonian context

Looking through the basic theoretical framework of identity politics, the Macedonian paradigm provides a representative model for most of the academic assumptions relating to it. The origins of the Macedonian identity question have been substantiated through the work of Georgi Pulevski in the late 19th century whose writings dealt with the continuity of a Balkan populace. Of course, the narrative of the historical continuum and therefore the assertions for the factual identity of Slavic—Macedonian peoples goes further back in time to the 18th century with the writings of the monk Spyridon Gabrovski or even earlier through the claims of Jordanes in the 6th century, who argued the kinship of Alexander the Great with the Bulgarians, the Illyrians and even the Bavarians (Mishkova 2011). However, these historical complications, debates, assumptions and vindications are not unique to the Macedonian case and stand for any modern Balkan state. Besides manifold countries throughout the globe especially during the 19th century shaped or re-shaped their identity according to their own political, economic or military scope. Be that as it may, the notion of "who-was-here-first" has tantalized Macedonian affairs and Balkan regional relations for over two centuries, but the particular issue has been rather popularized in the contemporary era after the Macedonian declaration of independence from Yugoslavia in 1991 and through the name dispute with Greece.

The sum of the documented Balkan historical landscape seems vague and somewhat turbid, nevertheless this is inaccurate. Perhaps due to the fact that the Balkan peoples have so much more in common than they wish to admit, allows to the historical narrative, instead of being as objective and definite as possible, to be open to interpretation and susceptible to nationalistic aspirations. Even though, the artificiality of nationalism in the Balkans given their position as a *"polyglot ethnic kaleidoscope"*—as Mazower (2000: 102) describes them-is not the focus of this paper, it must be admitted that it has some powerful and homogenizing properties. Popular irredentism, for example, mobilized the unsuspecting public opinion in the Balkans from the 19th century and it still does (Mazower 2000: 104).

The potentially premeditated historical vacuum occurs when history oversteps its didactic attributes and develops into the necessary social proof. According to Wood, et al. (1994) social proof is the quintessence of minority influence or in this instance, of the political elites. The "minority" in order to influence, needs the social proof which should be flexible and appealing and apparently history provides the vital fertile ground for such practice. Also according to Kelman (1958), identification, meaning the influence stemming from a famous personality or a historical figure, as one of the main components of social influence, could provide the required social proof. Besides, social proof feeds from doubt or social incoherence.

The Balkan political idiosyncrasy manipulated the emerging nationalistic sentiment or the brewing national consciousness to shape mono-ethnic nation states. The application of such policies differs from country to country in the Balkan region, as some states could be more hostile towards minorities and others simply do not acknowledge their existence. Apparently the presence or the acknowledgment of ethnic and even social minorities may undermine the solidity of the emerging identity. In this perspective most of the Balkan states including Greece are very similar. However, Macedonia as a contemporary example with the intention to join international political and military entities with supranational characteristics like the European Union and NATO—at a lesser degree— makes us wonder why the political focus on identity is so important when re-integration has become the order of the day.

Macedonia emerged out of the ashes of Yugoslavia where the identity temperament of each federal state was barren and perhaps forcibly innocuous yet brisk due to the sporadic discontent for the federal government despite the ostensible constitutional protection (Solomon 2001). Perhaps the political elites in Macedonia are rather verdant as the strife for self-determination coupled with the widespread corruption and the low living standards did not permit the fermentations for the development of an experienced leadership. Nevertheless, there must be compelling elements that ascribe to the political elites such devotion on identity politics.

The aforementioned parameters displayed the theoretical modus operandi of identity politics; the following section will shed light on the reasoning of this tendency and subsequently it will examine its efficacy.

The political rationality of the identity values

Once the political elites acquire the necessary social proof they can decide whether to resolve the—in all likelihood-hypothetical problematic issue or to intensify it. In any case, the Macedonian political elites drum up support and solicit votes through identity based rhetoric and practices instead of focusing more on real sustainable development and policies that could revivify the economy. The truth is that it is rather undemanding to categorize racially, ethnically and even sexually, individuals or even entire societies. Through this process, which is not necessarily a result of a conscious mandate, the political elites elucidate their rationality and obtain the essential legitimacy which paves the way to social compliance.

Of course, the task to distinguish whether the social compliance is artificial or real is very difficult. Nevertheless, recent reports and policy briefs (Kolozova, et al. 2013) suggest that the governmental narrative differs drastically from the public opinion narrative regarding identity. In contrast, the present research revealed that the younger University-educated generations are rather political and strongly opinionated regarding the identity issues of the Macedonians and it has also been recorded that there is a remarkable alignment with the governmental narrative.[1] Interestingly though, leaving politics and aspirations aside, this research also presented a certain degree of moderation and the subcutaneous acknowledgement of a potential hyperbole in the political rhetoric. In this perspective the aforementioned policy brief is in concordance with the observations of this research. Albeit it seems unattainable to weigh the proclivity of the public in Macedonia (unless someone perceives as an unfailing indicator the electoral results) as the public opinion is apparently not exclusively monocular and one sided as has been occasionally projected.

The political elites perhaps assume that identity based politics will invigorate past glories as the country needs a kind of special empowerment even if it is desultory. Nevertheless, the political elites, especially from the VMRP-DPMNE[2], apart from the obvious canvassing purposes that the nationalistic rhetoric carries, have exposed their intention to galvanize the heritage and identity of Macedonia by means of the controversial *"Antikvizacija"* or the policy to confer a more classical and archaic outlook in the capital through the project Skopje 2014 (Graan 2013).Even though the supposed intention of the project is to bridge Macedonia with tourism and

---

[1] In order to meet the aims and objectives of this study a theoretical and empirical research strategy has been applied, because some of the conclusions have also been made on the basis of the empirical data, gathered from the primary research. The research is based on an inductive qualitative approach in order to understand and interpret social interactions and perceptions as part of the findings was based on the analysis of secondary literature. The qualitative data also included open-ended responses from a small sample (18 individuals approached in natural environment and social media) where the biases of the participants in the study were known to the researcher.

[2] Internal Macedonian Revolutionary Organization—Democratic Party for Macedonian National Unity

investments, it has sparked widespread domestic and international criticism due to the dissipation of funds to careless, vapid and leaden banalities that mostly encourage internal antagonism and intolerance, especially towards the Albanian minority. Although this is stating the obvious, it must be pointed out that it is rather naive for the local government to have expected that a mere facelift would amend such deeply embedded impressions and that there are realistic limitations for Macedonia regarding tourism and investments. Therefore the frenzy to secure funds for the completion of the project on the one hand depicts the potential determination of the government to fulfil its vision and on the other hand highlights the concerns regarding embezzlement and mismanagement of the funds (Pajaziti 2013).

Then again Macedonia unlike some of its neighbors has indeed the capacity to effortlessly attract considerable foreign investments and derive some benefit from the currently insignificant exports of its high quality domestic products such as meat and wine. However, the progress of such policies that would enable the aforementioned course of action is minimal and slow as the current political focus is on the preservation of power. Additionally the vulnerability of the country on the parameters mentioned above has several disconcerting elements as it has very limited mechanisms to withstand a persisting economic recession and the endemic corruption debilitates the prospects for any potential improvement.

However, in all fairness it must be noted that the resurgence of identity politics in Macedonia does not solely stem from the domestic political capriciousness. Greece and Bulgaria for example have their own share of responsibility for the resurgence of identity politics in Macedonia. The refusal by Greece and Bulgaria to acknowledge certain aspects of the Macedonian identity at the present state of the affairs and developments in the Balkan Peninsula only credits additional domestic support and therefore additional legitimacy to the Macedonian political elites.

Aspects of the current Greek and Bulgarian predisposition on Macedonia is analogous with biting one's own hand as they actually facilitate, with their approach, the replenishment of identity politics in Macedonia. On one hand according to Solomon (2001) *"the Bulgarians reject the notion of the Macedonian language as being anything other than Bulgarian, thus undermining the reasoning for a distinct Macedonian national identity"* and perceive the Macedonian approach as denial of their real Bulgarian identity

(Roudometof 2002: 66). On the other hand, the refusal of Greece to accept the name "Macedonia" among other claims, rejects almost any association with the historical background of the two countries, thus undercutting the whole concept of the Macedonian identity altogether. Even though members of the public in Macedonia do not necessarily align with the governmental course of action on identity, they decry that at least the political elites-despite their general ineffectiveness regarding the profound issues of the country-challenge aloud those who ignore their right to self-determination and identity. Although the exclusivity of the Macedonian peoples seems to be potentially inflicted by the state apparatus, it is irrelevant and beside the point for the average citizen as this situation stimulates self-protective mechanisms for the popular sentiment that in due course may temporarily be convenient for the prolongation of the political elites' aspirations.

What is more, the politics of identity within the Macedonian framework overlook the Albanian minority issues and promote the alienation from the accords of the Ohrid Agreement. Thus the present identity resurgence could gradually rebuff the Albanian minority which represents more than a quarter of the Macedonian population. At the same time the Albanian minority does not necessarily endorse identity based politics and is somewhat distrustful towards the governmental decisions (U.S. Department of State 2013). As a result, segments of the Macedonian political elites still perceive the ethnic Albanians in the country as a destabilizing parameter (Templar 2012). Therefore, as the national consciousness of the Albanian minority seems difficult to be won over, despite the ostensible improvements in the Albanian representation in Macedonia after the Ohrid Agreement, the reality remains perplexed. The government deduces that given a new opportunity the Albanian minority will once again demand more self-rule rights through a referendum like they did for example several years ago. Thus the government according to what is being observed has to ensure that such development will not occur and it needs to debase the possibility of losing territory and demoralize the additional enhancement of the already strong westward ties of the Albanian minority.

Therefore, we may assume that the Macedonian political elites have been acting pre-emptively in this perspective by implementing all the aforementioned policies towards a robust and incontrovertible identity in order to clear out any elements that may destabilize the desirable internal "imbalance". On the one hand, the elites estimate that the attainment of an unequivocal and seemingly problem-free Macedonian state will secure, for example, the smooth accession to the European Union. On the other hand, if the identity issues have not being crystallized yet, but Macedonia satisfies the conditions for integration, a potential accession will routinely resolve or quieten many problematic issues within Macedonia, as more than likely everyone's real focus in such eventuality will be more on the financial aspects and less on the identity issues.

Thus, is identity after all a means to an end for Macedonia? For the political elites judging from the aforementioned analysis it seems that it is, not only for the petty political interests but for the wider political aims and objectives. However, for the grassroots of Macedonia—despite the potential appeal—it will only really matter if the rhetoric in the long run becomes more tolerable, leading to greater employment, less corruption and sustainable development.

Domestic and regional after-effects; the impact on the European Union perspective

The previous sections established the "how" and the "why" of identity politics in Macedonia. The present section will attempt to shed light on the efficacy and consequences of identity politics derived by reasoning from the aforementioned observed facts upon the domestic and regional backdrop.

Although identity and regionalism are not necessarily mutually exclusive concepts, the case of Macedonia poses certain compromises. Macedonia had very limited regional identity values as part of Yugoslavia and as a country that still ceaselessly endeavors to formulate and figure out its national domestic identity, is it really ready to proceed towards regional entities that will require certain concessions? From this point of view, it is unequivocally ready, as the European Union itself does not have a coherent regional identity, but that is not the problem and practically never was. Besides the similarity of the Balkan peoples in terms of the elements that could constitute a regional identity, such as culture and historical experience (Bechev 2004), with the exception of language, there are remarkable similarities.

Therefore the problems for Macedonia are far more complex and substantial. The perennial internal fragmentation and ethnic division, coupled with the uneven birth rate between the ethnic Albanians and the Macedonians will continue to shake the foundations of identity in the country. Despite the governmental attempts from 2008 to improve the Macedonian birth rate by giving incentives, especially towards regions of the country with the biggest fertility problems, the forecast has not changed significantly (Buechsenschuetz 2005; Marusic 2011). The main question for the political elites of Macedonia is whether this situation will further agitate the internal friction or will the antipathy eventually fade out and bring assimilation. Therefore, for the time being the tremendous lack of respect for most—if not all—the ethnic and social minorities will remain a stumbling block towards the European perspective. It will take many years of cognitive acclimatization and profound educational reforms to reverse the indifference imposed by identity politics and the prevalent societal conservatism in order to bring tangible results, but until then the existing course of action may have already backfired.

Perhaps the aforementioned dilemma is not adequate to single-handedly undermine the European accession in full, but it is indeed precarious for the domestic composure independent of any integration process. However, in the case of Macedonia the accumulation of the domestic negative consequences of identity politics has the ability to procrastinate and suspend the regional opening up of the country. More specifically, Macedonia also lacks the means and the resources—or as Luctick (2002) mentions, the constitutional mechanisms—to sustain a satisfactory level of democratic standards. Besides, the sustainability of multicultural democratic states is undermined by political movements that demand or subtly promote clear nationalistic features with ethnocentric character. According to Lustick's (2000 and 2002) agent-based model of collective identities, identity politics channeled by self-determination factions are in the end prone to resort to violence, intimidation or fully-fledged turmoil that will even pave the way to partition. The democratic standards in Macedonia are punctured and this situation alone could challenge the European perspective, and identity politics does not assist in the minimization of this confusion but quite the opposite. Also the democratic shortfalls offer an opportunity to unburden Greece from the spotlight of the *veto* due to the name dispute.[3]

In addition, irredentism for many academics is part and parcel of identity politics (Roudometof 1996; Kornprobst 2008). Despite the fact that conventional wisdom suggests that irredentist views have significantly subsided in the region, the Balkan countries as Mazower (2000) mentions, had always overestimated their own irredentist capacities. Of course, the overvalued assessments go vice versa, as Greece for example once felt threatened by Macedonia. As some diplomatic sources have previously claimed that, even when Greece realized that Macedonia apparently did not possess the wherewithal to push forward its alleged irredentist pretentions, it was still alarmed against all odds, logic and legitimacy due to the probable alliances Macedonia may form irredentist claims, even though both sides know that realistically they are out of the question, and are also convenient for Macedonia as well as for Greece. For the former, those supposed claims kindle the emerging Macedonian national consciousness, while for the latter provide a first-rate excuse to justify the foreign policy towards Macedonia.

Macedonia once again is on the threshold of a critical crossroads having to choose between a promising moderate political and democratic landscape and an outmoded, corrupt and intolerant state, which may be inherent and inevitable without due diligence. The simplicity for the achievement of a transcendentally pragmatist and positive future for Macedonia is obvious but not easy. The political elites may have to re-adjust their strategy and their long term assumptions upon the results of identity based policies. The elites also need to realize for their own benefit that the current approach deepens the domestic predicaments and also generates new obstacles distancing Macedonia from a future of stability and security. Apparently the European accession or a NATO membership should not be an end in itself for Macedonia nor does such an eventuality guarantee an untroubled future. Without doubt extrinsic and intrinsic factors, unrelated to the basis of identity and self-determination, prohibit Macedonia from accomplishing imperative objectives for the sustainability and growth of the country. Unfortunately Macedonia seems unable to fully

---

[3] Greece has repeatedly stated that it will exercise the right of veto in order to block Macedonia's membership to the EU or NATO unless the dispute over the constitutional name is resolved.

utilize the impetus given by the EU candidacy status. Even though nothing extremely significant materialized regarding the regional perspective or the participation of Macedonia to international organizations like NATO, several stimulating developments have taken place over the years.

It may be prosaic but the path towards a broader regional perspective is quintessential for the improvement of the state apparatus, the democratic standards and the welfare of the Macedonian public. Corruption and informal economy under the aegis of all three branches of government only serves to hinder the macro-economic development and the political sophistication of the country.

The straightforwardness of identity based politics may offer a short cut to political consolidation and its intensity has the potential to attain a certain degree of social conformity. However, it has certain limitations as its prolongation in a country with the multilateralism of Macedonia will eventually alienate instead of pull together the population.

The political elites could protract their endurance and maintain their niche without the controversial auspices of identity politics, and without the deterioration of democratic standards, while the entire populace enjoys greater freedom and respect.

Conclusion

The Balkan peoples whether they want to admit it or not, have remarkable similarities in terms of regional identity characteristics such as culture and historical experience (Bechev 2004). However it seems that these resemblances render the historical narrative susceptible to local and regional interpretation. The political elites in Macedonia cash in on identity politics to pursue a versatile agenda with results that have not fully surfaced yet.

How is this happening? Due to the tendency to overinflate glory stemming from the Balkan historical void, history has overstepped its didactic attributes and developed into the necessary social proof. This social proof armed with flexibility and appeal is a vital component for influencing the public through identity politics. Throughout history, political idiosyncrasy in the Balkans has manipulated the emerging nationalistic sentiment or the brewing national consciousness to shape mono-ethnic nation states. Macedonia displayed a relative temperance with its identity assumptions as part of Yugoslavia as it was compelled to be innocuous; nevertheless it was always subcutaneously vigorous. The rejuvenation of identity politics in the country is mostly a political construct, as the unripe elites preoccupied with the friction for self-determination coupled with the widespread corruption and the low living standards did not permit the fermentations for the development of an experienced leadership.

Why is this happening? The political elites, especially from the VMRP-DPMNE, perhaps assumed that identity based politics will invigorate past glories as the country required a kind of special empowerment even if that was desultory. More realistically though identity politics, apart from the obvious canvassing purposes that the nationalistic rhetoric carries and the consolidation of power it potentially offers, has also showed the political intention to galvanize a homogenized and coercive Macedonian heritage and identity that will be the centre of attention for tourism, investments and even for the European Union. However, it must be pointed out that the resurgence of identity politics in Macedonia does not solely stem from the domestic political capriciousness, as the refusal of acknowledgement of certain aspects of the Macedonian identity on behalf of the Greeks and the Bulgarians, stimulated the regional tensions but also provided additional credit and domestic support, and therefore additional legitimacy and arguments for the Macedonian political elites.

At the same time the politics of identity has a propensity of overlooking the ethnic Albanian minority issues as a potential destabilizing parameter (Templar 2012) and promoting the alienation from the accords of the Ohrid Agreement. All things considered, the political elites in Macedonia utilized identity politics to achieve their petty political interests as well as the broader political aims and objectives.

What is this going to do in the end? As identity politics nourishes the internal fragmentation and the ethnic division in addition to the uneven birth rate between the ethnic Albanians and the Macedonians, the question has been raised whether this situation will further agitate the domestic friction or will the antipathy eventually fade out and bring assimilation. Also as Lustick (2000) suggests, identity politics channeled by self-determination and nationalistic movements are ultimately prone to resort to violence, intimidation or fully-fledged turmoil, and in all probability will pave the way to partition. The democratic standards in Macedonia have relapsed and the chimera of irredentism, even though it is evident for everyone that Macedonia does not possess the wherewithal to pursuit it, is a convenient pretext for the Macedonian narrative as well as for the adjacent countries as it legitimizes their stance towards Macedonia.

Also it seems that identity politics has deteriorated the democratic standards and the polyphony in the country. The situation is assisted by the poor living conditions of the Macedonian public coupled with the endemic corruption and the augmenting informal economy which under the aegis of all three branches of government hinders the macro-economic development and the political sophistication of the country. Therefore, this situation challenges the European perspective and potentially the participation in international organizations like NATO. When all is said and done, identity politics does not function towards the minimization of these domestic and regional perplexities, but neutralize the small steps that Macedonia makes forward.

References

Bechev, D. 2004. *Contested Borders, Contested Identity: The Case of Regionalism in South East Europe.* Journal of Southeast European and Black Sea Studies, 4 (1), pp. 77–96.

Buechsenschuetz, U. 2005, June 5. *Macedonia: A Political Pact To Regulate Demography?* Retrieved April 30, 2014, from Radio Free Europe/Radio Liberty: www.unpo.org/article/2646#sthash.7DootbB6.dpuf

Graan, A. 2013. *Counterfating the nation? Skopje 2014 and the Politics of Nation Branding in Macedonia.* Cultural Anthropology, 28 (1), pp. 161–179.

Kelman, H. 1958. *Compliance, identification, and internalization: Three processes of attitude change.* Journal of Conflict Resolution, 1, pp. 51–60.

Kolozova, K., Lecevska, K., Borovska, V., & Blazeva, A. 2013. *Skopje 2014: Project and its Effects Skopje 2014 Project and its Effects on the Perception of Macedonian Identity Among the Citizens of Skopje.* Skopje: Institute of social sciences and humanities.

Kornprobst, M. 2008. Irredentism in European Politics: Argumentation, Compromise and Norms. Cambridge: Cambridge University Press.

Lustick, I. 2000, Arpil 22. *Globalization and the Resurgence of Identity Politics.* Paper presented to LiCEP workshop . Duke University.

Lustick, I. 2002. PS-I: *A User-Friendly Agent-Based Modeling Platform for Testing Theories of Political Identity and Political Stability*. Journal of Artificial Societies and Social Simulation, 5 (3).

Marusic, S. J. 2011, February 11. *Macedonians Shrink as Ethnic Albanians Expand*. Retrieved April 30, 2014, from Balkan Insight: www.balkaninsight.com

Mazower, M. 2000. The Balkans. London: Phoenix.

Mishkova, D. 2011. *Differentiation in Entanglment: Debates on Antiquitity, Ethnogenesis and Identity in the 19th century Bulgaria*. In O. G. Gábor Klaniczay, Multiple Antiquities—Multiple Modernities: Ancient Histories in Nineteenth Century European Cultures, pp. 213–246. Frankfurt: Campus Verlag.

Pajaziti, N. 2013, August 12. *Government illegaly allocated 58 million Euros for "Skopje 2014" project* . Retrieved April 25, 2014, from Independent Balkan News Agency: http://www.balkaneu.com/

Roudometof, V. 2002. Collective Memory, National Identity, and Ethnic Conflict: Greece, Bulgaria and the Macedonian question. Westport: Praeger.

Roudometof, V. 1996. *Nationalism and Identity Politics in the Balkans: Greece and the Macedonian Question*. Journal of Modern Greek Studies, 14 (2), 253–301.

Solomon, D. 2001. *Identity crisis: A briefing on Balkans key issues*. Geneva: Henry Dunant Centre pour le dialogue humanitaire.

Templar, M. 2012. *Skopje contributes to its own instability*. Retrieved April 27, 2014, from Research Institute for European and American Studies: http://www.rieas.gr/research-areas/greek-studies/678.html

U.S. Department of State. 2013. *Country Reports on Human Rights Practices for 2013*. Washington D.C.: U.S. Department of State, Bureau of Democracy, Human Rights and Labor.

Wood, W., Lundgren, S., Ouellette, J., Busceme, S., & Blackstone, T. 1994. *Minority Influence: A Meta-Analytic Review of Social Influence Processes*. Psychological Bulletin, 115 (3), pp. 323–345.

TONKA KOSTADINOVA

Reinventing the Past: Politics of Memory in the Post-Conflict Reconstruction of Cultural Heritage in Bosnia and Herzegovina

The paper will analyze the politics of public remembering as in the (re)construction of cultural heritage in post-war Bosnia and Herzegovina. The term politics of memory in the study refers to the institutionalized efforts of the international community to reconstruct the notion of peaceful cohabitation between Serbs, Croats and Muslims in Bosnia and Herzegovina after the end of the war in 1995. Through the analysis of two case-studies (the renovation of the National Museum in Sarajevo and the reconstruction of the Old Bridge in Mostar) the paper will argue that trans-national actors over-promoted representations of the common Bosnian history while neglecting other, less symbolically charged sites, thus changing the meaning of the Bosnian cultural heritage. The study will approach the trans-national politics of memory in the post-conflict society of Bosnia and Herzegovina by taking into account developments in the field on European, regional and domestic levels. It will touch on crucial questions related to the phenomenon of collective memory and its instrumentalization for the legitimization of power.

Keywords: Bosnia and Herzegovina, memory, cultural heritage, international community.

Dr. Tonka Kostadinova is an assistant professor of contemporary history at the Bulgarian National Museum of Military History. She holds a PhD in International history and has been an Advanced Academia Fellow at the Center for Advanced Study Sofia and a research fellow at the Department of General History at Charles University, Prague.

Politics of memory: the state of the debate

What we call memory is in fact the gigantic and breathtaking storehouse of a material stock of what it would be impossible for us to remember, an unlimitted repertoire of what might need to be recalled.

Pierr Nora (1989: 13)

The Western solution to the problem of Europe's troublesome memories has been to fix them, quite literally, in stone.

Tony Judt (2010: 826)

In August 2014 the world will mark the 100th anniversary of the outbreak of World War I, which began in Sarajevo. The centenary provides particularly interesting insights on the European memory map and reveals phenomena that go beyond the need to (re)evaluate the course of world history and to remember the past. The issue of the celebration appears to be a highly contested political matter with the European Union having rejected several Bosnian requests to make Sarajevo the central place of the anniversary events. The eventual project on the commemorations in the Bosnian capital belongs to, and is financed by Germany and France, thus bearing strong symbolism and sending a political message of reconciliation to the three ethnic groups in Bosnia and Herzegovina. The occasion raised hopes that the country would now have a political project that would be supported by the three communities for the first time since the end of the Bosnian war in 1995. Instead, Germany and France were accused of "partiality" and the Bosnian Serb President, Milorad Dodik, banned all people from Republika Srpska from participating in the events planned for 2014[1]. The reason was the different interpretation of WWI history in the European and Bosnian Serb memory narratives:—while Europe considers Gavrillo Prinćip a terrorist, Serbia commemorates him as a fighter for liberty and independence.

The issue of the WWI centenary accounts for at least two colliding phenomena: on a supranational level it reflects the progress achieved in terms of creating a European identity and a common European memory map that unites the diverse and often conflicting national readings of world history; on a micro-political level it reveals the very fragmented memory

---

[1] "French Embassy dismisses Dodik's accusations", Dalje.com report, 19 April 2013, http://dalje.com/en-world/french-embassy-dismisses-dodiks-accusations/464396 [Accessed 5 July 2013].

landscape in Bosnia and Herzegovina and the failed attempts on creating a supra-ethnic Bosnian identity based on the three ethnic groups' common history and shared past.

The materialization of history for the sake of public remembering has flourished on European soil in the last two decades. The process of formation of a European identity, particularly accelerated after the 1993 Maastricht Treaty, triggered the necessity for European political elites to publicly address Europe's troublesome past, and to incorporate the legacy of WWI, the 1930s, the Second World War and the Holocaust into a common European history and memory narrative. The political dealing with the past, has become both a prerequisite for entering "the family of Europe", and proof of belonging to the European culture and values, hence—a cultural identification tool. In the post-1989 period, the process of EU enlargement implied that all new members of the union should recognize "national" crimes conducted in the past and adjust their historical narratives to the common European memory map. Romania, Hungary, and even Poland had to acknowledge their own role in the Holocaust in order to proceed to EU membership. Croatia and Serbia have been given the prospect of EU membership only after publicly confessing guilt for the Yugoslav wars of the 1990s and proving themselves ready to cooperate with the International Criminal Tribunal for the Former Yugoslavia (ICTY). Dealing with the legacy of the past now bears a strong political charge that no country can afford to ignore.

The intensive politics of memory triggered the forgetting of the fact that remembering was a vague social process in post-war Europe. According to Tony Judt it took nearly four decades for Europe to overcome its "Vichy syndrome", defined by the French historian Henry Russo as the "decades-long difficulty of acknowledging what had really happened during the war and the overwhelming desire to block the memory or to recast it in a usable way that would not corrode the fragile bonds of post-war society" (2010: 808).

In the process of European integration numerous symbols and tangible images came to compensate for the "memory deficit" and to prove that Europe, in fact, does remember. In the last two decades memories of wartime events were fixed in memorials, monuments and museums such as the Holocaust Memorial in Paris, the Memorial to the Murdered Jews in Europe in Berlin, the Institute of National Memory in Warsaw, and the

House of Terror in Budapest. The over-production of places of remembering led to a compensatory surplus of memory, that, along with institutionalized public remembering, has become the very foundation of collective identity as a constructive myth of Europe (Judt 2010: 826, 829).

Historians and social scientists responded to the political "surplus of memory" by providing conceptual and empirical analyses of top-down approaches to coping with the past and the socio-political construction of memory. The field that emerged is today known as *politics of memory* and deals with the institutionalized efforts to recast the past and to embed its constructed symbols and significance into the public remembering of the society. Politics of memory includes the establishment of museums and memorials, changes in museums' expositions or school curriculums, the erection or the destruction of monuments, the (re)naming of geographical areas and towns and other forms of attaching symbolism to the past.

From a sociological perspective, politics of memory problematizes the notion of group thinking, group remembering and collective memory as set in the German and French historic-philosophical traditions. Already at the end of the 19th century the German historian Dilthey introduced the idea of collective subjects (*Gesamtsubjekte*) that, apart from the individual, can also bear the meaning of historical events (Kohli-Kunz 1972: 31). Habermas further developed the concept of group thinking (*Gruppenmeinen*) as a reflection of the inter-subjectivity of understanding, claiming that interpretations can be considered real only if they posses inter-subjective validity, or in other words, they are recognized and "thought" by a group or society (Habermas 1968: 222). In Halbwachs pioneering study *On Collective Memory* the notion of collective memory crystallizes as a social construct that can exist and develop only within social frames such as the family, the neighborhood, the nation, the culture. Introducing the idea of *places of common memory* Halbwachs stresses the role of spatial images as central to the formation of collective memory and argues that the individual and the group can recapture the past only by understanding how it is preserved by the relevant physical surroundings (1992: 7). The French historian Pierr Nora has provided perhaps the most detailed study on the interaction between memory and history within the so called *realms of memory* (*lieux de mémoire*) claiming that there is no spontaneous memory, and that we must deliberately create archives, museums and monuments so that history would not sweep memory away (1989:12). Today it is widely known that memory is framed by spatial reference points like places, sites, buildings, streets, and that the material construction or alteration of these places can lead to the substantial modification of our memories, and even their disappearance (Truc 2011:148). Political sociologists argue that even though institutions and larger social groups do not have a memory, they are able to create one for themselves with the aid of memorial signs, symbols, texts, images, rites, places and monuments (Assman 2008: 55).

One of the significant contributions of memory studies has thus been to explore how the construction of the past, through a process of invention and appropriation, affected the relationship of power within society (Confino 1997: 1393). Even though there is a wide consensus on the role of institutions in creating and modelling public remembering, politics of memory remains a slippery theoretical and methodological ground. Richard Lebow categorizes several types of public memory and defines the term "institutional memory" as the "efforts of the political elites, their supporters and their opponents to construct meaning of the past and propagate them more widely or impose them on other members of the society" (2006: 13). Peter Verovšek further conceptualizes politics of memory placing the focus of research on the level of political elites and governmental institutions and their use of contested interpretations of the past (2012: 21). In terms of functionality, memory politics refers to "a field of action where different memory entrepreneurs—political and social stakeholders such as governmental structures, political parties, interest groups and intellectuals—use public discourses and practices, such as the erection of monuments, to construct collective narratives on the past in order to support the legitimation of political action, the cementation of group cohesion and the development of a collective identity" (Moll 2012: 3).

The brief overview of the existing literature conceptualizing politics of memory shows that on-going debates focus predominately on the forms, acts and representations of public remembering[2]. This paper will suggest another level of analysis. In "creating" public memory institutions imply an act of public forgetting as well, since they choose to promote only these fragments of the past that fit the political considerations of the present. Museums, memorials, monuments and historical sites thus constitute not

---

[2] The overview encompasses only attempts at conceptualization in the field, and does not account for the extensive case-studies that fall within the purview of politics of memory.

only places of common memory, but also places of social forgetting, as they represent a past that is subjectively selected and politically imposed. History is "remembered" because it is embedded in symbols, monuments, sites and routines of life, which aim to remind the individuals of their belonging to a group/community/nation/state. These routines are so numerous and have become such a familiar part of the social environment that they operate mindlessly, rather than mindfully (Billig 1995: 38). Politics of memory thus maneuvers in the interplay between public remembering and social forgetting. The process is most evident in post-conflict societies where the need to forget the "immediate" violent past becomes the foundation of sustainable peace, and public memory is automatically projected to the more "distant" past, which could provide the ground for post-war recovery and reconciliation.

This paper will research the politics of public remembering and forgetting as they are seen in the (re)construction of sites of memory in post-war Bosnia and Herzegovina. The term politics of memory in the study refers to the institutionalized efforts of the international community to reconstruct the notion of peaceful cohabitation between Serbs, Croats and Muslims in the country. Politics of memory inspired by forces external to a nation can be conceptualized as international (when performed by other states), transnational (interventions by organizations or organized groups) and cross-national (activities by citizens who travel abroad and are exposed to different interpretations of the past) (Lebow 2006: 25–26). For the purposes of the current research, the paper will adopt the trans-national perspective in the analysis of the institutionalized efforts to recast the past as in the policy of major international organizations like UNESCO, the Council of Europe, the European Union and the World Bank[3]. These institutions constitute the main instigators of the heritage reconstruction projects in Bosnia and Herzegovina even though the financial aid for their implementation has often been provided by national governments—an issue that will be addressed later in this paper. The research will focus on top-down approaches to the interaction between history and memory and its instrumentalization in the present through symbolically charged signs such as commemorations, public holidays, monuments, museums, cultural sites.

---

[3] The international governmental organizations involved in Bosnia and Herzegovina are here referred to as "the international community".

As stated above the singularity of the Bosnian case-study lies in the predominantly transnational dimension of politics of memory[4]. Foreign cultural heritage management and the politics of memory have been researched by Musi (2012), Hajdarpśić (2008), Donia (2007), Landry (2002) and Grodach (2002). Hajdarpaśić (2010) and Mall (2012) have provided an outstanding analysis of the domestic aspects of the fragmented Bosnian memory landscape and the conflicting incorporation of Bosnia's past in the national discourses of the Bosnian Croats, Serbs and Bosniaks. The paper will contribute to debates on the role of external factors in the memory landscape of Bosnia and Herzegovina by contextualizing that role in two empirical case studies — the renovation of the National Museum in Sarajevo and the reconstruction of the Old Bridge (Stari Most) in Mostar. It will argue that in attempting to achieve sustainable peace, trans-national actors over-promoted representations of the Bosnian common past, and neglected other, less symbolically charged sites thus changing the meaning of the Bosnian cultural heritage.

Construction and destruction of the shared past in former Yugoslavia

Here, history is always in danger of becoming a myth. It appropriates specific historical events into monuments, while it abuses the past.

Zala Volcić (2009:16)

Notions of South Slavic common culture and shared history became the founding myth of the Socialist Federative Republic of Yugoslavia and the cornerstones of the "brotherhood and unity "concept central to the creation a single Yugoslavian nation. Tito's attempts to unify the diverse cultural and ethnic backgrounds in Yugoslavia relied mainly on the

---

[4] It should be pointed out that the transnational efforts to reinvent Bosnian common history coincided with significant structural changes in the international relations system manifesting in the multiplying cases of state-failure and inter-ethnic conflicts. Of the 111 conflicts that occurred between the end of the Cold War and the beginning of the new century, 95 were purely intrastate and pressed for outside actors and international institutions to intervene (Nye 2003: 150). In the new world order foreign agencies were tasked not only to prevent violence and maintain peace, but also to address local roots of conflict, to reverse the consequences of war, and to reconstruct the social symbiosis that had held war-affected societies together. The process was particularly evident in Bosnia and Herzegovina where the public authority was dismantled between two fragile state entities and a solid ad hoc international institution (the Office of the High Representative for Bosnia and Herzegovina).

memorialization of different WW II events and the common fights against fascism. The experiences shared by the different ethnic groups of Yugoslavia during the Second World War were memorilized through realms of memory aiming to promote the perception of a monolithic Yugoslavian community, and places of remembrance of the anti-fascist struggles became the cornerstones of the Yugoslav state (Zahović & Zulumović 2012: 249–250). As soon as time blurred the need of unification against a common enemy, however, the different historical trajectories of the Yugoslav peoples stood out again in a political struggle to legitimize power. The rise of ethno-nationalism in the 1980s emphasized the different religious and cultural backgrounds and quickly demolished the fragile bonds of common history in Yugoslavia.

Belligerent elements in the Yugoslav wars defined themselves entirely along ethnic and cultural lines and sought to justify their own existence and to (re)map their "ethno-national" territory by demolishing or suppressing the identity of "the other". In this process, the destruction of the cultural heritage served not only as an ethnic cleansing tool, but also as a means to break the materialized memories of a shared past so persistently promoted during the Tito's regime. According to UNESCO's estimates, the wars in Slovenia, Croatia, Bosnia-Herzegovina and Kosovo damaged nearly 75% of the common heritage and became a cultural catastrophe for all of the communities involved in war.

The process was particularly intense in Bosnia and Herzegovina, where the leaders of the Bosnian Serbs, Croats and Muslims aimed at the creation of ethnically homogeneous areas and sought to demolish any tangible evidence of other ethnic groups residing in the contested areas. Military actions burned or destroyed more than 1.500 religious sites and nearly 1000 other cultural sites in Bosnia and Herzegovina. Other sites of memory, such as the National and University Library, the Oriental Institute and the National Museum of Bosnia and Herzegovina survived the war but suffered substantial losses, with more than one million volumes of their collections burned or destroyed (Riedlmayer 1995:1).

The burning National Library in Sarajevo, August 1992

These numbers justify arguments that the wartime destruction of cultural heritage in Bosnia and Herzegovina attacked not only the cultural identity of "the other", but also the memories of the peaceful co-habitation between the three ethnic groups. Andreas Riedlmayer states that throughout Bosnia libraries, archives, museums and cultural institutions have been targeted for destruction, in an attempt to eliminate the material evidence that could remind future generations that different ethnic groups and religious traditions once shared a common heritage (1995: 8).

Mosque destruction during the 1992–1995 war

The fragmentation of the state set up in the Dayton Peace Agreement prefigured the further inability of the Bosnian authorities to cope with the broken narratives of the once shared Bosnian past. Closing down sites of memory established during the Tito's period represented yet another, milder manifestation of the destruction of collective memory in post-Dayton Bosnia and Herzegovina. The process of strengthening ethno-national consciousness sought to distance the people from the socially inclusive history of brotherhood and unity, hence an understanding of cultural heritage emphasizing a common Yugoslav identity was often perceived as threatening to the narrative of "national awakening" of the Bosnian Serbs, Croats and Muslims (Sahović & Zulumović 2012: 246, 253). Sites of memory from the recent past became politically irrelevant and, quite literally, disappeared from the memory map of the country. Hajdarpaśić, referring to the Museum of the 1984 Winter Olympic Games and the Museum of Literary and Theatrical Arts in Sarajevo, notes that;

> Before the war, those places were living, functioning parts of city life; they reflected historical influences and cultural experiences that could not be categorized solely in religious terms, no matter how flexible those terms might be. Since the war, those places—even though they could represent perhaps some of the closest approximations of prewar Sarajevo—have been left shattered (2008: 128).

Numerous UN reports evaluated that the 1992–1995 war did break the "shared identity" within the Bosnian society and emphasized the importance of recreating the memory of a shared Bosnian past as central in the process of post-conflict recovery and reconciliation[5]. Externally imported projects on reconstruction of cultural heritage, incorporated developing interpretations of the Bosnian history through the prism of the country's *traditional* multi-ethnicity and multi-culturalism. In re-casting the past, trans-national politics of memory relied mainly on symbols and tangible representations emphasizing previous forms of multicultural cohabitation. To support this argument I will address two case studies of post-war reconstruction policies:—the rehabilitation of the National Museum of Bosnia and Herzegovina in Sarajevo, and the recovery of the famous Old Bridge in Mostar.

---

[5] http://www.undp.ba [Accessed 5 July 2013]

(Re)inventing common history through the reconstruction of museum institutions and historical sites

> *The past is not preserved but it is socially constructed through archives, museums, school curricula, monuments, and public displays.*
>
> Brayan Osborne (2001:45)

The National Museum of Bosnia and Herzegovina

The role of museum institutions as instruments of politics of memory is a relatively new field of research. In his study *Imagined Communities* Benedict Anderson referred to museums as one of the three main components of civic nationalism (together with the map and the census) and defined them as instruments of power that are "profoundly political" (1991: 163, 178). James Clifford further developed the concept of museums as *contact zones* with the potential to serve not only as spaces for cultural encounter, but also as places for political negotiations. According to Clifford, museums cannot claim political neutrality and should be held accountable for the activities of their public and private sponsors (1997: 206). Museums, along with national institutions such as archives and universities, remain a relevant analytical category that provides insights into the complex political context in which these institutions operate (Hajdarpašić 2008: 109).

This is particularly relevant in the case-study of the National Museum of Bosnia and Herzegovina (NMBH), whose history reflects the instrumentalization of memory in accordance to the relevant historical and political context. During the communist regime in former Yugoslavia the institution functioned according to the slogan "brotherhood and unity" and primarily hosted exhibitions intended to foster a common Yugoslav identity (Lozić 2011: 77). After the war the international community perceived the museum as the only "national" institution that could operate beyond the boundaries of ethnic division. The NMBH reconstruction was funded by the EU and aimed to underline the history of a monolithic Bosnian community dating back from the ancient Roman period.

Perhaps a few words on the contemporary expositions in the museum will make clear the focus of the ongoing policies towards reinvention of the common Bosnian past. The anthropological house of the museum nowadays hosts only objects of Ancient Rome and the Medieval Bosnia period while there is no material representation of daily life and religious plurality during these periods. The ethnology building displays life in BiH during the Ottoman and the Austria-Hungarian period, as well as contemporary aspects of the Bosnian culture. In all expositions the people of Bosnia are referred to as "Bosnian" without a single reference to the terms "Croat", "Serb", or "Bosniak". The NMBH now projects a single national identity that includes all Bosnian people and overlooks the different cultural patters that had shaped the identity of Serbs, Croats and Muslims on the territory of Bosnia and Herzegovina (Taylor 2012: 10–12). Moreover, transnational aid primarily targets neutral components of Bosnian history that can emphasize the notion of a monolithic community and a shared past. The rehabilitation of the famous Sarajevo *Haggadah* (a fourteenth-century Jewish manuscript brought to Bosnia and Herzegovina more than 500 years ago) is an example of this process[6]. The manuscript, today perceived as one of the greatest Bosnian cultural treasures, was not publicly exhibited and didn't have the role of the main cultural item of the museum before the break-up of Yugoslavia (Lozić 2011: 78). During the 1992–1995 war, the book became a symbol of the "shattered dream of multiethnic harmony in Bosnia", and was conveniently embedded in the political interpretations of the Balkans as a region of diversity and multiculturalism[7].

The attempts to cast new symbolic meaning to the Bosnian past focused on the *Haggadah* for two main reasons. First, the manuscript was Jewish and hence unlikely to provoke conflicting ethnic interests; and second, — it had survived several armed conflicts and could thus easily be endorsed as a paradigm of the endurance of religious coexistence in the face of war (Hajdarpaśić 2008: 111). To the two main arguments drawn by Hajdarpaśić I would suggest another level of analysis: — the *Haggadah* represents one of the world's most famous Jewish manuscripts, and its restoration fell within the context of the pan-European process of incorporating Jewish legacy and history into a common European memory map, as noted at the beginning of this paper.

The Sarajevo *Haggadah* transformed into the main exhibit item in the National Museum of Bosnia and Herzegovina. In 2003, the United Nations Mission in Bosnia and Herzegovina (UNMBH) contributed $ 50,000 to the renovation of a separate room to accommodate and exhibit the manuscript.

---

[6] The interesting history of the manuscript's survival throughout the centuries and during the 1992–1995 war is examined by (Donia 2007: 396–397).

[7] "Sarajevo Haggadah Restored", 10 June 2012, http://www.jewishfederations.org/page.aspx?id=26463 [Accessed 20 May 2013]

The Jewish book, more than any other object of the museum, was targeted to both domestic and international audiences:—the Haggadah exhibition was accompanied by an interactive computer terminal providing information in several languages, and conveying a message of tolerance and cultural survival after war, apparently formulated for political purposes (Taylor 2012: 11).

The renovated Haggadah exhibition room

By promoting only neutral fragments of the Bosnian history and neglecting the differences in the cultural trajectories that had shaped the identity of the three ethnic groups, trans-national politics of memory attempted to create the notion of an ancient monolithic Bosnian society that had moved unchanged across time. In fact, it was the Bosnian Muslims' vision of a unified Bosnian nation that was embraced by the international community in its efforts to promote the notion of "traditional" multicultural co-existence and cross-religious tolerance in the country. Bosnian Serbs and Croats tend to distance themselves from the idea of a monolithic Bosnian community and to associate themselves with the historical and cultural patterns of Serbia and Croatia, respectively.

This explains why today Bosnian Serbs and Croats tend to perceive all "national" institutions based in Sarajevo as Bosniak. The appeals towards national unification are seen as a form of Bosniak nationalism and are strongly rejected by the other two ethnic groups in Bosnia and Herzegovina (Engelstoft ed 2001: 960). The Sarajevo *Haggadah* case study illustrates the short-term, superficial cultivation of representations of multiculturalism and religious tolerance to the detriment of carefully elaborated cultural policy in the region. Apart from the Jewish manuscript the international community didn't introduce any comprehensive program for the renovation of the National Museum in Sarajevo. Hundreds of artifacts and items from Habsburg archaeological exhibitions and natural science collections, as well as rare books remained unattended, and the museum remained closed for more than six years (2004–2010). In 2010 NMBH reopened only to reveal the shortage of any common cultural policy in Bosnia and Herzegovina, and closed down again in October 2012 due to the lack of any financing at the state or international level.[8]

Contextualized in a broader historical perspective the National Museum of Bosnia and Herzegovina reflects the growing uncertainty about the role of museum institutions in societies in transition. The demise of their functions as ethno or ideology-consolidating institutions can be observed throughout Eastern Europe. According to Vukov, an overview of history museums in the region in the last decades uncovers the shift from their role as centers of ideological and public activity to "a condition of dissolved narratives, unsystematic policies towards their maintenance and functions, and lack of public consensus about their meaning" (2009: 3). Politics of memory in post-socialist states inevitably relates to issues of transitional justice, lustration and legitimacy of state power. Sites of public memory, especially monuments of the socialist past, became the object of intense and controversial public debates, while new notions of the national past inspired by the process of "westernization" (and Europeanization) of cultural heritage emerged. The analysis of politics of memory, as in the reconstruction of NMBH should take into account both the specific domestic factors that hamper the museum's development, and the broader process of the difficult re-evaluation of the past in transition countries in the region and worldwide.

The Old Bridge (Stari Most) in Mostar

Politics of memory regarding the (re)construction of historical sites in Bosnia and Herzegovina followed a similar pattern and prioritized sites

---

[8] The recent rejection of the plea made by the New York Metropolitan Museum to temporarily host and exhibit the Sarajevo *Haggadah* due to the unsettled political and financial status of the museum reveals the extent to which the museum's objects and collections have been sacrificed to the fragmented political and memory landscape in Bosnia. For more see: Jukic, E. *Bosnia Rejects New York Plea to Host Haggadah*, 7 February 2013, http://www.balkaninsight.com/en/article/bosnia-prevents-sarajevo-haggadah-transfer-to-new-york [Accessed 15 February 2013].

symbolizing the Bosnian multicultural past. This is evident in the reconstruction policies towards one of the most significant cultural monuments in Bosnia and Herzegovina—the Old Bridge (*Stari Most*) in Mostar. The 16th century Ottoman site was fully destroyed by Croat units during the Bosnian war, when Mostar had become a politically contested place between Muslims and Croats. Contemporary discourses interpret the destruction of the bridge as a means to erase Mostar's multicultural identity, but in the pre-war period neither the bridge nor the town was perceived as a symbol of multiculturalism in the Balkans.

After the war, the notion of *Stari Most* as a symbol of peaceful multicultural coexistence appeared in countless articles and discourses on the Yugoslav wars (Grodach 2002: 76). Various projects for reconstruction of the bridge, such as the creation of a memorial or the construction of an entirely new, modern bridge were debated, but were eventually rejected to the benefit of the international community's political projects on reconciliation and post-war recovery (Armakolas 2012). It was decided that the very same Ottoman bridge would be reproduced as "a national unity symbol" intended to emphasize the peaceful cross-ethnic cohabitation during the Ottoman period.

Reconstruction plans were introduced in 1993 as part of the international project *Mostar 2004*, which foresaw the renovation of the entire old town within ten years. In 1994, the UNESCO International Committee of Experts, established to manage the reconstruction process, decided to rebuild the Old Bridge last, not first, so that "its completion would mark the renewal of a multicultural Mostar" (Bing 2001:242). The political importance of the site as an "instrument of reconciliation" became evident in the decision of UNESCO Ministers of Culture to meet in Mostar four days before the Old Bridge opening ceremony and to announce the beginning of a new global project titled "*Cultural Heritage—a Bridge Towards a Shared Future*", in which UNESCO member-states committed "to further work on the conversion of Southeast Europe into a region of tolerance, reconciliation and cultural inter-community dialogue"[9].

The reconstruction of the Old Bridge reveals the reinterpretation of myths of the past and their attachment to material culture in order to serve the political considerations of the present (Grodach 2002: 62.) The new symbolic meaning attributed to the bridge accounts for the role of the

---

[9] http://whc.unesco.org/en/list/946 [Accessed 17 April 2011].

political context in the manipulation of public remembering: before the war, the Ottoman heritage was interpreted mainly through the prism of the national liberation struggles and the battles against the foreign invaders; in post-Dayton Bosnia it came to represent the shared public life of the Bosnian religious and ethnic groups.

Even though mention of the bridge as evidence of Bosnia's multiculturalism had not appeared until after its destruction, today the Old Bridge is officially presented on the UNESCO website as "a symbol of reconciliation, international cooperation and of the co-existence of diverse cultural, ethnic and religious communities"[10]. Yet, the people in Mostar continue to live in ethnically homogeneous enclaves separated by invisible walls. Mostar remains a divided city whose citizens appear unsusceptible to foreign policies of reconciliation. It is interesting to note that even though *Stari Most* is internationally heralded as a symbol of the reunion between the Croat and the Bosniak parts of the town, the bridge is located in the Eastern (Bosniak) part and hence does not reconnect the Croat and the Muslim communities. Croats in Mostar continue to perceive the bridge merely as a Muslim site, which is not part of their history, and even point to it as evidence of the enhanced Muslim presence in the town.

A "Don't forget" message near the reconstructed Old Bridge in Mostar

---

[10] "Old Bridge Area of the Old City of Mostar", http://whc.unesco.org/en/list/946 [Accessed 18 May 2013].

Trans-national politics of memory in Bosnia and Herzegovina: lessons from the past and challenges for the future

The dissolution of Yugoslavia and the violent disintegration of the memory of the common past necessitated the (re)framing of history through the construction of narratives in which symbols and events were attributed with new meaning. In the first post-war decade, transnational politics of memory focused exclusively on the reconstruction of cultural sites as a means for the (re)invention of the common past. Places and sites were treated as tools for the re-interpretation of history through the fixation of public remembering upon fragments of the past that fitted the political context of the present.

The politics of memory in Bosnia and Herzegovina reflected the shortcomings of contemporary trans-national state—and society—building approaches to the Balkans. The need of integration of the Western Balkans into a common European narrative, which became evident after the introduction of the Stability Pact in 1999, gave rise to political generalizations aimed at overcoming the prevailing negative stereotypes of the Balkans as Europe's powder keg. This brings up another interesting pattern of analysis—the political language of the international community and the trans-national discursive framing of the Balkan history and past. Terms like "multi-culturalism", "reconciliation", "tolerance" and "co-existence" are a new discursive phenomenon, which seeks to create a specific image of the Balkans suitable to the region's European and transatlantic integration. Conceptual historians define those words as "collective reference terms" (*Kollektive Referenzbestimmungen*): terms in which the speaker develops theoretically a unit and implies that this unit must bear the idea of the group, the notion of the "collective" for the sake of homogenization (Kosseleck 2004: 27). Thus political discourses often address Southeastern Europe with idealized notions that overemphasized the idea of the common past and the Balkan 'traditional' multi-culturalism. The attempts to rhetorically imply contemporary politial language upon past developments in the region significantly differ from domestic realities and every-day life. There is an obvious tension between the meanings of the terms used to promote peace (e.g. multi-culturalism, reconciliation, co-existence) and the socio-politial context in which these meanings exist. The (mis)use of political language raises the question about the untested transfer of contemporary expressions to the past and calls for a critical conceptual history approach when analyzing the failed efforts on the creation of a supra-ethnic identity in Bosnia and Herzegovina. The blind projection of these terms onto the past without a diachronic analysis taking into account political and socio-anthropological aspects of previous forms of co-habitation in the Balkans, is not only bound to bring limited results, but can also prove to be counter-productive.

Another source of concern is the politicization of culture in the institutionalization of memory. Despite the pompous rhetoric emphasizing a common cultural past, international policies financed and reconstructed mostly ethnic heritage and religious sites. The extensive aid provided by Muslim governments is often interpreted as cultural policy aiming to promote Islam and Islamism through means that go beyond the capacity of conventional diplomacy. These claims have been triggered by the particularly intense (re)construction of mosques in Bosnia and Herzegovina: according to data of the Center for Islamic Architecture of the Bosnian Islamic Community, by 2008 3/4 of the destroyed or damaged mosques had been renovated with the help of the international community and different Muslim states[11]. The Turkish government is one of the most proactive sponsors of UNESCO's projects on the reconstruction of Ottoman heritage sites, including the Old Bridge in Mostar. Moreover, Bosnia and Herzegovina currently hosts many newly constructed mosques, whose size and artistic style resembles the environment in Dubai and Saudi Arabia more than the traditional Ottoman heritage of the Balkans. Many NGO activists report that the restoration of mosques in Bosnia and Herzegovina is often "ideologically inspired", and results in the transformation of those mosques into forms more appropriate to the organizations that funded restorations than to the congregations and communities that used them (Herscher 2007:11–12). According to Aksamija, the post-war construction of mosques in Bosnia has become a catalyst for the Muslim quest for national identity, and those who survived ethnic cleansing built or rebuilt Mosques as a means of asserting material evidence of their existence while simultaneously recovering from traumatic experience (2008:7).

Conversely, the restoration of churches in the country took place at a much slower pace. The Church of the Holy Trinity in Mostar, which is the biggest Orthodox church in Bosnia and Herzegovina and one of the most

---

[11] https://thebosnianwarfactstimelinehistorygenocidecriminals.wordpress.com/tag/remembering-over-1000-destroyed-and-damaged-mosques-in/, [Accessed 17 April 2011].

important Orthodox monuments in the Balkans, remained unattended for more than 16 years due to the lack of any foreign (or domestic) aid to provide for its renovation.

Newly constructed mosque in BiH   *Traditional Ottoman mosque in BiH*

Today, the mapping of ethnic territory and the channelling of foreign political interests through cultural strategies remains a widely spread phenomenon in Bosnia and Herzegovina. The memory landscape in the country remains fragmented and competed by conflicting local narratives, especially at the practices of commemoration and monument building (Moll 2012: 1). Politics of memory tend to be based on a priori constructed definitions and security interests rather than on the wider understanding of the social, cultural and economic aspects of the domestic environment. The number of renovated sites in Bosnia and Herzegovina shows that politics of memory succeeded in the tangible rebuilding of cultural heritage. Unaccomplished remains the reconstruction of the memory of the prewar cohabitation between the different ethnic groups. In this regard, the key challenge to the international community remains the same as it was in mid-1990s:—is it possible to reunite societies divided by traumas of war, to (re)build a sustainable peace and to re-create common identity/memory by importing foreign reconciliation policies based on external political discourses and mechanisms?

References

Anderson, B. 1991. Imagined Communities: Reflections on the Origin and Spread of Nationalism. London: Verso.

Aksamija, A. 2008. *(Re) Constructing History: Post-Socialist Mosque Architecture in Bosnia-Herzegovina*, In: Divided God. Project of Intercultural Dialogue, 11 June 2008, http://www.pozitiv.si/dividedgod/index.php?option=com_content&task=view&id=212&Itemid=68 [Accessed 17 April 2011].

Armakolas, I. 2012. *Mostar: Heritage Reconstruction in a Divided City*, CRIC Project, http://www.academia.edu/3164290/Mostar_heritage_reconstruction_in_a_divided_city [Accessed January 15 2013].

Assmann, A. 2008. *Transformation between History and Memory*. Social Research: an International Quarterly, Vol. 75, N 1, pp. 49–72.

Billig, M. 1995. Banal Nationalism, London: Sage Publications.

Bing, J. 2001. *Ideas and Realities: Rebuilding in Postwar Mostar*, Journal of Architectural Education, May, 2001, ACSA, pp. 238–249.

Clifford, J. 1997. Routes. Travel and Translation in the late 20th century. Harvard: Harvard University Press.

Confino, A. 1997. *Collective Memory and Cultural History: Problems of Method*, The American Historical Review, vol.102, No 5, pp. 1386–1403.

Cordero, G. 2006. "*Solutions for Northern Kosovo. Lessons Learned in Mostar, Eastern Slavonia and Brcko*", http://gmu.academia.edu/MelissaSinclair/Papers/313419/ [Accessed 15 May 2011].

Donia, R. 2007. *The New Masters of Memory: Libraries, Archives and Museums in Post-Communist Bosnia and Herzegovina*. In: Fr. Blouin and W. Rosenberg (eds) Archives, Documentation and Institutions of Social Memory: Essays from the Sawyer Seminar. Michigan: University of Michigan Press, pp. 393–402.

Engelstoft, S., Prodic, A. and Robinson., G. 2001. *Remaking Sarajevo: Bosnian Nationalism After the Dayton Accord*, Political Geography, 2001, 20(8), pp. 957–980.

Grodach, C. 2002. *Reconstituting Identity and History in Post-war Mostar. CPY*, Vol.6, No1, pp. 61–83.

Habermas, J. 1968. Erkenntnis und Interesse. Frankfurt am Main: Suhrkamp.

Hajdarpašić, E. 2010. *But my Memory Betrayes me: National Master Narratives and the Ambiguities of History in Bosnia and Herzegovina*. In Petritsch, W. and Dzihic V. (eds) Conflict and Memory: Bridging Past and Future in Southeast Europe, Baden-Baden: Nomos Verlag, pp. 201–214.

Hajdarpašić, E. 2008. *Museums, Multiculturalism and the Remaking of Postwar Sarajevo*. In R. Ostow (eds) (Re) Visualizing National History: Museums and National Identities in Europe in the New Millenium. Toronto: University of Toronto Press, pp. 109–139.

Halbwachs, M. 1992. On Collective Memory, Chicago: Chicago University Press.

Herscher, A. 2007. *Heritage in the After-war*. In: A. Herscher (eds) Heritage after War. The Hadum Mosque Restoration, pp. 9–15.

Hladić, J. 2001. *Protection of Cultural Heritage during Hostilities*, Museums International (UNESCO Paris), N. 211, Vol.53, No 3, pp. 65–67.

Judt, T. 2010. Postwar: A History of Europe since 1945, London: Penguin.

Koselleck, R. 2004. *Gibt es ein kollektives Gedächtnis?*, Divinatio:Studia Culturologica Series, 19/2004, pp. 23–29.

Kunz-Kohli, A. 1972. Errinern und Vergessen. Das Gegenwärtigkeit des Vergangenen als Grundproblem historischer Wissenschaft. Berlin: Duncker und Humblot.

Landry, C. 2002. *Togetherness in Difference: Culture at the Crossroads in Bosnia and Herzegovina*, http://www.coe.int/t/dg4/cultureheritage/culture/reviews/CDCULT200217BBosnie_EN.pdf [Accessed 2 October 2012].

Lebow, R. 2006. *The Memory of Politics in Postwar Europe*, in: Lebow, R.,

Kansteiner, W., Fogu, C. (eds), The Politics of Memory in Postwar Europe, Duke University Press, pp. 1–40.

Lozić, V. 2011. "*National Museums in Bosnia and Herzegovina and Slovenia: a Story of Making 'Us'*", Conference Proceedings from European National Museums: Identity Politics, the Use of the Past, and the European Citizen, Bologna, 28–30 April 2011, http://www.ep.liuse/ecp/064/005/ecp64005.pdf [Accessed 3 June 2013].

Moll, N. 2013. *Fragmented Memories in a Fragmented Country: Memory Competition and Political Identity-building in Today's Bosnia and Herzegovina*, Nationalities Papers: The Journal of Nationalism and Ethnicity, pp. 1–27.

Mussi, M. 2012. *The International Heritage Doctrine and the Management of Heritage in Sarajevo, Bosnia and Herzegovina: the Case of the Commission to Preserve National Monuments*, 27 July 2012, International Journal of Heritage Studies, http://dx.doi.org/10.1080/13527258.2012.709191 [Accessed 3 June 2013]

Norra, P. 1989. *Between history and memory: les lieux de mémoire*. Representations No 26, pp. 7–24.

Nye, J. 2003. Understanding International Conflicts. An Introduction to Theory and History, New York: Longman.

Osborne, B. 2001 *Landscapes, Memory, Monuments and Commemorations: Putting Identity in its Place*, Canadian Ethnic Studies Journal, 33(3), pp. 36–77.

Perry, V. 2002. *ECMY Civil Society Project in Bosnia and Herzegovina: Ensuring Effective Implementation of Annex 8 though the Establishment of a Cultural Heritage Association*. European Center for Minority Issues Report No36, 2002.

Riedlmayer, A. 1995. *Libraries are not for burning: International Librarianship and the Recovery of the Destroyed Heritage of Bosnia and Herzegovina*, Middle East Studies Association Bulletin, Vol.29, No1, pp. 7–12.

Sahović, D. and Zulumović, D. 2012. *Obsolete Cultural Heritage in Post-Conflict Environments. The Case of AVNOJ Museum in Jajce, Bosnia Herzegovina*, Journal of Balkan and Near Eastern Studies, 14:2, pp. 245–262.

Taylor, E. 2012. *Museums Narrating the Nation: Case-Studies from Greece and Bosnia and Herzegovina*, Totem: The University of Western Ontario Journal of Anthropology, Vol. 20/1, available at: http://ir.lib.uwo.ca/totem/vol 20/iss1/4 [Accessed 17 July 2012].

Teijgeler, R. 2011. *Archeologist under Pressure: Neutral or Cooperative in Wartime*. In: P. Stone, ed., Cultural Heritage, Ethics, and the Military, Woodbridge: The Boydell Press, pp. 86–109.

Truc, G. 2011. *Memory of Places and Places of Memory: for a Halbwachsian Socio-Ethnography of Collective Memory*, International Social Science Journal, No 203–204, pp. 147–159.

Verovśek, P. 2013. *The Politics of Memory: a Conceptual Approach to the Study of Memory in Politics*, http://www.yale.edu/macmillan/ocvprogram/conf_papers/Verovsek.pdf [Accessed 27 July 2013].

Volcić, Z. 2009. *Neither "East" nor "West": The Past and Present Life of Yugoslav Identity*, CAS Working Papers Series 2, CAS: Sofia, 2009, www.cas.bg [Accessed 3 December 2013]

Vukov, N. 2009. *Visualization of the Past in Transition: Museum Representations in Hungary, Romania, and Bulgaria after 1989*, CAS Working Papers Series 2, CAS: Sofia, 2009, www.cas.bg [Accessed 3 February 2014].

ANASTAS VANGELI

On the Growing Cooperation Between China and the Western Balkans[1]

As one of the central themes of contemporary world affairs, the rise of China is part of the process of the global redistribution of power. China has assumed a pro-active international role and its cooperation with countries all around the globe has been steadily increasing. The countries of the Western Balkans have not been an exception to this trend. The paper first provides a historical overview, discussing the relations between China and the Balkans before 1989, in the early post-communist period, and finally, in the last several years. The Sino-Balkan relationship today is examined through the lenses of China's Going Out policy, the Sino-European strategic partnership and the new platform for cooperation between China and the countries of Central, East and Southeast Europe. The paper discusses the current state and the future prospects of the Sino-Balkan relations, in particular the questions regarding the China-EU-Balkans triangle.

Key Words: Sino-Balkan relations, economic diplomacy, regional cooperation, political conditionality.

Anastas Vangeli is a PhD student at the Graduate School for Social Research at the Polish Academy of Science in Warsaw.

Introduction

The rise of China over the last three decades is one of the most important developments humankind has ever witnessed. As one of the central themes of contemporary world affairs, it is part of the process of the global redistribution of power. Many analysts in fact, have argued that China is poised to take on a leading role in global affairs (Jacques 2009).

How can the region of the Western Balkans adjust to this new reality? China, at least in the mainstream view, has been portrayed as distant—not only geographically, but also discursively. China runs on a political model

---

[1] This paper is part of a larger scale research project on the relations between China and the countries of Central, East and Southeast Europe with a special focus on Macedonia, supported by the Center for Research and Policy Making (CRPM) in Skopje.

that the Balkan countries had ultimately dissociated with by the early 1990s. On the other hand, the countries in the region themselves have been "inward-looking" and busy with the processes of political and economic consolidation, not having time to focus on emerging powers elsewhere in the world. Their foreign relations have primarily been concerned with regional affairs and their double integration in the European Union and NATO.

Furthermore, the disparity in size between the Balkans and China is astonishing. In terms of population, the Western Balkans countries combined equal the population of Beijing; while in terms of GDP they stand between the province of Yunnan and the Autonomous Region of Xinjiang, which rank 24th and 25th out of all of the administrative units of China in 2012 (see Table 1). Such miniscule size, and the troublesome experience of transition, could potentially render the Western Balkans insignificant in the eyes of global players such as China.

	Population	GDP in 2012 (billion USD)
Albania	3,162,000	12.65
Bosnia	3,834,000	17.47
Croatia	4.267.000	59.23
Macedonia	2,106,000	9.613
Montenegro	621,100	4.373
Serbia	7,224,000	37.49
Kosovo	1,806,000	6.445
Western Balkans	**18,753,100**	**147.271**
Chinese comparison	Beijing (roughly 19 million)	Between 24 and 25 place (Yunnan and Xinjiang)
China total	1,351,000,000	8,227.000

Table 1. Comparison between the Western Balkans and China. Sources: The World Bank; China Briefing (on provincial data).

Nonetheless, by the second decade of the twenty-first century, China has assumed a pro-active international role and its cooperation with countries all around the globe has been steadily increasing. The countries of the Western Balkans have not been an exception to this trend, and have swiftly gained prominence in the eyes of Chinese diplomats in the last few years.

Historical background

While economic interests and trends shape the overall direction, the details and the nuances of the relationship are of great importance in the process of crafting mutual trust, and in refining the political aspects of the relations between China and the Balkan countries.

Communist legacy

The history of bilateral relations between the two sides, although rich, does not extend to the very distant past. Before the second half of the twentieth century, China and the periphery of Europe—and particularly the Balkans—had had barely any contact, either political or economic.[2] This changed when they all emerged as parts of the "socialist community" in the aftermath of the Second World War. However, at that historical juncture, the relationship between China and the countries that now constitute the Western Balkans—and back then were Yugoslavia and Albania—was a function of their respective relations with the USSR, the stronghold of communism during the Cold War (Bailes 1990; Yahuda 1995).

The relationship between China and the USSR, on the other hand, has been highly unpredictable and turbulent (Yahuda 1990; Johnson 1971). Initially, after proclaiming the People's Republic, China pursued a "leaning on one side" policy, which meant full and unconditional commitment to the alliance with the USSR. To prove its loyalty to Moscow, China in the first place adopted an anti-American line, and got involved in the Korean War; pursued "fraternalism" with the Soviet satellite regimes in Europe, and strongly condemned Yugoslav "revisionism."

Albania, on the other hand, emerged not only as China's ally during the 1960s and much of the 70s, but also as a follower of Mao Zedong Thought during the Enver Hoxha regime, in what analysts labelled a "Sino-Albanian entente" (Tertiak 1962; Prifti 1968). After the Sino-Soviet split in the early 1960s, both China and Albania were isolated from the rest of the communist world and opposed to the "evil empire" image that USSR had acquired by that time.

---

[2] This is a matter of dispute. Croatia has recently claimed Marco Polo, the famous Venetian merchant that traveled to China in the thirteenth century, as part of its heritage, which caused furious reactions in Italy (Squires, 2011).

The growing perception of the USSR as a threat in the wake of the invasion of Czechoslovakia in 1968, and later on the rapprochement with the United States and Western Europe, also contributed to the improvement of the relations between Beijing and most of the other communist governments in Europe, and in particular with Yugoslavia (Andelman 1979). In 1978, the Chairman of the CCP, Hua Guofeng, after hosting Josip Broz-Tito the year before, travelled to Yugoslavia and Romania, which marked the first trip abroad of a top Chinese statesman since the 1950s. In the Balkans, Hua was allegedly impressed when he saw the potential benefits of economic experimentation and foreign trade, a lesson that would eventually reinforce the pursuit of economic reforms in China in the following years (Vogel 2011: 163). He also spoke on the infamous Macedonian Question, using it as a proxy venue to retaliate to the USSR regarding the events in Southeast Asia (Sfetas 2012). Paradoxically, while 1978 marked a breakthrough in the Sino-Yugoslav relationship, it also happened to be the year of the Sino-Albanian split, after Hoxha refuted the new Chinese leadership and opted for a policy of self-sufficiency (Biberaj 1986). After the death of Tito, Sino-Yugoslav relations remained mostly ceremonial; Albania had slowly started to normalize relations with China by the late 1980s.

In conclusion, the role of the communist legacy is limited, yet significant for the further advancement of Sino-Balkan relations. Unlike most of Europe and many other countries in the world, Albania and Yugoslavia recognized the People's Republic of China right after its foundation.[3] Albania and the Yugoslav successor countries have therefore increased symbolic capital in China. Their importance was recognized, for instance, during a recent retrospective exhibition in the National Museum of China which featured historical images of the cooperation of China and the countries of Central, East and Southeast Europe (National Museum of China 2013).[4]

---

[3] Yugoslavia was among the first countries to recognize the establishment of the PRC in October 1949. Since the relations between Beijing and Belgrade in the subsequent period were tense, primarily because of the ideological discrepancies, the state-to-state relations were formally functional, whilst the Party-to-Party relationship was inconsistent and for periods of time non-existent.

[4] For an example of using communist-era relations as a pretext for boosting contemporary cooperation with Albania, see Qin (2013). However, some of the Balkan countries might not be too proud of this aspect of their relations with China, as it

Post-communist scars

With little meaningful contact during the 1980s, the relations between China and the Balkans were once again set back with the developments of 1989, the most eventful year in the history of the "socialist community." After the Tiananmen Square events in June that year, China found itself estranged from by the international community. The Yugoslav federal government, which at the time had liberal orientations, sharply condemned the crackdown on the protestors (The Register Guard 1989: 5A). As later on communists lost power in the Balkans, most of the countries saw the rise of ideologically charged anti-communist elites—albeit less intensively anti-communist in comparison to their peers in Central Europe. However, the rejection of communism coupled with strong pro-Western attitudes had prevented any closer or strategic relationship with China. This new reality of the former communist states, now becoming Western allies and withering away from China, was described as a "new divide" by Michael Yahuda (1995).

One exception from this trend was the Federal Republic of Yugoslav led by Slobodan Milošević, which in China found sympathy and support in the face of growing pressure from the West. Beijing also had an interest in pushing for the preservation of Yugoslav borders and preventing the secession of Kosovo, both because of its non-interventionism principle and the renewed tensions in Tibet and in the Taiwan Strait which jeopardized China's territorial integrity. China therefore maintained very close cooperation with FR Yugoslavia and, after the Serbo-Montenegrin split, with the Republic of Serbia—its only strategic partner in the region. The warm political relations of the past have been reflected in contemporary cooperation. Serbia has more large-scale infrastructural cooperation projects with China than any other country in the Western Balkans and is also the largest trader with China in the region (gbtimes.com 2013).

In 1999 China was a fierce opponent of the NATO operation against FR Yugoslavia. As a permanent member of the United Nations Security Council, it protested against the breach of international law and protected the Milošević regime and Yugoslavia's territorial integrity. During the NATO air raids, the Chinese embassy in Belgrade was bombed. This inspired vigorous anti-American sentiment in China, that went on to define

---

proves counterproductive vis a vis the recent efforts of some individual Balkan countries, such as Macedonia, to condemn their communist past (see Vangeli, 2011).

the new identity of the People's Republic (Gries, 2005). At the same time, the rest of the Balkan countries supported the intervention against Milošević's regime while some of them also provided logistical support for NATO troops (e.g. Macedonia and Albania). After these developments, China—back then still pursuing a "low profile" foreign policy—had little interest in stepping up its involvement in the region.

Another burning issue that stood in the way of advancing relations between China and many of the governments in Europe at the turn of the century was Taiwan. Under the DPP government, Taiwan pursued an economic charm offensive in Europe, and in particular in the post-communist countries, trying to "shop for allies" and secure recognition via economic means (Tubilewicz 2007). Throughout the 1990s, most of the countries in the region expanded their cooperation with Taiwan and flirted with the idea of recognizing its independence. However, it was only Macedonia that did actually recognize Taiwan in 1999, thus rendering the relationship between Beijing and the region even more turbulent (Tubilewicz 2007: 177–179). The recognition of Taiwan provoked China to retaliate with a veto on the mandate on the United Nations Preventive Deployment Force in Macedonia. The withdrawal of the blue helmets from the country preceded the spill over conflict in 2001. In the meantime, the political elite were split on the Taiwan deal, preventing it from fully materialising. While Macedonia quickly restored its relationship with Beijing in less than two years after the breach, bilateral relations have remained scarred. The Taiwan experience has been singled out as an obstacle in terms of restoring the trust of China in Macedonia (Telegraf 2014).

Finally, China has remained a staunch opponent of Kosovan independence, and to date has not recognized it. Its relations with Bosnia and Croatia and, after its independence, Montenegro, have thus far had no significant ups and downs.[5]

---

[5] Another event that occurred later on was the Sino-Albanian Guantanamo prisoners' crisis, the one point where the pro-American orientation of the countries in the region was at odds with the relations with China. In 2007, Albania, a devout US ally in the War on Terror, accepted a deal with the US that resulted in Tirana offering to grant asylum to five ethnic Uyghurs, former detainees from the Guantanamo Bay prison, who were suspected of international terrorism. Official Beijing, facing its own woes over terrorism in the Xinjiang Autonomous Region, had insisted that the five men

The move forward

In the last several years—approximately from 2008/9 onwards—the relations between China and the Balkan countries have been substantially improving, and the so called "divide" has been gradually refashioned into a very promising relationship of mutual benefit.

China's rise and "going out"

China's rise as well as its future economic development is inevitably rooted in its relations with the rest of the world. Foreign trade and investment have been at the heart of China's growth from 1978 onwards, and, alongside ideology and normative values, have defined China's profile as a global actor. China overtook the US to become the largest global exporter of goods in 2009, earning the title of "factory of the world". Around the same time it became the second-leading importer of goods, after the US. In early 2014, it overtook the US as the country with the largest total trade volume of goods in the world (BBC 2014) and during the period of its rise China has also become the largest recipient of foreign direct investment.[6]

China has also become the largest holder of foreign reserves and is increasingly active in terms of OFDI and development aid. By 2014, China has amassed a record $3.82 trillion of foreign reserves (Bloomberg News 2014).

As a result, China has promoted a new approach to handling large amounts of capital, by actively promoting outward investment. In fact, outward investment is now considered to be of equal importance for China's future growth as attracting FDIs. This is the guiding attitude of the so called "Going Out/Going Global Policy" (*zouchuqu zhanlue*). As the 12th Five Year Plan (2010–2015)—the policy guideline for the Chinese government—states, China will

> "continue the combination of the strategies 'bringing in' and 'going out' and [will] pay equal attention to both foreign investment in China and Chinese investments abroad in order to increase safe and effective use of the two markets and their resources (Bernasconi-Osterwalder et al., 2013: 12)."

---

should be deported back to China to face justice; however Tirana, following the pro-American line, opted to keep the refugees in Albania (Golden, 2007).

[6] On the condition and prospects of the Chinese economy see Morrison (2014).

To do so, Chinese policy-makers prioritize stepping up "overseas investment cooperation in an orderly manner."

The resolve of such a robust economy to invest abroad is felt in all corners of the globe. While some voices abroad have warned that China's ambitious "Going Out" might be an attempt to gain the upper hand in the developing world, or even an attempt at colonialism (on this debate, see for instance Jauch 2011)—a more reasonable explanation is that, at the end of the day, China's "Going Out" is primarily rooted in the need to sustain a large and growing economy and to advance the competitiveness and the international profile of Chinese state-owned enterprises. In particular, as Sauvant and Chen (2013) argue:

> "For the national economy, broadening the scope and geography of investment means more options for economic restructuring and resource allocation optimisation. OFDI thus provides more resources and opportunities for economic growth. In addition, OFDI provides access to tangible and intangible resources directly relevant to China's development effort, beginning with raw materials but also including technology, brand names and others."

While its rise was originally founded on labor-intensive, export-oriented production, China, especially in the era of the leadership of Xi Jinping and Li Keqiang is aiming at a shift towards a model of economic development based primarily on domestic market forces. This process is to be accompanied by large-scale urbanization and a larger share of the tertiary sector in the economy (Drysdale 2013).

China–Europe relations

While China does business in every corner of the planet, official Beijing sees Europe as one of its most important partners. By the same token, China in recent years has gained one of the highest spots on the agenda of the EU, as well its member states, but also of European countries that are not members of the EU.

China and the EU are strategic partners; 2013 marked the tenth anniversary of the establishment of their partnership. In the early 2000s the relations between Brussels and Beijing were defined by a steady rise in economic cooperation and in finding common political stances (such as opposition to the invasion of Iraq and American militant unilateralism); among analysts on China–EU relations this period is referred to as the "honeymoon" (Shambaugh 1997). Yet soon after their relationship took a more bumpy turn (Shambaugh 2010), facing trade disputes (e.g. the numerous anti-dumping measures EU has been imposing on Chinese exports, the latest one being the solar panel crisis of 2013); collision over politically sensitive issues (such as Tibetan unrest, and the EU's reaction in the wake of the Beijing Olympics in 2008 and the on-and-off contention over human rights) and lack of coordination on global issues (such as the fiasco at the Copenhagen climate change COP in 2009).[7] Yet China and Europe have remained devout partners, and have succeeded in many areas of cooperation: they are still backbones to each other's growth; they both support multilateralism; they work together on achieving greener and more sustainable models of development, and work actively on people-to-people contact and cultural exchange (Austermann et al. 2013). By the end of 2013 they formulated the ambitious Strategic Agenda 2020, which is expected to have tangible policy outcomes.

While they still prioritize their own domestic imperatives, they try to avoid sensitive and conflicting situations and to expand opportunities for cooperation. Using Henry Kissinger's terminology, they essentially maintain a relationship of "co-evolution" (Austermann et al. 2013).

Moreover, the tone of the China–EU relationship since 2009 has been set by the global financial crisis. Europe came out of the crisis more vulnerable than ever, as its common currency and economic stability have been in constant jeopardy. Much of its domestic, as well as foreign policy have been directed towards mitigating the adverse effects of the crisis. China, on the other hand, went through the crisis with much less serious consequences, thus emerging as one of the most significant (or most hoped for) partners assisting European recovery.

At the same time, China maintains equal if not more intense bilateral relations with individual member states. Of special importance is the example of Germany and the so called "special relationship" between Beijing and Berlin (Kudnani and Parello-Plesner 2012). It is grounded on strong economic cooperation, as the Sino-German two-way trade accounts for about a third of the total volume of the exchange between China and the EU.

Beijing does not only look to the founding countries of the EU, but also the "new" and the "future" members as well. An actual outcome of this

---

[7] For a historical overview of Sino-European relations 2003–2013 see Wong (2013).

approach has been the establishment of the platform CEE16+1, which refers to the 16 European countries: Albania, Bosnia and Herzegovina, Bulgaria, Croatia, the Czech Republic, Estonia, Hungary, Latvia, Lithuania, Macedonia, Montenegro, Poland, Romania, Serbia, Slovakia and Slovenia; and China.[8] Out of these sixteen countries, only eleven are current EU member states, the rest being in different stages of accession.

In addition to the advancement of Sino-European relations beyond the China–EU platform in post-communist Europe, a great advancement in 2013 for China was the finalization of the free trade talks with Switzerland and Iceland, both European countries that are not members of the EU. These deals were important for demonstrating that China is not a protectionist trader (Y. Zhang 2013). Zhou Hong (2013) has therefore argued that this reflects China's pro-active and comprehensive approach to Europe.

China–CEE16 relations

In the last few years, China has stepped up its involvement in the post-communist countries of Europe. Moreover, for the first time in history, it is not Washington, Brussels, or Moscow, but Beijing that has established a platform for cooperation with the countries of Central, East and Southeast Europe.

The cornerstone of the CEE16+1 platform was set during the "China-Central and Eastern European Countries Economic and Trade Forum," held in Budapest, 2011 (China Daily 2011). After a year of preparations, in April 2012, during the "China-Central and Eastern Europe Business Forum" the then Premier of the State Council of China, Wen Jiabao, announced the so-called "twelve-point action plan" that aimed to significantly advance the relations between China and CEE16 (China Daily 2012).

The first of these twelve points referred to the establishment of the so-called Secretariat for Cooperation between China and the CEE16 countries, based within the Chinese Ministry of Foreign Affairs and chaired by the Chinese Vice-Minister for Foreign Affairs.

The Secretariat held its inaugural session on September 6, 2012 (Ministry of Foreign Affairs of the People's Republic of China, September 7, 2012).

---

[8] While the official terminology describes them as "Central and Eastern European (CEE) Countries," in this paper I use the term CEE16, and CEE16+1 when I add China to the group.

The rest of the goals outlined by Wen during the Warsaw meeting were as follows ("China's Twelve Measures for Promoting Friendly Cooperation with Central and Eastern European Countries," 2012):

> 2) Establishment of a US $10 billion special credit line for the CEE16 countries;
> 3) Setting up an investment cooperation fund between China and CEE16 countries with the goal of raising US $500 million in the first stage;
> 4) Increase of the total trade volume between China and CEE16 to US $100 billion by 2015;
> 5) Stimulation of Chinese enterprises to invest in special economic and technology zones in CEE16;
> 6) Exploration of potential financial cooperation such as "currency swap, local currency settlement for cross-border trade, and establishment of bank branches in each other's countries";
> 7) Establishment of an expert advisory committee on the construction of transportation network between China and CEE16 countries (e.g. regional highway or railway through joint venture, joint contracting and other means);
> 8) Expansion of cultural cooperation;
> 9) Provision of scholarships to the CEE16 countries and support of the Confucius Institutes and Confucius Classrooms programs, and invitation of Chinese language students to China;
> 10) Establishment of a tourism promotion alliance between China and CEE16 countries, coordinated by the China Tourism Administration;
> 11) Establishment of a research fund on relations between China and CEE16;
> 12) Hosting of the first young political leaders forum of China and CEE16 in 2013.

As Justyna Szczudlik-Tatar (2013) argues, the platform for cooperation, although announced with great fanfare, it is in fact more of a pragmatic arrangement for China to deal with all the sixteen countries at once. In this sense, the block of sixteen countries is somewhat arbitrarily created by China (currently there is no other platform that unites the Baltic, the Visegrad and the Balkan states as a subregion), primarily due to the shared communist past and the historical legacy of bilateral ties. However, the countries are diverse from each other, and have different orientations. This leads us to Szczudlik-Tatar's second point, that there is no common CEE16 policy towards China, but many individual agendas, which are sometimes competitive. Thirdly, annual forums are not "summits" in the classical sense, but primarily a format of simultaneous bilateral meetings between representatives of the CEE16 countries with the Chinese Premier. Last but not least, such cooperation also fosters intra-CEE16 competition for grabbing a large share of the resources plans to invest in the region.

Ever since the announcement of its work in September 2012, the Secretariat has organized several important meetings, initiating cooperation in the following fields:

- Promotion Event of Tourism Products of China and countries of CEE16;
- Cultural Cooperation Forum (coupled with a retrospective exhibition of the cooperation between CEE16 and China in the National Museum of China)
- An Education Policy Dialogue.

In terms of major meetings, the Meeting of Local Leaders in Chongqing took place during the summer of 2013, (Wang 2013). The meeting had high-level attendance as well as a significant number of business delegations, and resulted in the signing of the Chongqing Declaration which, among other things, speaks of the further advancement of the infrastructure projects that constitute the second corridor of the aforementioned "Eurasian Land Bridge" or the "New Silk Road."

In November 2013 the third summit took place in Bucharest, Romania. The host country was in the spotlight, announcing deals such as the construction of high-speed rail, nuclear reactors and power plants (Zhao 2013).

The Bucharest meeting was attended by the heads of states of the Western Balkans countries, and was used to reiterate the commitment of China towards their mutual partnership. Moreover, they specified further guidelines for trade and investment, designating 2014 as the "China-CEEC Investment and Business Promotion Year." The declaration from the Summit also specified a detailed point on "enhancing cooperation in connectivity" which consists of the following measures (The Bucharest Guidelines, 2013):

- Actively discuss the possibility of building an international railway
- Transportation corridor connecting China with CEECs and encourage businesses to establish bonded areas and distribution centers along the railway routes to build a new logistics passage between China and Europe.
- Strengthen cooperation in infrastructure development, such as construction of roads, railways, ports and airports based on the principle of mutual benefit.
- Support the establishment of a China-CEEC association on infrastructure cooperation and relevant Chinese and CEEC agencies and businesses are welcome to join on a voluntary basis.
- Welcome a high-level conference on transport, logistics and trade routes connecting Asia with Europe to be held in 2014 in Riga, Latvia.

The Summit declaration also introduced new provisions on cooperation in science, technology, innovation, environmental protection and energy The most important of these provisions is the commitment of China "to step up cooperation with CEECs on nuclear power, wind power, hydro power, solar power and other sources of clean power for mutual benefit and common development" as well as on upgrading the rusty old coal plants (The Bucharest Guidelines 2013).

Locating the Balkans on the Chinese radar

Contemporary Sino-Balkans relations are primarily a function of the CEE16+1 framework. While China's main partners in the group of CEE16+1 have been Hungary, Poland, the Czech Republic, Romania and Bulgaria, the Western Balkans are slowly gaining prominence on the agenda of the CEE16+1 platform.

As with the rest of China's foreign policy, the China-Balkans cooperation rests on the "mutual benefit" or "win-win" approach. The Balkans countries expect to get more loans, investments and trade opportunities, as well as support for large-scale infrastructure projects. China—in the Balkans as elsewhere on the European periphery (e.g. Ukraine)—is sticking to its formula that has already succeeded in the developing world. Firstly, it is willing to provide loans "without any normative strings attached" (aside from recognizing one-China policy and being a friend of China). Secondly, it is looking for opportunities to profitably invest its foreign reserves, to be present in the (wider) European market, and of course, to benefit both the host countries' economy, but also its own economic portfolio.

In this sense, political relations in the form of high and lower level diplomacy mostly play a "supporting role in achieving economic goals;" cultural exchanges, by the same token, serve as "soft power tools" aimed at painting a more appealing image of China in the region (Szczudlik-Tatar 2011).

However, unlike the developing countries of Africa, Central Asia and Latin America, or Ukraine, one of China's major partners in Wider Europe, the Balkans, is not rich in resources, and is miniscule in comparison to China. Unlike the majority of CEE16, except for Croatia, no other Balkans country is not part of the common European market. Yet the most important reason that China considers the Balkan countries as potential business partners is that the countries in the region have demonstrated a chronic and growingly indiscriminate thirst for foreign capital, both in terms of investment and development aid.

Most of the governments in the region, ever since the early phase of their economic transitions, have worked towards securing a more favorable climate for foreign investors, which at the same time would secure support among their electorates. Yet the FDIs attracted so far have only partially met expectations. The reason for this lies not only in the above mentioned exogenous factors such as size or distance, but also in the quality of their institutions (Saul and Uvalic 2013).

In the aftermath of the global financial crisis, the traditional investors in the region—in the first place the EU—have had limited capacity to inspire positive economic trends, or at least are being perceived as such (Bechev 2013). Therefore, other sources of capital are warmly welcome. In addition, China seeks very little in return for economic cooperation and focuses primarily on mutual benefit and tangible business outcomes.

The Balkan countries also still need core infrastructure. Brokering and implementing infrastructure deals are something that China has perfected both at home and abroad, by engaging in large-scale projects in the transportation and energy sector. As we see in the next section, the majority of Chinese FDIs in the Balkans, in place or in progress, are either in the energy or transportation infrastructure sector.

At the same time, Chinese companies working on infrastructure in the Balkans, while building on their experience at home and in the developing world, get a chance, as Pavlicevic (2011: 5.8) suggests, to improve and "achieve compliance with European standards and gain maturity to enter regulated and competitive EU markets."

This is related to the third point of interest for China, which is the Balkans' potential role as a de facto European "backdoor." For China, it is invaluable that Balkan countries are projected to join the common European market in the future (as Croatia already has). While not being as attractive partners as the most developed European states, the Balkans have comparatively lower production costs, lower barriers and less competition, while providing more benefits and demonstrating strong political will for cooperation. More cooperation with the Balkans adds to the already high intensity of cooperation with the EU that China has achieved in the last decade, but is also an investment that might pay off in the future by securing a permanent Chinese presence in the common market once the Balkan countries join the EU (Pavlicevic 2011: 5.3–5.4).

Fourthly, while physically distant from the main EU markets, the Balkans has a peculiar geographic location, which fits into China's broader vision of establishing trade routes across Asia and Europe. China has already invested significantly in developing three Eurasian Landbridges (Lin 2011):

- the first one joins the existing Trans-Siberian Rail (passes through Mongolia, Russia, Belarus, Poland, before reaching Germany);
- the second one spans from Eastern and Central China, to Chongqing, and then to Xinjiang, before passing through Kazakhstan, Russia, Belarus and Poland and finally reaching Germany;
- the third one is the southern route, which starts from Guangdong, spans through South and West Asia to Turkey (with a branch line towards the Middle East), and then through the Balkans to the rest of Europe.

While the Baltic countries and Poland are key to Landbridges I and II, the Balkans is an important region for the third one. The large scale investment in infrastructure in Turkey, in the Greek seaports and in road infrastructure in the Western Balkans, certainly reinforce the impression that China has a strong interest in further contributing to the development of regional transportation infrastructure. In addition to emphasising transportation as a key sector in cooperation during the Bucharest summit, and committing to the construction of high-speed rail in Romania, China has also committed to upgrading the Belgrade-Budapest rail link.

As of recently, Chinese SOEs have shown interest in a major river-transportation project that would link the Danube, Morava and Vardar through canals (an idea dating back to the 19 century).

Advancement of China–Balkans relations

Trade

In recent years every single one of the CEE16 countries, including the Balkan countries, saw a rise in their economic exchange with China. The dramatic increase in the two-way trade between China and the countries of the Western Balkans can be seen in Chart 1.

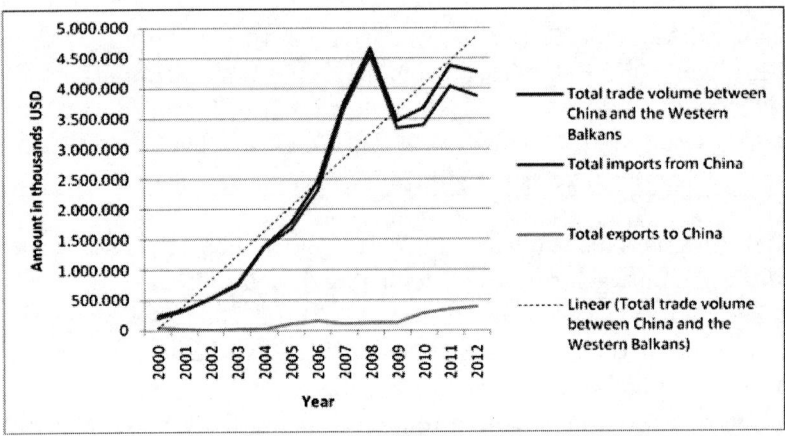

Chart 1. Trade between the Western Balkan countries and China 2000–2012. The data until 2007 is aggregated for Albania, Bosnia and Herzegovina, Croatia, Macedonia and FR Yugoslavia, later called Serbia and Montenegro. From 2008 onwards, the data is aggregated for Albania, Bosnia and Herzegovina, Croatia, Macedonia, Montenegro and Serbia. Source: UNCTADstat.

The two-way trade between China and the Western Balkans countries has been constantly rising. While the total two-way merchandise trade volume in 2000 was less than USD 0.25 billion, in 2008 it peaked at more than USD 4.5 billion. However, in 2009 it fell significantly, as a result of the global financial crisis. Since then, the pace of trade has been restored.

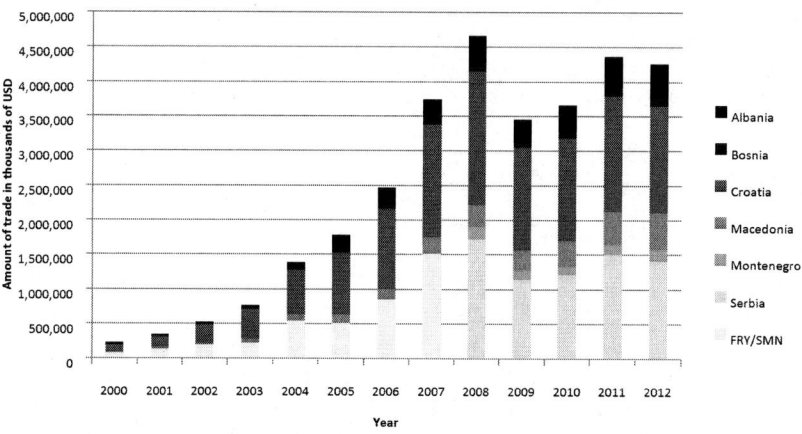

Chart 2. Trade between the Western Balkan countries and China 2000–2012, by country. Source: UNCTADstat.

However, not all countries trade equally. As we see in Chart 2, Croatia and Serbia are the leading traders with China in the region. More important is to note that Balkan countries have a very high trade deficit in their relations with China. Even though exports have increased in the last three years, the two-way trade is significantly asymmetrical. This can be seen in detail in Table 2.

Total imports from China in thousands of dollars, annual, 2008–2012					
	2008	2009	2010	2011	2012
Albania	316,269.249	281,786.160	264,781.131	339,012.723	364,208.663
Bosnia	124,665.830	67,608.948	78,405.149	91,581.311	91,325.750
Croatia	1,885,833.301	1,441,495.746	1,440,729.319	1,604,811.743	1,487,851.145
Macedonia	314,773.568	289,409.300	288,781.531	354,650.660	374,766.854
Montenegro	182,649.262	126,333.240	117,014.840	143,831.310	167,629.541
Serbia	1,719,046.969	1,135,316.185	1,202,476.189	1,488,491.950	1,386,698.608
WB Total imports	4,543,238.17	3,341,949.57	3,392,188.15	4,022,379.69	3,872,480.56

Total exports to China in thousands of dollars, annual, 2008–2012					
	2008	2009	2010	2011	2012
Albania	66,106.691	47,848.359	125,003.375	119,611.910	138,056.581
Bosnia	6,611.343	14,121.624	18,224.000	30,859.740	22,357.681
Croatia	35,263.636	41,090.655	37,695.204	54,692.458	45,866.130
Macedonia	3,342.181	3,243.627	89,177.970	127,460.025	158,846.262
Montenegro	225.500	133.103	197.112	1,038.909	4,884.060
Serbia	5,777.250	8,954.988	7,258.518	15,257.557	20,264.677
WB Total exports	117,326.601	115,392.356	277,556.179	348,920.599	390,275.391
Total trade volume, annual, 2008–2012					
	2008	2009	2010	2011	2012
Albania	382,375.940	329,634.519	389,784.506	458,624.633	502,265.244
Bosnia	131,277.173	81,730.572	96,629.149	122,441.051	113,683.431
Croatia	1,921,096.937	1,482,586.401	1,478,424.523	1,659,504.201	1,533,717.275
Macedonia	318,115.749	292,652.927	377,959.501	482,110.685	533,613.116
Montenegro	182,874.762	126,466.343	117,211.952	144,870.219	172,513.601
Serbia	1,724,824.219	1,144,271.173	1,209,734.707	1,503,749.507	1,406,963.285
WB Total trade	4,660,564.780	3,457,341.935	3,669,744.338	4,371,300.296	4,262,755.952
Trade balance, annual, 2008–2012					
	2008	2009	2010	2011	2012
Albania	-250,162.56	-233,937.80	-139,777.76	-219,400.81	-226,152.08
Bosnia	-118,054.49	-53,487.32	-60,181.15	-60,721.57	-68,968.07
Croatia	-1,850,569.67	-1,400,405.09	-1,403,034.12	-1,550,119.29	-1,441,985.02
Macedonia	-311,431.39	-286,165.67	-199,603.56	-227,190.64	-215,920.59
Montenegro	-182,423.76	-126,200.14	-116,817.73	-142,792.40	-162,745.48
Serbia	-1,713,269.72	-1,126,361.20	-1,195,217.67	-1,473,234.39	-1,366,433.93
WB Total	-4,425,911.58	-3,226,557.22	-3,114,631.98	-3,673,459.10	-3,482,205.17

Table 2. Two-way trade between the Western Balkan countries and China in detail. Source: UNCTADstat.

As far as the composition of the trade by products is concerned, there is a uniform trend that the Balkans countries primarily export mined raw materials and ores, while they import products such as textiles, electronics or miscellaneous (Table 3).

Year: 2011	Albania	Bosnia	Croatia	Macedonia	Montenegro	Serbia
Main exports	Chromium ore, Gold content	Textiles, Lead ores	Electronics, Minerals	Ferroalloys, Lead ores	Zinc ores, Chromium ores	Zinc ores, Ferroalloys
Main imports	Textiles, Miscellaneous	Textiles, Electronics	Electronics, textiles	Electronics	Electronics, textiles	Electronics, textiles

Table 3. Main products traded between the countries of the Western Balkans and China in 2011. Source: MIT Economic Complexity Observatory.

However, despite the rise in bilateral trade, China is still not a major trading partner of any single one of the Western Balkan countries, as they still trade mostly with the EU and between each other. China, though, does emerge as the most significant non-European trading partner, alongside Russia and Turkey. The Western Balkans, in this sense, has a long way to go in order to catch up with the rest of CEE16, and the EU28 as a whole, which is China's number one trading partner. Yet two-way trade between the Balkans and China is expected to grow in the future, especially since 2014 was announced as "China-CEEC Investment and Business Promotion Year" throughout which officials are supposed to actively encourage further growth of economic exchange.

Investment

Chinese investments in the Balkans, as noted above, come primarily in the form of transportation infrastructure, in the first place railroads and highways and in energy projects, primarily electricity production capacities.

Table 4 shows a list of eleven major ongoing projects undertaken by Chinese SOEs in the Balkans. The total cost of these projects is close to USD 6.9 billion.

Year	Country	Amount (million USD)	Chinese Partner/Contractor	Sector	Project
2010	Bosnia	710	Dongfang Electric	Energy (Coal)	Development of a new thermal plant near the Stanari coal mine.

2010	Serbia	344	China National Machinery and Equipment Import and Export Corp.	Energy (Coal)	Reconstruction of the Kostolac coal fired power station (completed).
2010	Serbia	260	China Road and Bridge Corporation (CRBC)	Transportation (Bridge)	Construction of a landmark 1.5km Zemum-Borca bridge in Belgrade (to be completed by the end of 2014).
2012	Croatia	415	China International Investment Stock Ltd	Industry; Energy (geothermal)	Construction of a paper mill in Croatia with local PAN Papirna Industrija d.o.o, powered by a geothermal plant, in Slatin.
2012	Serbia	1,500	Environmental Energy Holdings and the Shenzhen Energy Group	Energy (Coal)	Developing the Nikola Tesla coal power plant.
2013	Bosnia	280	Sepco III Electric Power Construction Corp	Energy (Gas)	Construction of a 390 megawatt (MW) gas-fired power plant in Zenica.
2013	Macedonia	400	Power Construction Corp	Transportation (Highways)	Construction of two stretches of highway linking Kicevo-Ohrid and Miladinovci-Stip, 56.7km and 53km long, respectively.

2013	Montenegro	1,070	Chinese Communications Construction Company (CCCC), and its subsidiary China Road and Bridge Corporation (CRBC)	Transportation (Highways)	Construction of the first 41 km section of the planned Bar-Boljare highway.
2013	Serbia	850	China Road and Bridge Corporation	Transportation (Motorways)	Construction of a 110-kilometer motorway from Pojate to Preljina and a 27-kilometer motorway from Novi Sad to Ruma.
2013	Serbia	330	Shandong Gaosu	Transportation (Highways)	Construction of portions of section of Corridor 11 through Western Serbia.
2013	Serbia	720	China National Machinery and Equipment Import and Export Corp.	Energy (Coal)	Further work in Kostolac.
Total	Two projects in Bosnia, one in Croatia, Macedonia and Montenegro each, and six projects in Serbia.	6,879		Six energy projects; five transportation projects.	

Table 1. Major Chinese investments in the Balkans. Own research, combined with data from Heritage Global Chinese Investment Tracker.

However, as in any other segment, Chinese involvement in the region is happening incrementally and less spectacularly than some might envision. In practice, the cooperation is still far from smooth or living up to the expectations of both sides. The differing managerial cultures and the diverging visions of running businesses in general, as well as some institutional constraints and human errors, have often led to cancellation of projects and loss of resources.

A prevailing problem is that Balkan officials, aiming to boost their public image, often hyperbolize the state of affairs regarding Chinese potential investments or involvement in large-scale projects. This is more often than not conflicted with the Chinese approach, which is cautious, technocratic and not overly enthusiastic about communicating details in the early stages.

Political and cultural cooperation

The economic cooperation has been accompanied by a growingly favorable political climate, primarily through increased diplomatic activity between China and the Balkan countries. First and second track diplomatic exchanges are more frequent than ever, and so are multilateral summits—primarily within the CEE16 framework—in which Chinese representatives meet delegations from several, if not all the countries from the region. There has been military cooperation as well, with high representatives of the People's Liberation Army visiting the region on several occasions.

Furthermore, four countries in the region now host Confucius Institutes (Albania, Croatia, Macedonia and Serbia, which hosts two). Confucius Institutes serve as the cornerstone of Chinese cultural diplomacy and soft power abroad.

	Year opened	Host institution	Chinese partner institution
Albania	2013	University of Tirana	Beijing Foreign Studies University
Croatia	2012	University of Zagreb	Shanghai Institute for International Trade
Macedonia	2013	University Ss Cyril and Methodius, Skopje	Southwestern University of Finance and Economics, Chengdu
Serbia	2006	University of Belgrade	Communication University of China, Beijing
	2013	University of Novi Sad	Zhejiang University of Technology

Table 5. *Confucius Institutes in the Western Balkans.*

The China–EU–Balkans triangle

China as an actor in Europe

In the EU, there are growing perceptions of China as an economic threat. This is mostly due to the intertwining of business and politics when China is in question; as well as Beijing's multi-level foreign policy approach towards Europe. China's economic interest, and as a consequence its presence in Europe, has been more visible since the onset of the European sovereign debt crisis (Austermann et al. 2013).

China has become an economic actor inside Europe through the actual increase of Chinese investments in the EU, but also due to the promises, expectations and speculations about potential future investments. If not the reality, then the narrative of the coming of China has substantially increased debate, and by the same token, the suspicion of the potential influence of Beijing in the Union and on the continent in general. Since it comes at a time of crisis, many Europeans see it as a signal of the decline of the West, and frequently couple it with unpleasant and dystopian visions of the future in which Europe "kowtows" in front of Beijing, losing all its grace, dignity, culture and values (Scurati 2011; Fox and Godement 2009).

China's multi-level approach towards Europe is another issue for worry in Brussels. Working with both the Union and the member states has had an impact on the success (or lack thereof) of the common European policy on China. The European Council on Foreign Relations (ECFR) has argued that many countries in Europe are now adopting much more flexible attitudes towards China on issues critical to Brussels as a result of the growing interest in cooperation and the increase in effective cooperation.

A few years ago, European countries could be divided into four camps with regards to their attitude on Sino-European relations—a) those closely following the common EU policy ("European followers"); b) those that were tough on Chinese unfair trade and dumping ("accommodating mercantilists"); c) those who were pushing for further opening of the Chinese market to European companies ("ideological free-traders"); and d) those who were critical towards China in terms of both economic and political issues ("assertive industrialists"; see Fox and Godement 2009). By 2011 the landscape was drastically different. Only a few "frustrated market-openers" had maintained their attitudes in line with the Union's and would not shy away from criticism when necessary. The majority of EU countries, however, struck by the crisis, have put the priority on attracting Chinese deals, while neglecting issues that might lead to confrontation with Beijing. Especially important was the formation of the block of "cash-strapped deal seekers" which has become mute on the points of contention between Brussels and Beijing (including political issues), fulfilling the expectation that strong business ties with China imply mostly ceremonial politics, and certainly avoidance of critical issues (Godement et al. 2011).

It is important, however, to note that the favoritism of business over politics has not only been present among the crisis-struck countries on the periphery of Europe, but also at the very core of it. The most obvious example is Germany. Some voices in Europe have increasingly portrayed China and Germany as two complementary actors, or "conjoined twins" (Saunders 2013). China often prefers Berlin over Brussels when it wants to talk to Europe, while Germany has acted as a mediator in the recent disputes between China and the EU over the import of solar panels (Donahue and Nicola 2013). On the other hand, Germany has significantly toned down its criticism on topics such as human rights (Handelsblatt 2013). Other big players, such as the UK, have also tried to craft a closer business relationship with China by neglecting political conditionality, which has resulted in David Cameron being blamed for "kowtowing" by domestic media (Ren 2013).

Is the Sino-Balkans relationship anti-EU?

In Brussels, the skeptical attitude towards Chinese economic involvement has greatly shaped the attitude towards increased CEE16+1 activity in general. By choosing a sub-regional approach, and most importantly choosing Warsaw, Budapest and Bucharest as the centers for cooperation, many EU diplomats see the CEE16+1 platform as an attempt to circumvent Brussels—and by some, it is even deemed as a covert attempt to "divide and conquer" the continent, and to replicate China's model of cooperation devised in the developing world (Bolzen and Erling 2013). In the aftermath of the Bucharest CEE16+1 Summit, for instance, the Trade Commissioner Karl de Gucht had sent a letter "expressing irritation" to the EU countries involved (Chiriac 2013). As opposed to this, Chinese foreign policy analysts labelled the collaboration with the CEE16 a "highlight" of the whole of Sino-European relations. Outside the CEE16+1 platform, China also pursued cooperation with European states that are not part of the EU (Ukraine and

Moldova, as well as Belarus), extending its "project" in the wider Europe area.

The potential implications of an economically active China inside Europe have been a major concern for analysts in the EU. Timothy Garton Ash (2011) was among the more influential voices to warn of potential "informal colonization," and moreover the emergence of a "Chinese lobby" within the EU, comprised of states indebted to China, willing to stand for or at least not obstruct, Chinese interests in the EU. With regards to the Balkans, only one of the countries is by now a full EU member state, whilst the rest are in different stages of accession. In that sense, they could not be considered as a potential "Chinese lobby," at least until the day they have a vote in the European Council.

However, one might argue that being too close to China could be reflected in various forms on the road to EU integration. One of the root causes of concern is the belief that China might become a dominant economic force in the region, and consequently diminish the influence of the EU.

The EU has traditionally tied its economic aid investment to certain standards and political norms, based on its liberal-democratic, pro-human-rights exceptionalism. In the Balkans, the EU has had a transformative role, and has played a crucial role in the establishment and the maintenance of democratic institutions. Moreover, the European dream of the Balkan countries is one of a prosperous economy at least as much as it is one of liberal democracy. Thus the question is: if the EU's relative contribution to the economic development of the region is being partially replaced by the influence of outside actors such as China, would domestic elites (and the citizens) still pursue the rest of the European dream? A significant portion of pro-EU sentiment in the Balkans has been lost in the aftermath of the economic crisis, complemented by the dissatisfaction with the tortuous ending of the transition process (Bechev 2013), as well as the permanent presence of nationalism. The promise that economic prosperity is achievable without bothering with the rest of EU integration, could lead to further decline of European ideals in the region.

Moreover, dealing with China is about business with no strings attached. Unlike the other major traders and investors in the world—the US and the EU—China discriminates much less regarding whom it deals with; unlike the US and the EU, it leaves normative conditionality outside the deal (however, there is a political conditioning in terms of recognizing the One-China Policy and not challenging China on what Beijing deems "sensitive issues" and "core interests," i.e. Taiwan, Tibet, Xinjiang). In fact, such an approach—and cooperation with countries that have difficult relations with the West (e.g. Iran, Zimbabwe) has also led to controversies. This is partially why some progressives in the Balkans fear that China could one day partner with non-democratic leaders and dictators, should they emerge.

However, there are two factors that suggest that these fears are exaggerated. Firstly, regardless of how interested it is in the region, China has no real ambitions—nor has it the potential to replace traditional economic partners. The Balkans is still comparatively less attractive than other post-communist countries in Europe, such as Hungary, Poland, the Czech Republic, Romania or Bulgaria, which have higher potential, are bigger markets, and are part of the EU already. Unlike them, the Western Balkans countries are further away from the big EU markets, and as much as the relative underdevelopment and lack of infrastructure opens "developmental" opportunities for China, it also prevents engagement in more advanced and profitable ventures. As stated previously, China's "Going Out" is strongly guided by the quest for the sustainability of the domestic economy, and in this sense it prefers regions that are rich in resources, or partners that can offer advanced technologies, two things that the Balkans cannot offer. That means that the level of cooperation is going to sooner or later plateau.

Secondly, China's interest is not to subvert democracy and the EU integration of the Balkans, but to actually support them—albeit, one could argue, from a pragmatic standpoint. China is becoming more involved in the Balkans precisely because of its European future. The Western Balkan countries therefore, would still have to advance their EU-membership prospects in order to become more relevant partners for China; Beijing has little interest in cooperating with small countries that have no access to the common European market. Moreover, a hypothetical departure from democracy and the European path in the Balkan context, almost without exception, would be either a cause or a consequence of destabilization and increased political risk, and would even attract potential international sanctions; while China is not overly concerned with norms and values, it pays close attention to the political climate and the stability of institutions prior to advancing economic cooperation, and regulates investment through Bilateral Investment Agreements (BITs) — currently, it has signed more BITs than any other country in the world (Bowman et al. 2013). Should some of the countries in the region fail to Europeanize or experience democratic backsliding, they will likely remain isolated islands, significantly limiting the potential return from investing and trading with them even to such an indiscriminate partner like China.

Furthermore, while stimulating intra-CEE16, and by the same token, intra-Balkans competition for grabbing a larger share of the newly available Chinese deals, Beijing might also inspire regional cooperation. The gradual shift of the focus towards transportation infrastructure projects would require cross-border collaboration and overall good neighborly relations. This could also contribute towards advancing the relations between the Balkan countries and their neighbors, in particular the ones that are already EU member states. The hypothetical undertaking of projects such as the announced upgrade of the Budapest-Belgrade link, or finding an effective way to link Macedonia and Serbia through their rivers with the Aegean coast, could prove to be instances in which China could facilitate cooperation between the Western Balkans and the EU.

In fact, to a great extent, the CEE16+1 platform and the role the Western Balkans plays in China's strategy towards Europe, could be seen as a process that passively and inadvertently elevates the status of the Balkan countries within the continent. During the CEE16+1 meetings, the Albanian, Bosnian, Macedonian, Montenegrin and Serbian representatives are treated equally as their counterparts from the rest of the CEE16 EU-member states, among which there are powerful players, such as Poland. This new reality certainly could have emancipating effects in terms of the Western Balkan countries stepping out on the international scene. It also poses the challenge of pursuing a more mature foreign policy that would have to tread carefully between strategic orientations and doing business, and discern between political interest on one hand, and economic benefit on the other.

References

Andelman, D. A. 1979. *China's Balkan Strategy,* International Security 4 (3), pp. 60–79.

Ash, T. G. 2011. *Europe's Crisis Is China's Opportunity. No Wonder Nice Mr Wen Is on His Way.* The Guardian, June 22. http://www.theguardian.com/commentisfree/2011/jun/22/europes-crisis-is-chinas-opportunity.

Austermann, F., Vangeli, An. and Wang, X. (eds) forthcoming. China and Europe in 21st Century Global Politics: Partnership, Competition or Co-Evolution? Cambridge: Cambridge Scholars Publishing.

Bailes, Alyson J. K. 1990. *China and Eastern Europe: A Judgement on the 'Socialist Community.* The Pacific Review 3 (3), pp. 222–42. doi:10.1080/09512749008718871.

BBC News - China 'Overtakes' US as World's Largest Goods Trader. 2014. Accessed March 1. http://www.bbc.com/news/business-25678415.

Bechev, D. 2013. *The Periphery of the Periphery: The Western Balkans and the Euro Crisis.* Policy Brief 60. London: European Council on Foreign Relations. http://ecfr.eu/content/entry/the_periphery_of_the_periphery_the_western_balkans_and_the_euro_crisis.

Biberaj, E. 1986. Albania and China: A Study of an Unequal Alliance. Westview Press.

Bolzen, S, and Erling, J. 2013. *Divide, Conquer, Aim East: China Has A Sharp New European Trade Strategy.* Worldcrunch. Accessed July 24. http://www.worldcrunch.com/world-affairs/divide-conquer-aim-east-china-has-a-sharp-new-european-trade-strategy/eastern-europe-beijing-foreign-commerce/c1s10100/.

Bowman, M., Gilligan, G. and O'Brien, J.. 2013. *China: Investing in the World.* CLMR Working Paper 13-5. CLMR Research Paper Series. Centre for Law, Markets and Regulation. The University of New South Wales School of Law. http://www.clmr.unsw.edu.au/resource/risk/state-capitalism/clmr-working-paper-13-5-china-investing-world.

Bradford, An., and Posner E. A. 2011. *Universal Exceptionalism in International Law.* Harvard International Law Journal 52, pp. 1–40.

Briefing, China. 2014. *China's Provincial GDP Figures in 2012 | China Briefing News.* Accessed March 9. http://www.china-briefing.com/news/2013/05/16/chinas-provincial-gdp-figures-in-2012.html.

Buckley, N. 2012. *Beijing Wakes up to Eastern Europe.* Financial Times, May 17. http://www.ft.com/cms/s/0/03d93826-9f79-11e1-a255-00144feabdc0.html#axzz2cn6rX4GL.

China Global Investment Tracker Map. 2013. Heritage Foundation. http://www.heritage.org/research/projects/china-global-investment-tracker-interactive-map.

China's New Nationalism Pride, Politics, and Diplomacy. 2005. Princeton, N.J.: Recording for the Blind & Dyslexic.

China's Twelve Measures for Promoting Friendly Cooperation with Central and Eastern European Countries. 2012. Ministry of Foreign Affairs of the People's Republic of China. http://www.fmprc.gov.cn/eng/topics/wjbispg/t928567.shtml.

Chinese Firm to Build Highway in Southeast Europe|Companies|chinadaily.com.cn. 2014. Accessed March 1. http://europe.chinadaily.com.cn/business/2013-07/30/content_16852688.htm.

Chinese Investment into Serbia Set for Sea Change—BUSINESS NEW EUROPE. 2014. Accessed March 1. http://www.bne.eu/story3768/Chinese_investment_into_Serbia_set_for_sea_change.

Chiriac, M. 2013. *China Raises Its Game on Europe's Eastern Flank.* Balkan Insight, November 28. http://www.balkaninsight.com/en/article/china-raises-its-game-on-europe-s-eastern-flank.

Drysdale, P. 2013. *Likonomics and China's New Economic Strategy.* East Asia Forum, July 8. http://www.eastasiaforum.org/2013/07/08/likonomics-and-chinas-new-economic-strategy/.

Drysdale, P, and Shang-Jin, W. 2012. *The Rise of Chinese Foreign Investment.* East Asia Forum, June 11. http://www.eastasiaforum.org/2012/06/11/the-rise-of-chinese-foreign-investment/.

Economist. 2009. *China's 'Going out' Strategy.* The Economist Free Exchange Blog. http://www.economist.com/blogs/freeexchange/2009/07/chinas_going_out_strategy.

Estrin, S. and Uvalic, M. 2013. *Foreign Direct Investment into Transition Economies: Are the Balkans Different?* LEQS Paper No. 64/2013. LSE "Europe in Question" Discussion Paper Series. London: London School of Economy and Political Science. http://www.lse.ac.uk/europeanInstitute/LEQS/LEQSPaper64.pdf.

Godement, F. 2012. *China Goes for the New Europe in Warsaw—Be Our Guest—E!Sharp*. E!Sharp, April. http://esharp.eu/be-our-guest/17-china-goes-for-the-new-europe-in-warsaw/.

Godement, F., Parello-Plesner, J. and Richard, Al.. 2011. *The Scramble for Europe*. Policy Brief. London: European Council on Foreign Relations. http://www.ecfr.eu/page/-/ECFR37_Scramble_For_Europe_AW_v4.pdf.

Golden, T. 2007. *Chinese Leave Guantánamo for Albanian Limbo*. The New York Times, June 10, sec. International/Europe. http://www.nytimes.com/2007/06/10/world/europe/10resettle.html.

Golonka, M. 2012a. *Partners or Rivals? Chinese Investment in Central and East Europe*. CEED Report Part I. Warsaw: Central and Eastern Europe Development Institute.

———. 2012b. *Partners or Rivals? Chinese Investment in Central and East Europe*. CEED Report Part II. Warsaw: Central and Eastern Europe Development Institute.

Grzeszak, Ad. 2011. *Poland: The Motorway That China Couldn't Build*. Presseurop, June 16. http://www.presseurop.eu/en/content/article/716731-motorway-china-couldnt-build.

Handelsblatt. 2013. *Europäische Leisetreterei in China Muss Ein Ende Haben*. Handelsblatt. May 18. http://www.handelsblatt.com/politik/international/menschenrechtsbeauftragter-europaeische-leisetreterei-in-china-muss-ein-ende-haben/8225394.html.

Jauch, H. 2011. *Chinese Investments in Africa: Twenty-First Century Colonialism?* New Labor Forum 20 (2): 48–55.

Jiao, X., and Hu, H. 2013. *Education Policy Dialogue Between China and Central & Eastern European Countries Held in Chongqing*. Jiangsu Provincial Department of Education. http://english.jsjyt.gov.cn/news/keynews/folder612/2013/07/2013-07-032743.html.

Johnson, A. R. 1971. *The Sino-Soviet Relationship and Yugoslavia 1949–1971*. RAND Paper. Santa Monica, California: The RAND Corporation. http://www.rand.org/pubs/papers/P4591.html.

Kudnani, H. and Parello-Plesner, J. 2012. *China and Germany: Why the Emerging Special Relationship Matters for Europe*. Policy Brief. London: European Council on Foreign Relations. http://ecfr.eu/page/-/ECFR55_CHINA_GERMANY_BRIEF_AW.pdf.

Lin, C. 2011. *China's New Silk Road to the Mediterranean: The Eurasian Land Bridge and Return of Admiral Zheng He*. 165. ISPSW Strategy Series: Focus on Defense and International Security. Institute for Strategic, Political, Security and Economic Consultancy.

Liu, Z. 2013. *An EU Opening: China Stands Ready to Increase Investment in Central and Eastern European Countries*. Beijing Review, January 10. http://www.bjreview.com/world/txt/2013-01/07/content_510717.htm.

Local Leaders from China-Central and East European Countries (CEEC) Launched a 'Chongqing Initiative. 2013. Chongqing Municipal Government. http://en.cq.gov.cn/ChongqingToday/News/4021.htm.

Millner, C. 2012. *With 10 Billion Dollar Credit Line, China Deepens Presence in Central Europe*. Spiegel Online, May 18. http://www.spiegel.de/internatio nal/europe/with-10-billion-dollar-credit-line-china-deepens-presence-in-central-europe-a-833811.html.

Morrison, W. M. 2014. *China's Economic Rise: History, Trends, Challenges, and Implications for the United States*. 7-5700/RL33534. Congressional Research Service. https://www.fas.org/sgp/crs/row/RL33534.pdf.

MTI. 2014. *Hungary, Serbia, China Agree on Upgrading Budapest-Belgrade Railway*. Politics.hu. Accessed March 9. http://www.politics.hu/20131 126/hungary-serbia-china-agree-on-upgrading-budapest-belgrade-railway/.

Pantucci, R., and Petersen, Al. 2012. *China's Inadvertent Empire*. The National Interest, December. http://nationalinterest.org/article/chinas-inadvertent-empire-7615.

Pavlicevic, D. 2011. *The Sino-Serbian Strategic Partnership in a Sino-EU Relationship Context.* 68. Briefing Series. The University of Nottingham, China Policy Institute. http://www.nottingham.ac.uk/cpi/documents/briefings/briefing-68-sino-serbian-partnership.pdf.

Prifti, P. R. 1968. Albania's "Cultural Revolution. Cambridge :: Massachusetts Institute of Technology, Center for International Studies,.

Qin, Am. 2013. *A Friendship Is Rekindled With Albania* - NYTimes.com. New York Times. Sinosphere Blog., November 29. http://sinosphere.blogs.nytimes.com/2013/11/29/a-friendship-is-rekindled-with-albania/?_php=true&_type=blogs&_php=true&_type=blogs&_r=1.

Ren, Yuan. 2013. *Is Britain Kowtowing to China?* The Atlantic, November 14. http://www.theatlantic.com/china/archive/2013/11/is-britain-kowtowing-to-china/281479/.

Retrospective Exhibition on Cultural Exchanges between China and Central and Eastern European Countries Opens. 2013. National Museum of China. http://en.chnmuseum.cn/Default.aspx?TabId=521&InfoID=91718&frtid=500&AspxAutoDetectCookieSupport=1.

Šambevski Dade Otčet Za Srabotenoto. 2014. Telegraf. February 28. http://www.telegraf.mk/aktuelno/makedonija/112465-sambevski-dade-otcet-za-srabotenoto-vo-kina.

Sauvant, K., and Zitian Chen, V. 2013. *China Invests Overseas to Develop Domestically*, 5 (3), pp. 32–34.

Sfetas, S. 2012. *The Bulgarian-Yugoslav Dispute over the Macedonian Question as a Reflection of the Soviet-Yugoslav Controversy (1968–1980).* Balcanica, no. 43, pp. 241–71. doi:10.2298/BALC1243241S.

Shambaugh, D. 2007. *The 'China Honeymoon' Is over.* New York Times. November 26. http://www.nytimes.com/2007/11/26/opinion/26iht-edshambaugh.1.8482459.html?_r=0.

Soare, S. R. 2012. *Beijing's Central and Eastern European Charm Offensive: The Implications of China's Growing Presence in the New Europe.* In Navigating Uncertainty. US—Central European Relations 2012, edited by Jakub J. G., Kron, R., Mitchel, A. W. and Paskova, G., pp. 64–73. Washington: Center for European Policy Analysis.

Squires, N. 16:44. *Italians Furious as Croatia Lays Claim to Marco Polo.* Telegraph.co.uk, sec. worldnews. http://www.telegraph.co.uk/news/worldnews/europe/italy/8471174/Italians-furious-as-Croatia-lays-claim-to-Marco-Polo.html.

Szczudlik-Tatar, J. 2011a. *China's Policy towards Central and Eastern Europe.* Bulletin No. 44 (261). The Polish Institute of International Affairs.

———. 2011b. *China's Policy Towards Non-EU 'New Eastern Europe'.* Bulletin No. 103 (320). The Polish Institute of International Affairs.

The Bucharest Guidelines for Cooperation between China and Central and Eastern European Countries. 2014. Accessed March 9. http://gov.ro/en/news/the-bucharest-guidelines-for-cooperation-between-china-and-central-and-eastern-european-countries.

The First China-Central & Eastern Europe Cultural Cooperation Forum. 2013. Embassy of the Republic of Poland in Beijing. http://beijing.mfa.gov.pl/en/news/the_first_china_central___eastern_europe_cultural_cooperation_forum.

The Globalization of Chinese Capital.

The Inaugural Conference of China-CEE Cooperation Secretariat and the First National Coordinators' Meeting Are Held in Beijing. 2012. Ministry of Foreign Affairs of the People's Republic of China. http://www.fmprc.gov.cn/ce/ceuk/eng/zgyw/t969490.htm.

The Unbreakable Connection between Serbia and China. 2013. Gbtimes.com, August 6. http://gbtimes.com/world/unbreakable-connection-between-serbia-and-china.

Tretiak, D. 1962. *The Founding of the Sino-Albanian Entente.* The China Quarterly 10, pp. 123–43. doi:10.1017/S0305741000002824.

Tubilewicz, C. 2007. Shopping for Allies: Taiwan and Post-Communist Europe. London; New York: Routledge.

Vangeli, An. 2012. *Beijing via Warsaw: The Growing Importance of China—CESEE Relations.* Perspectives Internationales, May 12. http://perspectivesinternationales.com/?p=511.

Vice Foreign Minister Song Tao Meets with Leading Officials of Tourism Departments of Central and Eastern European Countries. 2012. Ministry of Foreign Affairs of the People's Republic of China. http://www.fmprc.gov.cn/eng/zxxx/t991771.shtml.

Vogel, Ez. 2011. Deng Xiaoping and the Transformation of China. Harvard University Press.

Voss, H., and Clegg, L. J. 2011. *Understanding the Chinese-EU Investment Relationship.* East Asia Forum, February. http://www.eastasiaforum.org/2011/02/02/understanding-the-chinese-eu-investment-relationship/.

Wang, W. 2013. *Local Level Coop to Be a New Pillar of China-CEEC Coop.* China Radio International. July 4. http://english.cri.cn/6909/2013/07/04/2361s773929.htm.

Wong, R. 2013. *The Issue of Identity in the EU-China Relationship.* Politique Européenne n° 39 (1), pp. 158–85.

World Condemns Tiananmen Bloodshed. 1989. The Register Guard, June 5.

Xinhua. 2011. *Wen Proposes More Cooperation with Europe.* China Daily. June 26. http://www.chinadaily.com.cn/china/2011weneurope/2011-06-26/content_12777273.htm.

———. 2012. *Wen Calls for Deepening Ties with Central, Eastern Europe.* China Daily, April 26. http://www.chinadaily.com.cn/bizchina/2012-04-26/content_15153189.htm.

Yahuda, M. B. 1995. *China and Europe: The Significance of A Secondary Relationship.* In Chinese Foreign Policy: Theory and Practice, edited by Thomas Robinson and David Shambaugh, pp. 266–82. Oxford University Press.

Zhang, Yuan'an. 2013. *Closer Look: In Germany and Switzerland, Li Chooses His Friends Carefully.* Caixin. May 27. http://english.caixin.com/2013-05-27/100533383.html.

Zhao, Yinan. 2013. *China, Romania Seal Deals - Chinadaily.com.cn.* China Daily, November 26. http://www.chinadaily.com.cn/china/2013livisiteuasia/2013-11/26/content_17130655.htm.

ALMA VARDARI-KESLER

Statehood Without Sovereignty: Risky Negotiations in Post-Independence Kosovo[1]

Since the Dayton Agreement (1995) all the countries belonging to the "Western Balkans' basket" have been subjugated to the unified Western political and economic "tool-kit" advancing the prospects of democracy, market-economy and multiculturalism. Lumping together the regional societies has facilitated an EU policy-making and a regional research agenda that mutes the cultural, historical, political and economic traits of the local societies and current state institutions. In an attempt to amend the conceptual silence and to draw attention to the domestic voices, this paper focuses on the negotiation process between Kosovo and Serbia as situated in the context of Kosovo's supervised statehood. But, opposing the institutional mindset, this work embraces a bottom-up approach that explores the local contention and enables focus to fall on the emergent discourses and practices (2010–2013). While the EU state-builders and the local politicians present the negotiations as crucial to "the normalization process of the regional relations", this paper argues that the domestic contenders frame them as "imposed and risky", because they undermine Kosovo's sovereignty.

Keywords: Kosovo, supervision regime, negotiations, EU policy-making.

Alma Vardari-Kesler is currently completing her doctoral studies in the Department of Sociology and Anthropology at Tel-Aviv University.

---

[1] I would like to thank the peer reviewers for their useful comments on an earlier draft of this paper. Responsibility for all possible mistakes in this work remains mine.

Introduction

> *The flight from Vienna to Belgrade was nearly an hour, but due to my long anticipation to finally meet the city and its people, it seemed longer. I approached the counter and the border officer took my passport. Her silent face for some reason became annoyed and with a heavy accent asked me: 'Where do you come from?' I answered shortly: "From Vienna" and without really hearing my answer started to put an 'ANULLE' stamp on each border stamp of Kosovo's authorities in my Israeli passport. I didn't react at all, just kept watching her. Probably disappointed by my deliberate silence, she kept looking obsessively for the stamps in every page of my passport to annul them, while irately saying: "There is no state of Kosovo" and in Serbian added through her teeth: 'Kosovo je Serbia', Serbian for 'Kosovo is Serbia'. After 'invalidating Kosovo's statehood' she finally put the stamp of the Serbian authority, dating September 25, 2011. Now I was allowed to enter Serbia, and so I did."*

The officer's practice of annulling Kosovo's statehood, even in a foreign passport, demonstrates the complex viewpoints, the far-stretching practices and the assiduous mental maps engaged in the thorny negotiation process between Kosovo and Serbia, imposed pungently by the European Union.

The body of literature produced by scholars and policy-makers, attempting to research the consequences of the fall of communism and to resolve the conflicts in former Yugoslavia, have concocted a monolithic image of the reconstruction needed for Balkan states. Since the Dayton Agreement (1995), all the countries belonging to the "Western Balkans' basket" have been subjugated to the unified Western political and economic "tool-kit", advancing the prospects of democracy, market-economy and multiculturalism. Lumping together these regional societies has, on one hand, indicated an EU commitment to be involved in the local political and economic processes, while on the other, it has facilitated a policy-making and research agenda that mutes the cultural, historical, political and economic traits of the local societies and current state institutions.

In an attempt to amend the conceptual silence and draw attention to the domestic voices, this paper focuses on the negotiation process between Prishtina and Belgrade as situated in the context of contemporary Kosovo. To that end, the conventional perception of the international involvement in Kosovo as state-building is being challenged and comprehended instead as a supervision regime. Recognizing the supervised nature of the newborn state paves the way to an analytical approach that identifies new connections between structures and actors and provides an alternative understanding of the emerging context. By 'supervision regime' I refer to the international conceptual (discourse) and pragmatic (mechanisms of policy-making) dictation that are constantly impacting on all aspects of the state-building process, while disregarding local interests and systematically imposing a foreign-led decision-making process that alienates local opposing actors and their agendas. In the case of Kosovo or that of Bosnia and Herzegovina for that matter, this dictation is reinforced by the physical presence of the international authorities[2], marking a new pattern of international state-building practice that has been largely overlooked so far.

Secondly, this work challenges the existing institutional and academic mindset by embracing a bottom-up approach. Instead of focusing on the democratization process, the procedures of state-building or market liberalization, this study explores the politics of contention in supervised Kosovo. Taking into account the local contention highlights new from-below-insights about the relationships between national, regional, international and supranational actors interlocked in political, social and economic processes. Those relationships up to now are conceptually and empirically fragmented at best, or muted at worst by the top-down approaches of sociology[3], international relations and political studies.[4]

This paper seeks neither to explain international state-building in contemporary Kosovo nor to study democratization procedures as such. Rather it seeks to establish a different understanding of the emerging configuration of power; the interplay between the local challengers, the newborn state institutions and the Western authorities, as well as the mutual impacts they have on each-other. Hence, the negotiation process provides us with an empirical site that incorporates multiple actors and their competing agendas regarding state-building in Kosovo in a changing socio-political environment.

---

[2] A detailed analysis of the international presence in Kosovo will be provided further on in the study.

[3] The sociology of social movements has been forged primarily in democratic contexts (Meyer 2004: 132), urging thus the need for empirical research and conceptual rethinking of contention politics in non-democratic settings.

[4] While in international studies in the last decade a critical rethinking of international interventions has led to new conceptualizations of sovereignty and statehood as reflected in the works of Zaum 2007, Chandler 2006, Ignatieff 2003 and more.

This work operationalizes two theoretical models in the study of contention: the *political opportunity structure* and the *collective action frames*.[5] The core idea of *political opportunity structures* derives from the emphasis put on the impact of the external context (mainly state institutions, political elites, changing alliances etc) on the emergence and development of social movements (Tilly 1978; McAdam 1982; Tarrow 1998). The key-concept of this theoretical model is "opportunities"—created, encouraged or restrained by the configuration of the political environment and the actors and structures within the state boundaries (Koopmans 1999; Mayer 2004). By political environment scholars have mainly referred to four clusters: 1) openness or closure of the state institutions, 2) presence or absence of elite allies, 3) stability or instability of the political alliances nurturing the polity and 4) state's capacity for repression (Della Porta & Diani 2006). In the context of the newborn state of Kosovo, I apply this analytical tool by referring to the declaration of independence (Feb. 2008) and the supervision regime established since, as two variables shaping the opportunities of local actors for collective action. This kind of conceptualization facilitates new approaches to the politics of contention. It broadens the application of the political opportunity concept beyond traditional nation-state structures, and emphasizes the impact of international actors and their alignments on the process of state-building.

State-building clearly presents an elaborate junction for competing actors and conflicting agendas. In this political process the multiple opportunities do not emerge as empirical facts but rather as sets of meanings perceived by the collective actors. Thus, the framing process as analyzed in the theories of social movements, serves as an analytical tool to elucidate the construction of those collective meanings. This approach sees collective action as rooted in the subjective interpretation that the "challengers" produce in light of the changes of the political reality (McAdam 1982). The notion of "collective action frames" adopted by Snow *et al.* (1986: 464) indicates the schemes of interpretations through which the members of the movements define and articulate their social situation, and grasp and signify their grievances. These schemes of interpretations comprise the source of legitimacy for the members' protest, justifying their very

---

[5] This analysis presents the Albanian contentious organizations in Kosovo, inviting further research regarding their Serbian counterparts and their interactive dynamics, especially intriguing after the declaration of independence.

collective action as a way of improving their conditions (Snow and Benford 1992; Benford and Snow 2000).

How can these approaches assist our understanding of contention politics in present-day Kosovo? While the EU state-builders and local politicians present the negotiation process between Kosovo and Serbia as essential to "the normalization process of the regional relations", domestic contenders frame it as "imposed and risky", because, to their reading, it undermines the sovereignty and thus the future of Kosovo. Moreover, the combined conceptualization of political opportunities and collective framing reveals the unique feature of the local contenders' action strategies which I call *the bifurcated contention*—pointing at a double target: foreign politicians and institutions (Pieter Feith, Catherine Ashton, Christopher Dell, EULEX & EU) on one hand, and current local politicians and government on the other.

The data presented in this study refer mainly to the action strategies and discourse produced by the Levizja Vetevendosje! (henceforth, VV), Albanian for the Movement for Self-determination. Since its establishment in 2005, VV's structure has changed from a grass-root core to an organized social movement. After the declaration of independence, its leading activists initiated the parliamentary group of VV, which emerged in the elections of 2010 and has maintained a fierce and persistent opposition in the Kuvend since then.

I am aware of the conceptual argument which might identify VV as a political party acting within the realm of institutional politics, rather than a contentious actor enhancing its action strategy. Since this study aims to reveal the local collective perspective often silenced so far, and since the members of the movement perceive themselves and their parliamentary work as an undivided part of their contentious praxis, I have decided to treat and explore it as such.

Setting the Kosovar scene—political opportunities and collective meanings

As previously mentioned, the POS approach is a primarily context-driven analytical tool (Koopmans 1999: 102), and is helpful in the attempt to perceive and explain contention politics. Following this logic, this part of the paper briefly presents a background of the historical events and political structures that have shaped the collective actions and meanings of the Albanian resistance in Kosovo.

The struggle for autonomy under the Yugoslav regime (1946–1989)

Kosovo constitutes a mixture of a post-communist society with a post-war reality, clouded by lingering ethnic animosities. The roots of the conflict between Albanians and Serbs in Kosovo are deeply seated in history. Both sides have diachronically advanced conflicting claims for the national "historic" rights over the Kosovo region, bestowed by the virtue of settlement by their forefathers. The annexation of Kosovo to the Kingdom of Croats, Serbs and Slovenes in 1918 and the Yugoslav federation in 1946, signified the main historical junctions when Albanians of Kosovo identified the Serbian hegemony as their chief enemy (Mertus 1999; Judah 2000).

The Yugoslav federation state structure, comprised of six republics, put Kosovo Albanians in a subordinate position within the Serbian federal unit, lacking independence and disconnected from Albania proper (Malcolm 1998: 215–319). The UDBa—secret police—headed by Alexander Rankovic[6] and its repressive practices simply contributed to the further ethnic polarization in Kosovo (Judah 2000: 34–6; Malcolm 1998: 320–3). Especially after the Yugoslav break with Moscow, "Rankovic's regime of state terror in Kosovo" heavily impacted on the post-war relations between Serbs and Albanians and the political life of the province (Glenny 1999: 579–580), leading to the persecution of the whole Albanian population which was perceived as "a potential nest of fifth-columnists and traitors" (Malcolm 1998: 320). As a result, at that period emerged several national organizations, protestations and illegal activities aimed at uniting Kosovo with Albania. During those two decades, thousands of Albanians in Kosovo were questioned, arrested and imprisoned repeatedly (Kecmezi-Basha 2003; Gashi 2010). The Serbian leadership defined those networks of people and activities as irredentist, and used organized state power to put an end to it.

Autonomy, granted to the province in 1974, was the result of the constitutional changes and decentralization policies initiated by Tito (Hayden 1992: 665). Kosovo was granted equal status to the other republics, representation in the highest Yugoslav institutions, recognition of Albanian as the official language, self-governance of the province, and the right to

---

[6] Aleksandar Rankovic Leka served as the Minister of Interior Affairs of Yugoslavia, Head of Military Intelligence (OZNA) and Secret Police (UDB) from 1946–1966.

issue an Albanian constitution (Malcolm 1998: 327). Yet, according to the legal definition, Albanians in Kosovo remain demarcated as *narodnost* (national minority, such as: Albanians, Hungarians etc) as opposed to *narod* (nation, like: Slovenes, Croats, Serbs, Montenegrins, Bosnians and Macedonians), denoting the lack of the constitutional nation's right to secede. (Hodson *et.al* 1994; Malcolm 1998: 328)

Although the 1974 constitution led to many organizational, political and cultural developments in Kosovo, the immense economic and social disparities between Kosovo and the rest of the Yugoslav republics resulted in the increasing perception of the Albanian national elite as "being the real losers of Yugoslavia" (Calic 2000: 25). The students of the University of Prishtina were the first to protest against their conditions in 1981, and soon the miners of Trepca followed (Kecmezi-Basha 2003; Malcolm 1998: 334–5). What first started as local complaints against the general work conditions and profits shifted quickly into an economic and social demonstration against "the Serbian manipulation and Yugoslav exploitation of Kosovo resources".[7]

The claims voiced during these demonstrations indicated the ethnic nature of collective grievances: "We are not Yugoslavs, we are Albanians", "Trepca is ours", "Kosova-Republic", "Long lived the union of the Albanian nation" (Kecmezi-Basha 2003: 66–7). While the demonstrations were in accordance with constitutional rights, the response of the regime was curfews and the declaration of a general state of emergency (Malcolm 1998: 335).[8]

The emergence of the peaceful & armed resistances (1989–1999)

The Kosovars' protests in 1981 were just one part of the overall social, economic and political vacuum that characterized the Yugoslav federation after Tito's death in 1980. Slobodan Milosevic—the rising political figure at the time—adopted a fierce nationalistic ideology. When Eastern Europe

---

[7] In various talks and interviews the author has held with former students and later soldiers of KLA or citizens there has emerged a recurrent narrative of exploitation, as expressed in their words: "Kosovo's natural resources served other republics while Albanians were the poorest region in former Yugoslavia".

[8] In this period more than 2,000 Albanians were arrested, massive *camera* trials were held, over 1,200 prison sentences were issued and more than 3,000 other were sent to jail for up to three months (Malcolm 1998: 335).

took down the Iron Curtain, Milosevic initiated massive protests against the abuse of Serbs' rights in Kosovo (Mertus 1999: 9). Kosovo has historically embodied the quest of the Serbian people for their identity and sovereignty, so it is no accident that in the time of the Yugoslav state collapse it re-emerged as the central narrative of the Serbian nationalist agenda (Calic 2000: 24; Anastasijevic 2000: 50). Hence, in 1989, in defence of the victimized Serbian national identity, Milosevic met the protesters in the "epic" Kosovo Polje (Kosovo field)[9], and abolished the autonomy of Kosovo, enabling the Serbs, who comprised less than 20% of Kosovo's population at the time, the right to rule over the Albanian majority (Demjaha 2000: 33).

The dissolution of Kosovo's autonomy led to the widespread dismissal of Albanians from their work places, resulting in the cleansing of the administrative, education and health systems; the closure of Albanian local media, and the prohibition of Albanian as the official language (Gashi 2010: 95; Malcolm 1998: 346–7). Following the aggravating reality, Albanians decided to disregard Serbian domination and initiated a parallel society, represented by the establishment of illegal education, health and welfare systems (Mertus 1999: 204; Kostovicova 2005). This socio-political configuration of powers is known as the "peaceful resistance" of the Albanians, and was advocated and headed by Ibrahim Rugova (Malcolm 1998: 347–9). "Underground" president of Kosovo since May 1992, he became the leader of what emerged first as a social movement, and was later transformed into a political party[10] known as LDK—"Lidhja Demokratike e Kosoves", Albanian for The Democratic League of Kosovo (Malcolm 1998: 348).

With the establishment of this shadow state, all contacts between the Albanian and Serb political elites and communities came to an end (Calic 2000: 27). In her comprehensive research of the education system during this period, Kostovicova argues that the very act of education became both an exercise in national resistance and an important contribution to the building of the independent Albanian state in Kosovo. According to her

---

[9] The Serbs narrative has constructed the site as historically important due to the story of Prince Lazar who fought the Ottomans there in 1389, defending the heavenly kingdom till his death, thus transforming Kosovo into the cradle of Serbian nationalism (Malcolm 1998: 61–62).

[10] Its membership was over 700.000, eclipsing any other party at the time (Malcolm 1998: 348).

"The sense of nationhood ceased being a matter of self-awareness. It became a daily practice" (Kostovicova 2005: 125).

Her analysis of the spatial division (Albanian homes-turned into schools) as a solution for the political segregation highlights a crucial process that contributed immensely to the future idea of sovereign statehood. The home-schooled generations and the nationalization of the school curricula since 1992 enabled educational autonomy (ibid: 131). Furthermore, "The idea of sovereign statehood and, thereby sovereign education, was graphically imprinted on all school certificates and diplomas. They bore the inscription of the 'Republic of Kosovo'" (ibid: 130). Therefore, the parallel education system in Kosovo taught the Kosovo Albanians "the lessons of nationhood" and designated the idea of sovereign statehood in their mental maps.

From my talks with various people in Kosovo, I became aware of the tension embodied in the idea of the peaceful resistance advocated by Rugova, since it perceived autonomy as a result of the international intervention. As Rexhep Selimi (of VV and a former KLA commander), has put it: "the 90's in Kosovo are the years tamed Albanians to identify domestic independence with dependence on the internationals".[11] In a more moderate point of view, Petrit Zogaj of FOL movement has recognized Rugova's policy as the "period that rooted the mentality of non-self-reliance" for the Albanians in Kosovo.[12]

Rugova's policy to 'internationalize' the issue of Kosovo through peaceful resistance was deeply challenged by the Dayton Agreement (1995), which ended the war in Bosnia and Herzegovina but totally disregarded the political reality in Kosovo (Malcolm 1998: 353). It was this disappointing event which led to the consolidation of the Albanian voices, which had been advocating for quite some time the need for an armed resistance against the Serbian regime. By the beginning of 1997, the organized armed struggle had intensified and "Ushtria Clirimtare e Kosoves", Albanian for the Kosovo Liberation Army (KLA) had openly accepted responsibility for various attacks on Serbian policemen (Malcolm 1998: 355). Meanwhile a growing number of Albanians in Kosovo gradually abandoned the idea of peaceful/passive resistance, and "fighting for freedom" became the prevailing narrative and practice in the society. The Serbian regime

---

[11] Interview with the author in March 2013, in Pristina.
[12] Interview with the author in August 2012, in Pristina.

perceived Albanians once more as "terrorists" and "separatists" victimizing the Kosovo Serbs (Anastasijevic 2000: 56) thus, legitimising the use of military power. The ensuing massacres of Likoshan and Qirez (February 1998) and Prekaz (March 1998) caused increased support of the local population for KLA, and attracted the attention of the international community.[13] It seems that for international public opinion, the massacre of Racak[14] (January 1999) was a turning point in the conflict. This was reflected in the condemnation of this act by the OSCE-led Kosovo Verification Mission, as a "crime against humanity" for which the Serbian army was responsible.[15]

Following the intervention of the international diplomatic corps, the sides met repeatedly in Rambouillet during January–March 1999, attempting to achieve an agreement between Kosovo Albanians and Serbs. The Kosovar political scene was divided between Rugova and his LDK party on one hand, and the KLA leaders: Hashim Thaçi, Ramush Haradinaj, Agim Ceku and many others who later became key players in Kosovo's political scene, on the other.

Following Milosevic' refusal to sign the Rambouillet agreement and to accept the NATO presence in the territory of the Federative Republic of Yugoslavia, NATO started its air strike over Serbia on March 24, 1999 (Demjaha 2000: 36). The military operation lasted for 72 days of destruction and violence, leading to 10,000 casualties and more than 800,000 displaced persons (Calic 2000: 29; Anastasijevic 2000: 57). Eventually a military agreement was reached on June 9 between NATO and the Yugoslav representatives, obliging the Serbian forces to withdraw from Kosovo. In its place an international presence was established, based on the UN Resolution 1244 of 10 June 1999.

---

[13] See: http://www.bndlg.de/~wplarre/year1998.htm, http://news.bbc.co.uk/2/hi/europe/453897.stm, http://www.ess.uwe.ac.uk/kosovo/Kosovo-Massacres5.htm, http://www.nytimes.com/1998/03/09/world/ravaged-kosovo-village-tells-of-a-nightmare-of-death.html, http://news.bbc.co.uk/2/hi/europe/674056.stm

[14] For more info see: http://news.bbc.co.uk/2/hi/europe/298131.stm, http://balkanwitness.glypx.com/racak.html

[15] See: http://www.un.org/News/Press/docs/1999/19990119.sc6628.html

Mapping the political structure of opportunities in supervised Kosovo

From UNMIK to EULEX

No representatives of the Albanian leadership (passive or active resistance) participated in the Komanovo military technical agreement[16] signed between KFOR and the Republic of Serbia, an event that would impact immensely on Kosovo's future political developments. For Kosovo Albanians, the end of both the peaceful and armed resistance came hand in hand with additional foreign interference and the loss of sovereignty. From numerous talks with members of different organizations, there is a hinted message of wounded pride, as expressed in these sentences: "We didn't earn the freedom"[17], or "It was NATO who liberated us"[18], resonating with the loss of self-reliance, leadership and autonomy.

Even the establishment of Provisional Institutions of Self-Government (PISG) in 2001 created an institution that lacked genuine authority and whose decision making was heavily dependent on UNMIK. Hence, after long national struggles, Kosovo Albanians found themselves free of Serbian domination but essentially subordinated to the Western authorities.

The NATO-led international intervention in 1999 resulted in the United Nations' civil interim administration, known as UNMIK. Many other international and supranational organizations[19], political, economic and diplomatic, followed. They all abided by UNMIK's logic of building Kosovo from scratch, aiming to bring Western 'civilization'[20] to the Balkan 'wilderness'. After experimenting with the 'Standards for Status' policy and many diplomatic attempts to solve the issue of Kosovo's status, it was Martii Ahtisaari's comprehensive proposal that suggested the establishment

---

[16] See: http://www.nato.int/kosovo/docu/a990609a.htm

[17] Author's interview with Ferdinand Nikolla (then of the Forum Initiative), June 2011, in Pristina.

[18] Author's interview with Loril Bajrami (of Stand-up! organization), March 2013, in Prishtina.

[19] Some of them are: European Union (EU), Organization for Security and Co-operation in Europe (OSCE), World Bank (WB), International Monetary Fund (IMF) and so on.

[20] The tremendous investments of the international community have been focused mainly on the reconstruction of the country, as opposed to the lack of sustained and systematic endeavor of reconciliation.

of the supervised statehood of Kosovo. Following Ahtisaari's[21] recommendation indicating that: "Kosovo's status should be independence supervised by the international community", a reconfiguration of powers was in order. Practically that meant the transfer of UNMIK's competencies to the civilian and political missions of the European Union. Ahtisaari's proposal also aimed at paving the way to consociational democracy through guaranteeing minority rights, protection and representation, essentially for the Serbian minority in Kosovo. On February 17, 2008 the-then and current PM Hashim Thaçi declared the independence of Kosovo.

While Artisaari's legal and political platform embodied a new opportunity for the pragmatic realization of the sovereignty of the new state of Kosovo it also cemented the regime of supervision endorsed by the international presence and authorities.

The succession of UNMIK's authorities by EULEX clearly illustrates the lack of traditional sovereignty, indicating the new international practices of state-building. To this day, Kosovo's government and Assembly are heavily influenced by the EU and the international diplomats residing in Prishtina; the judicial system, the police structure and the custom authorities are closely monitored by the EULEX (whose annual budget exceeds 200 million Euros), while the Kosovo Security Forces (KSF) are still under the control of Kosovo NATO's force (Kostovicova 2008; Pond 2008).

The first 'product' of the supervision regime was Kosovo's Constitution, a text which constitutes a replication of Ahtisaari's proposal (Tomson 2012; Tunheim 2009; Aucoin 2008). The constitution was the result of an internationally-supervised drafting process which cemented the pillars of a multi-cultural democratic state. But the institutional structure and the creation of divided communities along ethnic lines constitutes a Western, 'imported' political tool, that is empty of meaning for the local communities.

Framing the negotiations between Kosovo and Serbia as 'risky and imposed'

This section aims to identify the EU-brokered negotiations between Kosovo and Serbia as a source of political opportunity for contentious actors to

---

[21] United Nations Special envoy for Kosovo, and former Finnish President, Martti Ahtisaari presented his plan to the U.N. Secretary-General in March 2007, known as the Comprehensive Proposal for the Kosovo Status Settlement.

participate in the state-building process and articulate their meaning of sovereignty. In the context of economic and political collective grievances, the local actors frame the "risky negotiations" as the master scheme of interpretation through which its members define and articulate their social situation. The collective actors steer the frames of their contentious acts towards the protest, making it fit with the specific context, and basing it on the merger between the culture of the target group and their values and goals (Benford and Snow 2000). Frames are flexible packages of meanings and adaptable interpretative tools that do not occur in a political and social vacuum. Based on this conceptualization, master frames act as "broader models for mobilizing support that movements draw upon" (Glenn 2001: 50).

In my reading of the local contention regarding the negotiations, I identify three main narratives: the first is the '*Bosnian Cantonization of Kosovo*' and it emerges immediately after the DoI. The second one refers to the '*Undermining of Reciprocity*" imparted with the stage of the technical dialogue, while the third one '*Frozen State-building*' is clearly instructed by the 'upgrading' of the negotiations to the phase of the political dialogue between Prishtina and Belgrade. These three narratives have comprised over time the master frame of "risky negotiations" structured by the local contentious actors.

'*Stabilization of the region*' vs. '*Bosnian cantonization of Kosovo*' (2008–2009)

More than 5,000 protesters gathered in front of the National Library in Prishtina and marched towards the headquarters of UNMIK, to continue to the National Theatre in November 19, 2008. Many white sheets with the writing "S'BAN, S'KI, S'MUN", Albanian for "Don't, Mustn't, Can't" were held by the demonstrators. Various civil society organizations[22] came together to protest against the six-point plan suggested by the UN Secretary-General Ban Ki-moon's recommendations on the reorganization of the civil mission in Kosovo. This document, adopted eventually by the UN Security Council in late November 2008, cemented EULEX neutrality towards the newly declared independence of Kosovo. Furthermore, by subordinating the mission to the framework set by the Security Council Resolution 1244 (1999), and the status-neutral authority of the United

---

[22] The demonstration was organized by: VV, COHU, The Network of Kosovo Women, The Network of Kosovo Youth, Civic Action Fol '08, CBM-Mitrovice, The Initiative for Progress, etc.

Nations, it has assured the detachment of EULEX from the implementation of Ahtissari's agenda, strongly opposed by the Serbian Government.[23] Ban Ki-moon's plan instigated a number of protests due to the local interpretation of it as an obstruction to Kosovar independence.

"The President and the Prime Minister are lying. One compromise after the other, this evil is not stopping," Zogiani from COHU told protesters.[24] While Kurti of VV addressed the crowd: "Don't trust our politicians. It's the document that matters while politicians come and go. The recent document is the six-point plan which endorses Serbia's parallel structures in Kosovo". He also declared the head of UNMIK Lamberto Zannier as a "persona non grata" in Kosovo. In one of my meetings with Petrit Zogaj of FOL nearly two years later[25], he shared with me his opinion on the issue:

> "Recommending the subordination of police, customs, judiciary, transportation and infrastructure, administrative lines and Serbian cultural heritage in Serb majority areas under Serbia's authority and obliging Prishtina to enter the "dialogue with Belgrade" was a direct threat to our sovereignty and territorial integrity".

Liburn Aliu of VV shared with me in September 2010:

> "Finally encouraged by the DoI, Ban Ki-moon's negotiations with Serbia over Kosovo have served to prepare the strategy of institutional and territorial disintegration as we know it today. We have opposed EULEX presence in Kosovo and its agreements with the Serbs because it has attested to our formal independence".

In August 2009, EULEX signed a protocol of cooperation between its police and their Serbian counterpart within Kosovo. VV organized what they called a symbolic action (sic) in August 2009, throwing nearly 25 jeeps upside down, all property of EULEX, in order "to punish this institution for the tremendous injustice committed to the people and state of Kosovo" as stated in their newsletter.[26] Following the European requests[27] to reprimand these contentious acts and the cooperation of the local leaders, 22 activists

---

[23] See Woehrel's report 2010: *www.au.af.mil/au/awc/awcgate/crs/rs21721.pdf*

[24] See: *old.balkaninsight.com/en/main/news/15235/?tpl=297*

[25] Author's interview with Petrit Zogaj on September 2010, in Prishtina.

[26] See: VV weekly gazette, no. 214, October 12, 2009.

[27] Carl Buildt, the Swedish foreign minister at the time, and the EU security chief Javier Solana's spokeswoman Christina Galach, strongly condemned the actions of VV and demanded the rebuke of the local participants in this act.

of VV were arrested and imprisoned for two and a half months each. According to VV, the activists were "isolated from society as they were perceived as threatening to the Western neo-coloniser of Kosovo".[28]

Peiter Feith, then the chief of ICO and EU Special Representative was targeted as the international leader dictating a harmful agenda for Kosovo. Feith, as head of ICO, was the European leader in charge of the reconfiguration of the municipal borders and the reconstruction of the Serbian-inhabited areas, and was obliged to implement Ahtissari's proposal for the creation of five new municipalities with a Serbian majority. ICO under his lead was the international institution in charge of the "establishment of 45 exterritorial zones" in the name of the protection of Serbian heritage. That meant that the territories allocated to the Serbian Orthodox churches, cathedrals and monasteries, and subjugated to its authority, were carved up from the collective land of specific areas previously belonging to the Albanian population (see: Prizren, Peja, Hoca a Madhe, etc), and were once again establishing new territorial and political boundaries. What was presented by the international institutions (EULEX and ICO) as steps to stabilize the region, has been perceived by the local challengers as the 'Bosnian Cantonization of Kosovo'.

Another crucial international actor during that period was Tina Kaidanow, the US Ambassador in Kosovo, whose involvement in the political processes of Kosovo, according to the local actors, had by far exceeded the conventional powers of the head of a diplomatic mission. At the end of her mandate in Kosovo, in early July 2009, the local organizations 'asked' her to take along with her the two "obedient" local politicians, Hashim Thaçi at the time PM and leader of PDK[29] and Fatmir Sejdiu, then the leader of the LDK. The subsequent US ambassador, Christopher Dell, according to Zogiani of COHU has been following the same logic:

---

[28] See the speech of one of the arrested activists before the judges, VV weekly gazette, no. 215, October 19, 2009, pg. 4.
[29] PDK—Partia Demokratike e Kosoves, the Democratic Party of Kosovo.

"Dell thinks he is god in Kosovo. He would not dare to use in any Western country the language, deeds and methods he practices here, but we are not Western yet for him, are we? The most outrage case of all maybe, is his interference in the voting process which secured the presidency of Begjet Pacolli in Kosovo. The Reporters Without Borders were engaged as well when he even condemned the journalist and demanded their apology for revealing the facts to the public. Can you imagine his arrogance..?"[30]

The cooperation agreement between the Serbian police in Serbian inhabited areas in Kosovo[31], known as the 'Protocol', sidelining the Kosovar state-authorities and strengthening the Serbian factor, caused many demonstrations. "Feith NO MORE" and "EULEX made in Serbia" were the messages written in the posters glued in every corner of Prishtina during September 2009. One month later, a 'demonstration against decentralization' was organized in Gjilan by VV. The protesters expressed the collective demand that the foreign "autocrat" leave Kosovo.[32] "In his imposed representation of the new statehood and its people, he was very damaging because being guided by the Western agenda, he did neither understand nor acted for the domestic interest" Liburn Aliu told me in the same talk referred to earlier.

When asked about KFOR, he chose to remind me of the passive propensity that has characterized KFOR since the DoI. He then asked me: "Where was KFOR when Serb structures burned our borders only one month after the declaration of independence? Where was KFOR when the same structures at the same time occupied the legal and justice institutions in Mitrovica?" To add to that, when Serbia held the election campaign in May 2008, the Serbian politicians were secured by KFOR while entering Kosovo to meet with the Serbian communities in northern and other enclaves.[33] In mid-May that year, VV organized a symbolic action involving tens of activists throwing containers of garbage into the headquarters of

---

[30] The event has made too many headlines due to the various Kosovo journalists that used blown-up photos of text messages on a smartphone screen, documenting Dell's dictation of the voting procedure of the Kuvend, February 23, 2011, see: http://en.rsf.org/kosovo-us-ambassador-launches-01-03-2011,39649.html http://www.zeri.info/artikulli/1/1/22443/dell-deputete-rrini-ne-kuvend/

[31] For further info see: http://www.eulex-kosovo.eu/en/pressreleases/january-december-2009.php

[32] See: VV weekly gazette, no. 215, October 19, 2009.

[33] See: VV weekly gazette, No. 138, May 12, 2008.

UNMIK and some local institutions. In the activists' masks against the stench one could read: "Because UNMIK and the Government stink!"

ICO's implementation of Ahtisaari's plan is translated by the local Albanian collective actors as the policy that aims to secure Serbian communities located in various places within Kosovo. Thus, the local challengers have contested the reconfiguration of municipalities' borders and territories as an effort to establish new municipalities with a Serbian majority, and framed it as territorial disintegration of the new state of Kosovo. The above mentioned events illustrate the closure of the power order, leaving the VV activists with no channels of communications and with no options of influencing the decision-making process. Hence, the local contention clearly targets both the international and the local authorities, constantly reminding the Kosovo citizens of 1) the menacing partition and cantonization of their state, and 2) the subordinate role of their local leaders in the hierarchy of supervision. When reading these events, one should take into account the expectations of the collective actors after the DoI, regarding the sovereign performance of the new Kosovar state vis-a-vis the Serbian counterpart and the termination of the international dictation.

Technical dialogue—(establishing or) undermining reciprocity? (2011–2012)

The technical talks between Belgrade and Prishtina were launched in March 2011. Borislav Stefanovic, at the time Director of Ministry for Foreign Affairs, headed the negotiation team of Serbia and Edita Tahiri, Deputy Prime Minister headed the Kosovo team, mediated by the EU representative Robert Cooper. The "technical dialogue" and its ensuing agreements have evoked a lot of contention in Kosovo, organized by various local organizations. The challenging actors have embraced numerous forms of actions, from street demonstrations to media conferences; from public speeches in the Kuvend to symbolic actions targeting local leaders and institutions. In one of his speeches in the Kuvend, Albin Kurti, the leader of VV, has asserted:

> "The formal independence of Kosovo, truly awarded us with little as a state, but with these talks without a public agenda and with a leader of negotiations who lacks any platform for negotiations, all is in danger... while keeping the agenda concealed, the government of Kosovo demonstrates to us that the only non-negotiable thing is the negotiation process itself".[34]

He explicitly condemns the vagueness of the process and the prompt willingness of the local political leaders to participate in the negotiations without any previous institutional or public debate. Thus, according to him, the negotiations serve not the interest of Kosovo but the integration of Serbia in the EU. "On the contrary" he maintained, "with these talks we will be like Bosnia, whom is not being accepted by the EU because is too decentralized in order to claim sovereignty". He went on to remind the deputies of the Kuvend that "...the Ahtissari plan has planted already the seeds of the bosnization of Kosovo, which this government is applying further through these talks with Serbia".

The comparison of Kosovo to the Bosnian decentralization, says Visar Ymeri of VV, serves as a public warning of the "Serbian approach of securing their hegemony in the region".[35]

It was this alleged hegemony that was publicly protested in the streets of Prishtina in May 20, 2011, when Stefanovic came to Kosovo for an official meeting with the-then Kosovar Foreign Minister, Hajredin Kuci. Afterwards, in the TV program "Jeta ne Kosove" Albanian for "The life in Kosovo", when interviewed by Jeta Xharra, a very well-known journalist for her critical investigations[36], he repeatedly stated:

> "Serbia cannot and will not recognise Kosovo... Why do you insist in those symbols of sovereignty?... Give us a chance, our intentions are good... let's talk and see how we can normalise the relations without abandoning our state position of course".

Also the Serbian president, Boris Tadic explicitly maintained that the visit of Stefanovic means "to improve the atmosphere" and that "Serbia... under

---

[34] See; VV weekly gazette, No. 294, March 14, 2011.
[35] Interview with the author, March 2013, in Pristina.
[36] Jeta Xharra acts also as the Director of Balkan Investigative Reporting Network's (BIRN) in Kosovo. For the full interview see: http://www.jetanekosove.com/en/Interviews/Interview-with-Borislav-Stefanovic-Serbias-chief-negotiator-in-the-Kosovo-Serbia-dialogue-230

any condition will never recognize the independence of Kosovo".[37] Stefanovic' staunch representation of the Serbian categorical rejection of Kosovo's statehood was firmly evidenced in his later announcement regarding the intense negotiations on civil registry: "Giving up the originals would mean giving up sovereignty". The agreement eventually reached on the subject was that "Kosovo would receive copies of the civil registry and cadastres".[38] On a warm July afternoon that year, I met with some activists at the centre of VV in the neighborhood Pejton of Prishtina, and while discussing the negotiations, one of the activists cynically noted that "... instead of gaining sovereignty, now Kosovo has become a 'copy' republic".

In reaction to the Serbian delay regarding the anticipated agreement on custom stamps on July 19, 2011, which aimed to secure the free movement of goods in accordance with CEFTA[39], the government of Kosovo decided the day after to adopt "reciprocity measures" against Serbia, unrecognizing its custom stamps as well.[40] Five days later, Kosovo's prime minister sent the special police forces (ROSU) to the custom points 1 and 31 at the northern border to enforce reciprocity measures. As PM Thaçi himself stated in his speech to the press that day (July 25, 2011), the state of Kosovo intervened in order to "implement the statehood and protect sovereignty". The Serbian parallel structures led by radical nationalists fought back and built barricades which even today internationals have failed to remove.

The Kosovo Government initially heaped support on all the political parties as well as the local civil society organizations, including VV. But this political and public consensus melted away quickly with the death of an Albanian policeman and the withdrawal of the Special Forces, ensuing in the intervention of KFOR which is to this day in charge of security in the area. The mission that was meant to reinforce sovereignty, says Ferdinand Nikolla of FIQ, "resulted in an embarrassing fiasco for the Government of Kosovo because by further strengthening the Serbian parallel structures in north Kosovo has actually undermined our state-building". Furthermore, when talking with students of the University of Prishtina, statements such

---

[37] See: http://www.gazetaexpress.com/repository/docs/_911538.pdf, pg. 5
[38] See: http://www.euinside.eu/en/news/kosovo-serbia-dialogue-second-round
[39] See the KIPRED Report: "The Analysis of the Implementation of the Technical Agreements between Kosovo and Serbia", No. 2, June 2013. pg 8
[40] See the policy analysis of Group for Legal and Political Studies (GLPS), Kosovo-Serbia Dialogue: Windows of Opportunity or a House of Cards? By Agron Bajrami, No. 3, March 2013, p. 7.

as: "We cannot defend ourselves", "Not much has changed apparently since 1999" or "Without an army we cannot fight Serbia"[41], conveyed feelings of disappointment that arched back to the war period and the international intervention of KFOR, which has become emblematic of the perceived collective local powerlessness to protect itself.

The head of the Kosovar team, Edita Tahiri, has been personally seen as one of the key leaders responsible for these "concessions" as called by the local activists. In early September 2011 while back in Kosovo from one of the rounds of the negotiations, she was "welcomed" with rotten tomatoes on her way from the airport to Prishtina, by the protestors of VV. The activist Etleva Malushaj, who was arrested that day along with many others by the special units of Kosovo police, told me later: "Our protest aimed to block her and the concessions she is producing. The rotten tomatoes we threw on her were a symbol of her agreements which are constantly disintegrating our statehood".[42]

Another agreement was reached in February 2012[43] in the framework of the "technical dialogue"; that of the Regional Representation and Cooperation, ensuing Serbian efforts "to obstruct Kosovo's membership in international organizations" (Lehne 2012: 12). The negotiating teams concluded eventually that when participating in regional forums, Kosovo's nameplate would include an asterisk indicating that: "This designation is without prejudice to positions on status, and is in line with UNSC 1244 and the ICJ Opinion on the Kosovo Declaration of Independence".[44] This agreement, referred to in the local jargon as "the footnote", has evoked in the collective memory the post-war quandaries of the status of Kosovo. This accord, which validated the Serbian demand to use the name Kosovo without the designation 'Republic', was perceived by many Kosovo Albanians and expressed in Petrit Zogaj's words as a "treacherous return to the pre-independence phase, sabotaging the sovereignty of the new state".

Many agreements were reached during the nine rounds of the "technical dialogue" between Tahiri and Stefanovic in Brussels. Their tangible results

---

[41] The talks with the students were held by the author during July and August 2011 in Prishtina.
[42] Interview with the author, March 2013, in Prishtina.
[43] See the EU Press Statement *EU Facilitated Dialogue: Agreement on Regional Cooperation and IBM Protocol* at: http://www.consilium.europa.eu/uedocs/cms_Data/docs/press data/EN/foraff/128138.pdf
[44] See footnote no. 25.

took the form of the copies of civil registry books instead of the originals, the recognition of the custom stamps without the constitutional name "Republic", the asterisk in the nameplate of Kosovo representing it in regional forums and the lack of any symbols of state jurisdiction in the framework of integrated border management.[45] All these agreements have emerged in the local collective consciousness as the explicit insolence of Serbia towards Kosovo's independence, and as an obvious lack of sovereignty, further destabilizing Kosovo's statehood.

The issue of implementing reciprocity was fiercely contended in the Kuvend as well as at Kosovo's borders. In the name of "reciprocity principle and its protection", demonstrations were organized by VV in the northern border points with Serbia, in January 2012. The protestors' objective was to prevent goods coming in from Serbia by blocking the passage of arriving trucks. In my talk with Visar Ymeri a year later, he explained the protest:

> "Serbia is profiting from our market 400 million Euros yearly, while blocking our products not only in Serbia but in the region as well. Serbia is undermining our economy, politics and consequently our state-building, so we have every right to defend reciprocity as accorded in our constitution, even if it means with our bodies".

In order to halt the marching protesters at the border crossings, the Kosovo police used pepper spray, tear gas and water cannons. Many of them were brutally arrested. Some were even injured, resulting in a lot of media attention and public consideration of the issue of reciprocity. The brutality of police forces facilitated the emergence of a public consensus against the governmental reaction to the collective action.

Two days later, 25 civil organizations demonstrated in front of the Government building in Prishtina[46] "to condemn the brutal violence" exercised by the local police. "We have gathered today to express the deep indignation with the international community. Its position has legitimized the violence against the protesters" Lorik Bajrami of COHU told the demonstrators. Besnik Ramadaj from the Kosovo Democratic Institute addressed the participants also and stated that the protests of January 14 are "a manifestation of the will of citizens and a democratic method".

---

[45] See footnote no. 26, pg 12.
[46] See the article of Linda Karadaku for Southeastern Europe Times, titled *Protesting violence: Kosovo NGOs condemn police action*, at: www.setimes.com/features/2012/01/16/feature-01

It is remarkable to note how the support of civil society on the subject of reciprocity is carried out through the condemnation of police brutality. The concept of the citizens' right to protest outshines the citizens' actual readiness to protest. Despite the violent police methods, the activists went back on January 22, to maintain their peaceful-contentious presence at the border crossings of Dheu I Bardhe and Merdare. These events lucidly illustrated the profound political nature of the "technical dialogue". Stefan Lehne in his Carnegie Report (March 2012) titled *Kosovo and Serbia: Towards a Normal Relationship*, while outlining the development of the negotiations to date, notably indicated:

> "Despite its name, the dialogue was not technical but highly political in character, as each of the issues discussed had its status-sensitive aspects. And EU '"facilitation" was not facilitation at all but rather heavy-duty mediation, including setting the agenda, elaborating solutions, and using massive carrots and sticks to bring the parties on board".

His 'real-politik' reading of the realities on the ground is pointing clearly to the roles of each side, especially emphasizing that of the EU. His policy paper might be well perceived as the document which envisions the future steps of the international approach in the region:

> "The situation in northern Kosovo remains tense, and the mistrust between Belgrade and Pristina continues to be high. Therefore, no further time should be lost. Building on the success of the agreements reached in February 2012, the EU should move quickly to a more comprehensive and ambitious dialogue, which also tackles the key issue of the predominantly Serb North. The process presents both obstacles and opportunities, but it should bring Belgrade and Pristina a good deal closer to what must be the common objective—a normal and neighborly relationship". (Lehne 2012: 3, *italics mine*)

This paragraph is an unambiguous statement of the European perception of the political developments regarding the conflict in the region and its mindset toward Kosovo's statehood. As shown in the passage, the European community sees the technical dialogue and the agreements reached so far as a "success", thus the policymaker urges the EU leaders and diplomats to upgrade the process. This text demonstrates the EU's political manoeuvring which stubbornly advocates the "normalization of relations" while totally dismissing the local voices speaking decidedly of the "hostilization" of the relations.

From technical to oolitical dialogue—"frozen state-building" (2012–2013)

The upgrading of the technical dialogue to the political level paved the way to the meeting of two "old enemies"[47], the Serbian PM Ivica Dacic and his Kosovar counterpart Hashim Thaçi. On one hand, Dacic who had been Milosevic' spokesperson during the 1998–99 war in Kosovo, personifies in the Albanian collective memory the Serbian nationalist agenda and its war crimes. On the other hand, Serbia has issued an arrest warrant, still valid today, for Thaçi as a former political leader of the KLA.

Following the lack of public consensus regarding the "technical dialogue" and the need to cement and legitimatize the process, the Government asked the Kuvend to ratify the Agreement of the Resolution of Kosovo for the Normalization of Relations with Serbia.[48] During the séance of the resolution, Visar Ymeri and Liburn Aliu of VV both stood in front of the speaker's podium holding a banner reading: "The Resolution of Submission to Serbia".[49] Outside, the activists of VV demonstrated in front of the Kuvend calling for the end of the current negotiations. Inside the Kuvend, Kurti challenged the "normalization of relations" discourse with the cultural narrative of historical enmity:

> "The normalization of relations with Serbia means the normalization of relations with the criminals because they remain criminals as long as they do not regret their crimes and do nothing to stop it today. With this resolution, the victim is demanding in the name of the slayer... We all know that it is the slayer that is interested and demands to reconcile with the victim and not vice versa. The victim never demands to reconcile with the slayer. But in Kosovo is happening the opposite... the true normalization comes through the implementation of reciprocity... Do not vote this resolution which is a betrayal to the Republic of Kosovo".

This passage is rooted in the Albanian collective memory of the past ordeals inflicted by Serbian aggression, of reconstructing the relationship between victim-slayer and of opposing the image of "normal relations" featuring equal sides. The charged language of the collective victimization and the act of surrendering to the historical slayer is encapsulated in the accusation of

---

[47] See footnote no. 26.
[48] See: http://www.assembly-kosova.org/common/docs/Rezolute_Marredhenive_Kosova_Serbia.pdf in Oct. 18, 2012
[49] See VV weekly gazette, No. 358, October 22, 2012.

"betrayal of the national interest". Despite the manifold opposition of VV, inside and outside the Kuvend, in the late hours of the evening of October 18th, the resolution was eventually approved, unlocking the path for political dialogue and giving the green light for the meeting between Thaçi and Dacic.

The dual contentious presence of the VV within and outside the Kuvend is a lucid example of the increasing pressure applied by the movement. In addition, the collective strategy is clearly shifting away from Western targets, and instead is steadily infiltrating the state institutions. This alteration might be understood as a counterbalance to the heavy Western supervision of the Kosovo government and its leaders, expressed in the fast progress of the dialogue. On the other hand, VV's entrance into the formal political arena enables the movement to: 1) disrupt and affect the routine of state policy-making, 2) reach a broader audience and thus mobilize new public support, and 3) undermine the local coalitions between the political elites. Clearly not every contentious act bears the expected results, thus ensuing in the proliferation of collective actions for overcoming the inaccessible political configuration. In the process, the activists employ the local narratives of historical oppression, victimization and national betrayal to frame the risky negotiations endangering the future of the national collective.

The first historic meeting between Dacic and Thaçi (October 19, 2012) with the mediation of EU Foreign Affairs Chief, Catherine Ashton, was immediately followed by a mass demonstration (October 22, 2012) organized by the VV. The forefront lines of the protestors were seated in front of the Government building, while the others were standing and listening to the speeches held by the deputies and activists of VV. The motto of the protest was: "Unification with Albania, no bargains with Serbia" and the activists denounced the 'criminal' meeting.[50] The police forces again intervened very violently; Liburn Aliu (VV activist and deputy) was beaten by the special police forces, many others were arrested and several citizens and protestors ended up injured in the nearby hospital.[51]

---

[50] See: VV weekly gazette, No. 359, October 29, 2012.
[51] For further info see: http://www.setimes.com/cocoon/setimes/xhtml/en_GB/features/setimes/features/2012/10/23/feature-01

While framing the Thaçi-Dacic meetings as criminal, it is worth noting the shifting framing of the local leader. Hashim Thaçi—once the former-commander of KLA, the defender of the people and its freedom, is considered by many Albanians as the legitimate and charismatic leader of Kosovo. The activists and deputies of VV, in their protests, symbolic actions and speeches in Kuvend, are questioning his legacy and legitimacy by constantly framing his leadership mindset as corrupt, and disloyal to the national ideals of KLA. One illustration is the following event: after Thaçi's report regarding his third meeting with Dacic, Kurti referred to the dialogue as identifying with a one man show on Kosovo's part, constructing Thaçi as the only actor benefiting from the agreements:

> "We are actually living in a political debt with this dialogue. We will have to pay for it later. The relations are normalizing between Thaçi and Dacic, not between the Albanians and Serbs, not between the people of Kosovo and Serbia. This dialogue is formalizing and legitimizing Serbia within Kosovo".[52]

Kurti's message is twofold; the first is the identification of a secluded negotiation between two leaders speaking a common language, equalling Thaçi, the former KLA commander, to Dacic, locally referred to as the 'spokesperson of Milosevic". In the cultural and historical context this equation stirs up the narrative of collective resistance and sacrifice, associating the act of shaking hands with the enemy with a national betrayal. The second goal of this message, to my reading, is the shifting away of Thaçi from the citizens' interest, and from the state-building agenda, ensuring thus the erosion of the collective base of legitimacy of his authority.

As for the Serbian PM, Dacic, he has been following a pragmatic approach "skilfully meandering through Brussels' requests and domestic criticism".[53] When asked in December 2011 what is more important to him; Kosovo or the EU, he answered Serbia. In an interview for the Serbian Kurir, he declared that "Serbia will not be destroyed if it loses Kosovo".[54] This coming from the same man who two months before openly expressed:

---

[52] See: VV weekly gazette, No. 366, December 17, 2012.
[53] See: http://www.helsinki.org.rs/doc/HB-No94.pdf, pg. 2
[54] See: http://www.b92.net/eng/news/politics.php?yyyy=2011&mm=12&dd=31&nav_id=78066

"Excluding the war as an option would send the wrong message to Thaçi, as there has to be a balance of fear because of a security in the region. Thaçi has to know that if he attacks Serbs in Kosovo, he attacks Belgrade. Serbia cannot and will not stand still and watch".[55]

In April 2013, after rejecting the EU offered deal of reconciliation with Kosovo, Dacic affirmed: "The Serbian government cannot accept the proposed principles ... because they do not guarantee full security, survival and protection of human rights for the Serbs in Kosovo".[56] For many, Dacic' inconsistent messages reflect the ideological and political rifts that characterize Serbian society and the official divisions towards the Kosovo issue.

In addition to the EU officials who are heavily engaged in supervising the dialogue, the European ambassadors in the region are also strongly pushing forward the EU agenda. It was the German ambassador to Serbia, Heinz Wilhelm, who declared that Kosovo's membership in the UN could be a result of a political dialogue between Belgrade and Prishtina. Commenting on the meetings between Thaçi and Dacic, Štefan Füle, the EU's Enlargement Commissioner, while praising the courage both leaders were showing in difficult times, heavily played on the leverage of EU integration. On one hand, Kosovo has been lured with the possibility of the beginning of the Stability and Association Agreement (SAA) talks by the first half of 2013[57], on the other, the carrot offered to Serbia was the starting date of the EU accession process.[58]

The next level of the "normalization of relations" was the presidential meeting between Atifete Jahjaga and Tomislav Nikolic, in February 2013.[59] Prior to the meeting, the Kosovar president Jahjaga stated: "We are dedicated to this process and firmly determined not to pass all the

---

[55] See: Press online, Oct. 24, 2011.
[56] See: http://www.theguardian.com/world/2013/apr/08/serbia-eu-deadline-kosovo-independence
[57] See: http://www.b92.net/eng/news/politics.php?yyyy=2012&mm=10&dd=12&nav_id=82619
[58] See: http://www.b92.net/eng/news/politics.php?yyyy=2013&mm=05&dd=19&nav_id=86246
[59] Due to their ceremonial roles in the domestic politics, as opposed to the executive powers which reside with the PMs, the public opinion perceives this meeting as "an artificial ornament" of the dialogue as the Kosovo political analyst Belul Beqaj has putted. See: EUbusiness, Feb. 5, 2013.

animosities of the past to younger generations".[60] While her counterpart, in an interview with B92 right after their joint meeting on February 6, 2013, proclaimed: "Serbia's desire is completely clear—the last thing that I would do for as long as I live would be to agree, to accept Kosovo as an independent state." After the same meeting Ashton concluded: "I saw constructive engagement coming from both sides. Both presidents have assured me of their continued support and commitment to the dialogue and their respective European agendas.[61]

The discourse of the "normalization of relations" demands new spatial and temporal configurations of the past from both the Albanians and the Serbs. Whereas Kosovo Albanians are reimagining their community as sovereign, their Serb counterparts are forced to recognize themselves as a minority within a new political entity which reduces their own sovereignty. The top-down approach of the negotiation process is well reflected in the absence of any representative of the Serb community in Kosovo, which resembles the agreement between the UN and Serbia in 1999, which ignored the Kosovar leadership.

Adapting to the European agenda and the heavy personal involvement of Ashton, Thaçi and Dacic eventually agreed on the adoption of a 15-point agreement envisioning the establishment of the Association/Community of Serb Majority Municipalities and its broad powers.[62] This emerging polity is intriguing in itself as regards the ambivalent meanings it bears for each side, embedded in its dual naming. For the Serbs, the preferred meaning behind this new entity is that of the "community" (zajednica), indicating its independent nature and governing rights, whereas the Albanians refer to it as an "association" implying its coordinating function within the state order (Prelec 2013). In the European political imagination, the Association/Community is the product of the manoeuvring between the Serbian rhetoric of national heritage and rights, and the Kosovar Albanian discourse of sovereignty, while luring both sides with the carrot of EU membership.

---

[60] See: FINNCIAL, February 2, 2013
[61] See: B92 online, Feb 6, 2013.
[62] The agreement was signed in April 19, 2013. See: http://www.balkaninsight.com /en/article/kosovo-and-serbia-may-seal-eu-deal

Conclusions: statehood without sovereignty!

During my last visit in August 2013, besides the KFOR jeep constantly securing the bridge of Mitrovica, I saw green weeds growing on the barricade piled up in the middle of it. And I couldn't help thinking of the symbolic layers of the tangible and spatial divisions; the bridge which symbolically is alleged to connect both sides, for quite a long time has been the symbol of ethnic and political division in Mitrovica and Kosovo. And now, the barricade with the grass on it has emerged as the representation of the insurmountable divergence between the Albanian and the Serbs in Kosovo.

How can this study then shed light on the "barricaded" collective meanings as produced and performed by the contentious actions of Kosovo Albanians in the context of supervised Kosovo? From a particular case to a generalization of the theoretical insight, this study broadens the model of POS since it indicates a new context and identifies in it new external factors that affect and shape local collective action, enlarging the understanding of contemporary contention in non-Western democracies.

The conceptual contribution of this paper is reflected in two insights. The first is the realization of *bifurcated contention*, which to my interpretation is strongly shaped by the political structure and the opportunities perceived and mobilized by the collective actors. Mounting claims against both the international and the national authorities is a strategy affected by the closeness of the political structure of supervision. EULEX, although constantly monitoring and shaping the judiciary, police and custom sectors in Kosovo, is inaccessible for the collective actors. According to its establishing rationale, EULEX does not recognize the state of Kosovo, and is accountable to the Council of the EU, a body which represents all the EU Member states[63], including the five members that haven't recognized Kosovo yet.[64] Exposing and framing the clash between the interests of the newborn state, and the agenda that guides (implicitly or explicitly) the international actors and authorities, allows local contenders to go beyond the work of building public awareness. In the context of supervised statehood, they are active intruders of the state-monopoly over sovereignty

---

[63] For a detailed explanation see: http://www.eulex-kosovo.eu/docs/Accountability/EULEX-Accountability-05.01.2010.pdf

[64] The EU Member states that have not recognized the state of Kosovo are: Slovakia, Spain, Romania, Greece and Cyprus.

production; interfering in the process with the emergent practices of state-building.

The second insight is *the zoom-in targeting strategy* shaped by the structure of opportunities and facilitated by the framing process. The members of social movements, on one hand label the injustice, while on the other articulate the broader frames of meaning which are consistent with the cultural spirit of the society. As such, collective frames refer to the active process of the construction of meaning in a given cultural context (Snow and Benford 1992; Tarrow 1998). Frames are notable if they are consistent with the national myths, the cultural narrative and the political perceptions of society (Benford and Snow 2000).

Given this theoretical understanding I suggest that the collective actors engage the public frustration and channel its discontent with contemporary developments by addressing the international and local authorities for the perceived collective injustice. Operating thus on the narratives of 'national resistance', 'collective sacrifice' and 'self-reliance' has enabled the local challengers to construct the frame of "risky negotiations", aligning the local symbolic reservoir with the contested legitimacy of the foreign-led state building process. The political discourse through time, as shown in this study, has shaped a perception of national liberation as the key to the political freedom of the people, their future social wellbeing and economic welfare. Even after the war (1999) and the declaration of independence (2008), the society in Kosovo is still ethnically divided as reflected in the course of negotiations. This process imprints the political discourse with nationalist voices and messages. This work shows that the collective actors, VV among them, also incorporate nationalist logic when framing the risky process of international state-building. While many voices (the political parties, the international institutions and some local civic organizations) have criticized VV for their political manipulation of the Albanians' grievances, I tend to believe that the use of the nationalist agenda is historically embedded in local politics and is therefore utilized by all actors. In addition, the imposed international discourse of a multi-ethnic society which is conditioning the state-building process, although totally detached from the actual demographic of present-day Kosovo, reinforces deep-rooted existential fears, thus shaping the modern thinking and praxis of individual and collective actors.

With the DoI, many actors have been involved in the drama of state-building: be them international diplomats and European leaders (Ban-Ki-moon, Christopher Dell, Marti Ahtisaari, Pieter Feith and Catherine Ashton) or local leaders (Hashim Thaçi, Edita Tahiri). According to the contentious actors (VV, COHU, FOL etc) they have all been engaged in the agenda of destabilizing the welfare and future development of the domestic society, resulting in the weakening of the sovereignty of Kosovo. Therefore, both the local and the foreign authorities have been targeted as responsible for impeding Kosovo's state-building.

With the beginning of the technical dialogue, it is important to pay attention to the shift in the targets of contention, where the focus has narrowed from being primarily on the international authorities and then zooming in on local state-institutions and the domestic political leaders. By this I do not mean to say that the European factor has been completely disregarded, rather that the local authorities have been framed by the local challengers as the key actors accountable for obediently implementing the foreign agenda, constantly harming the interest of the citizens and of the state of Kosovo.

Also, this paper presents two complementary paths of contentious actions: collective protest in the streets, and organized disturbance in the Kuvend, the governmental institutions. The establishment of the electoral group of VV is perceived by activists as another channel of action; as an opportunity to overcome the repressive response of the government and the closure of the institutional routes of political impact. Since the options of affecting the international authorities and their policy-making are not viable, the local challengers zoom in on the state-institutions and the individual leaders.

To conclude, ignoring the contemporary polis in Kosovo might lead to a misunderstanding of the emergent power order, its structures and praxis. Acknowledging and accounting for the interactions between the international authorities, the state institutions and the local collective actors opens up new ways of understanding the politics of contention and offers us an alternative analytical approach for the understanding of the politics of international state-building in post-socialist and post-war settings.

References

Aminzade, R. *et al.* 2001. Silence and Voice in the Study of Contention Politics. Cambridge University Press.

Anastasijevic, D. 2000. *The Closing of Kosovo's Cycle: Victimization versus Responsibility* in Schnabel. A and Thakur. R, (eds), Kosovo and the Challenge of Humanitarian Intervention: Selective Indignation, Collective Action and International Citizenship. United Nation University Press, Tokyo & New York & Paris.

Aucoin, L. 2008. *On constitution Writing: The Case of Kosovo* in PRAXIS The fletcher Journal of Human Security. at: http://fletcher.tufts.edu/Praxis/Archives/~/media/EFB50A4BC05A482994D6E3D246D57309.pdf.

Benford, D. R. and Snow, D A. 2000. *Framing Process and Social Movements: An Overview and Assessment*. Annual Review of Sociology. Vol. 26, pp. 611–639.

Calic, M. J. 2000. *Kosovo in the Twentieth Century: A Historical Account* in Schnabel. A and Thakur. R, (eds). Kosovo and the Challenge of Humanitarian Intervention: Selective Indignation, Collective Action and International Citizenship. United Nation University Press, Tokyo & New York & Paris.

Chandler, D. 2006. Empire in Denial: the Politics of Statebuilding. Pluto Press.

Della Porta, D. and Diani, M. 2006. Social Movements: An Introduction. 2nd edition. Blackwell Publishing.

Demjaha, Ag. 2000. *The Kosovo Conflict: A Perspective from Inside* in Schnabel. A and Thakur. R, (eds), Kosovo and the Challenge of Humanitarian Intervention: Selective Indignation, Collective Action and International Citizenship. United Nation University Press, Tokyo & New York & Paris.

Diani, M. 1996. *Linking Mobilization Frames and Political Opportunities Insights from Regional Populism in Italy*. American Sociology Review. 61, pp. 1053–69.

Gashi, S. 2010. Adem Demaci—Unauthorized Biography. Prishtina: Rrokullia.

Glenny, M. 2001 (1999). The Balkans: Nationalism, War & the Great Powers, 1804–1999. Penguin Books.

Hayden, R. 1992. *Constitutional Nationalism in the Formerly Yugoslav Republic.* Slavic Review. Vol. 51, No. 4, pp. 654–673.

Ignatieff, M. 2003. Empire lite: Nation-building in Bosnia, Kosovo and Afghanistan. Vintage.

Judah, T. 2000. Kosovo, War and Revenge. New Haven & London: Yale University Press.

Kezmeci-Basha, S. 2003. OrganizatatdheGrupetIlegalene Kosove. 1981–1989. Institutii Historise. Prishtine.

Kostovicova, D. 2005. Kosovo: The Politics of Identity and Space. Routledge.

Kostovicova, D. 2008. *Legitimacy and International Administration: The Ahtisaari Settlement for Kosovo from a Human Security Perspective* in International Peacekeeping. Vol. 15, No. 5, pp. 631–647.

Lehne, S. 2012. *Kosovo and Serbia: Towards a Normal Relatioship*. Carnegie Report.

Malcolm, N. 1998.Kosovo: A Short History. Pan Books.

Mazower, M. 2000. The Balkans: A Short History. New York: The Modern Library.

McAdam, D. 1982. *The Classical Model of Social Movements Examined* in Buechler and Cylke, 1997, Social Movements: Perspectives and Issues. Mayfield Publishing Company, California & London & Toronto.

Mertus, A. J. 1999. Kosovo: How Myths and Truths Started a War. University of California Press, Berkley & Los Angeles & London.

Pond, El. 2008. *The EU's Test in Kosovo* in The Washington Quarterly. Vol. 31, No. 4, pp. 97–112.

Prelec, M. *Why Less is More*. at http://www.crisisgroupblogs.org/across-eurasia/2013/05/07/the-kosovo-serbia-agreement-why-less-is-more/

Snow, A D and Benford. D. R. 1992. *Master Frames and Cycles of Protest* in Buechler and Cylke (eds), 1997, Social Movements: Perspectives and Issues. Mayfield Publishing Company, California & London & Toronto.

Snow, A D., Rochford, E. B., Worden, S. and Benford, R. 1986. *Frame Alignment Processes, Micromobilization and Movement Participation.* American Sociological Review. Vol. 51, pp. 464–81.

Tarrow, S. 1998 (1994).Power in Movement: Social Movements, Collective Action and Politics, (2nd edition). New York/Cambridge: Cambridge University Press.

Tomson, D. 2012. *Constitution as Reconciliation? Exogenous Influences on Post-Conflict Kosovo* in the Yale Review of International Studies. Available at http://yris.yira.org/essays/762

Tunheim, J. 2009. *Rule of Law and the Kosovo Constitution*, Minnesota: Journal of International Law.Vol. 18.

Zaum, D. 2007. The Sovereignty Paradox. Oxford University Press.

TOM PHILLIPS

Western Europe, Western Balkans: Barriers to Cross-Cultural Encounter

The barriers to cross-cultural encounter between Western Europe and the Western Balkans are often theorized in terms of geo-political, ideological and economic imbalances. Whilst accepting that these imbalances undoubtedly have a role to play, this chapter argues that the accounts of cross-cultural encounter with Western Balkan culture in English-language travel writing and journalism suggest that the factors which have most bearing on the outcome of these encounters might best be classified as perceptual-circumstantial and conceptual. Whilst specific sets of paradigms, stereotypes and generalizations evidently distort and interrupt such encounters, it is also argued that discourses such as Balkanism originate in a particular way of conceptualising culture—and that, paradoxically, this may well also open up the possibility of a more profound and productive exchange, even though it initially appears to constitute another barrier.

Key words: Cross-cultural encounter, Western Balkans, Western Europe, English-language travel writing, Balkanism.

Dr Tom Phillips is a writer living in Bristol, UK. He holds a Ph.D. in creative writing from the University of Reading.

Introduction: the suntanned restaurateur

In his 1998 travel narrative *The Accursed Mountains,* Robert Carver describes an encounter with the unnamed Albanian owner of a fish restaurant on the shores of Lake Ohrid. He is accompanied by an interpreter, Gabriel, and a driver referred to only as Mr Slovki. Over the course of the encounter, Carver becomes increasingly suspicious of his companions. He fears that Gabriel and Mr Slovki are conspiring with the restaurateur to swindle him, by attempting to persuade him to invest in a property deal and by getting him to pay for food he didn't order. As his suspicions intensify, Carver decides that "these people were crooks who lied and fawned on you for advantage and then cheated on you when they lulled you into believing their lies". A catalogue of denigratory generalizations follows, and Carver goes on to claim that Albanians consider anything other than "honeyed phrases" to be "hostile"; that in Albania "foreigners were a source of both plunder and status, their 'culture' so admired was an object to possess"; that "Albanians themselves couldn't produce but could only fake"; that, during the communist era, the country had been "an imitation Soviet" and is now "an imitation of capitalism, a fun-fair democracy"; that, as a country, it operates "on clan and tribal lines"; and that "Whatever the ostensible system, the real basis of all Albanian endeavor was deceit, fraud and theft; a few pashas living on the backs of their slaving peons" (Carver 1998: 52–4).

For Carver, the value of this cross-cultural encounter is the knowledge which it enables him to produce about Albanian culture and an Albanian national character. Moreover, the generalizations he amasses appear to be authenticated by an assertion of his empirical trustworthiness and physical presence at the point of encounter. At the very beginning of the episode, he gives a brief description of the restaurateur as "short and muscular, with a shock of thick grey hair and a bold, brutal, suntanned face sporting a beaky nose: a tough commander of a Roman legion, an energetic provincial who with a bit of luck might rise high, even become Emperor" (Carver 1998: 52). As well as providing an introductory sketch of the restaurateur, Carver places himself in the scene as a participant-observer: the structure of the description mimics the movement of his gaze, first taking in the man's build and hair, then focusing in on his face and nose, before zooming out again. At the same time, the seemingly artless elements of the text—the dead metaphors in "shock of ... hair" and "beaky nose", the peculiar bathos of the sequence of adjectives "bold, brutal, suntanned"—suggest that these are the author's direct, unmediated first impressions.

Even in this opening description, however, the restaurateur is beginning to disappear into stereotype—"energetic provincial", "tough commander"—and this process accelerates as the episode develops. Gabriel and Mr Slovki (who rarely emerges from invisibility) also begin to lose any semblance of individuality until the three Albanians become almost allegorical figures, standing for the collective character traits which Carver believes to be common to all Albanians. Their specificity is transformed into typicality, and this transformation suggests two questions: what is Carver actually encountering in this episode (and *re*-encountering in the act of writing)? And what is the outcome of this encounter?

The first of these questions might be answered using Polish journalist and travel writer Ryszard Kapuściński's distinction between an enculturated and unenculturated self. According to him, each person "we meet along the road ... is in a way twofold ... One of these beings is a person like the rest of us: he has his joys and sorrows, his good and bad days ... The other being, who overlaps and is interwoven with the first, is a person as bearer of racial features, and as bearer of culture, beliefs and convictions" (Kapuściński 2008: 14). Carver, it would seem, only encounters the latter: the restaurateur, Gabriel and Mr Slovki are represented as bearers of culture, rather than as people "like the rest of us". As readers, of course, we can accept, question or reject their being 'typical' Albanians, but Carver himself appears convinced that what he has encountered here is a manifestation of an essential 'Albanian-ness'.

Kapuściński also offers a typology of cross-cultural encounter based on outcome. Derived from anthropological thinking and, in particular, the work of Bronislaw Malinowski, this model consists of three categories of encounter: conflict, withdrawal and exchange (Kapuściński 2008: 81). These categories can, of course, be further divided into any number of sub-categories and a single encounter may have a series of overlapping outcomes: it might begin as exchange, turn into conflict and result in withdrawal, or begin in conflict and result in exchange and so on. Nevertheless, as broad categories, they constitute a starting-point. "The three possibilities I have mentioned," Kapuściński continues, "have always stood before man when he has encountered an Other: he could choose war, he could fence himself in behind a wall or he could start a dialogue" (2008: 81).

Looked at in these terms, Carver's encounter with the fish restaurateur appears to result in exchange (of money, information, knowledge). Carver himself certainly presents it in such a way. The author's conviction that he has somehow come closer to essential qualities of Albanian culture, however, need not preclude an alternative interpretation: that Carver is, in fact, withdrawing from encounter with unpredictable individuals ("like the rest of us") here. Rather than 'discovering' the generalizations and stereotypes he reiterates, he is, in effect, retreating behind them, moving onto more secure terrain where an unknowable 'otherness' no longer need present a threat to his equanimity because it can be understood in terms of an already available or hastily improvised set of paradigms. What Carver encounters, in other words, is not so much a trio of individual Albanians as a reflection of his own generalized ideas about Albanian culture.

Carver, of course, is not alone among travel writers in presenting himself as an impartial, unencumbered participant-observer whilst at the same time inadvertently revealing that the encounters which give rise to his observations are themselves distorted, interrupted and even prevented, both by already-existing assumptions and preconceptions and by the conceptual habits of classifying individuals according to their typicality and of generalising from the specific. Narratives on the Western Balkans by West European travel writers from Rebecca West to Eric Newby, Dervla Murphy and Robin Hanbury-Tenison exhibit a similar contradiction between their authors' gestures of impartiality and the partiality (in both senses of the word) of their descriptions of travelling encounter. It is not, however, their partiality which is problematic. Partiality is inevitable: as Maurice Merleau-Ponty points out, without the ability to focus on particulars and without what he calls our individual "'world of thoughts', or a sediment left by our mental processes", we wouldn't be able to construct any knowledge of the world at all (1962: 148). On the contrary, in fact, it is the implicit denial of subjective partiality in assertions of empirical trustworthiness which is problematic—as is the associated belief that cross-cultural encounter can ever be unencumbered, uninhibited, or occur of 'neutral' ground.

My contention here, therefore, is that, whether designated as cross-cultural or not, any encounter is liable to be inhibited, distorted and interrupted to some degree and how it unfolds and how it is perceived, interpreted and evaluated will be subject to a complex of factors—some inhibitive, some facilitative. Compiling a comprehensive catalogue of these factors is beyond the scope of this paper, but it is possible to identify two principle categories of inhibition: the circumstantial and the conceptual. Examining how the effects of some of these factors can be detected in English-language writing on the Western Balkans will not only indicate how they can inhibit encounter, but also lead to the perhaps unexpected conclusion that they may well represent necessary stages in the overcoming of barriers to cross-cultural exchange.[1]

---

[1] Even though most of the examples I draw on relate to writings on and encounters with Albanian culture, much the same could be said about writings on and encounters with other cultures within the Western Balkans.

Circumstantial factors

Describing any factor which appears to inhibit encounter as wholly circumstantial is misleading. It implies that any such inhibitions objectively exist within the encountered culture and are, to some extent, unavoidable. Certainly, the political situation in a country may restrict opportunities for encounter. During the communist period, for example, it was difficult for West Europeans to get permission to enter Albania and the majority of those who did were only permitted to travel there as part of a closely monitored tour group: who and what they encountered—and how these encounters progressed—were controlled (if not always successfully) by guides, interpreters and other officials. Travel writers Eric Newby, Philip Ward and Anton Gill all pay great attention to the difficulties they faced obtaining a visa and to the restrictions placed on them as visitors to Albania in the early 1980s. Likewise, war and other catastrophic circumstances may play a significant role in determining the form and outcome of encounters between individuals. During the 1999 conflict in Kosova, for example, the identity of the individuals British journalists were able to contact and communicate with while reporting the war was at least partially determined by the situation around them: for much of the conflict, the British media focused on the experiences of refugees in Albania and Macedonia, largely because the fighting made it difficult—and dangerous—for all but the most hardy of journalists to travel into Kosova itself. Later, after NATO ground troops were deployed, the focus of reporting altered as different people became—or were made—'available' as witnesses and sources of information.

The kind of 'encounter management' attempted by governments and other institutions and the temporary boundaries between safety and danger, the accessible and the non-accessible, put up during wartime, however, no longer play as significant a role in the Western Balkans as they have done in the past. Institutions such as government tourist and culture ministries may still want to present West Europeans with a particular image of their respective country—by, for example, encouraging travellers to visit certain historical sites or eat in certain restaurants—but they are no longer in a position to impose an itinerary, a regime of encounter, except, of course, in those cases when visitors voluntarily accept the recommendations they suggest.

Nevertheless, the 'difficulty' of visiting the Western Balkans remains a trope in English-language travel writing—and circumstantial inhibitions to encounter which existed at certain times in the past persist in the form of what might be described as ongoing perceptual-circumstantial factors. Albania, for example, has been regarded as 'remote' and 'inaccessible' since the eighteenth century—i.e. long before the isolationist policies of the communist regime. Edward Gibbon, for example, described it as "A country in sight of Italy ... less known than the wilds of America"(1776–8: 217), Byron repeated that description in his notes to *Childe Harold's Pilgrimage* (1986: 87), and since then its remoteness and isolation have been amongst the first characteristics attributed to the country by a wide range of travel writers. As recently as 2010, Robin Hanbury-Tenison gave his book *Land of Eagles* the sub-title *Riding through Europe's Forgotten Country* and begins: "Albania is one of the poorest and least-known countries in Europe" (2010: xix)—its least-known status deriving from its supposed remoteness and isolation. In such narratives, encountering Albanian culture is always-already difficult because the country itself is supposedly difficult to reach—and, even when reached, difficult and, in some instances, dangerous to travel around: Dervla Murphy, for example, abandons her journey through Albania altogether after she is robbed by a group of children on a country road (2002: 209–227).

Although it is often used as if it were, remoteness is not a term which refers to a geographical fact. Remoteness is a matter of perspective, and while, like other parts of the Western Balkans, Albania may appear remote to some West Europeans, this perception owes more to the hegemonic image of the country in Western Europe than it does to the actual difficulty of getting to a place which is, in fact, only a three-hour flight from London. We might also question the claim that Albania is difficult to travel around: this is a claim, after all, which is often made by travellers who have chosen to travel through thinly populated parts of the country on horseback (like Carver, Hanbury-Tenison and Tessa de Loos) or bicycle (like Murphy). As these narratives progress, in fact, it becomes apparent that these supposed difficulties do not prevent their authors encountering individual Albanians or Albanian cultural phenomena.

Another frequently cited, potential hindrance to encounter is the so-called language barrier. Edward Lear—who described Albania in 1848 as "a puzzle of the highest order"—advised any traveller to the country that "A good dragoman, or interpreter, is absolutely necessary, however many languages you may be acquainted with. French, German and Italian are useless, and modern Greek nearly as much if you travel higher than Macedonia. Bulgarian, Albanian, Turkish and Sclavonic are your requisites in this Babel" (2008: xv). Even transliterating Albanian eluded Lear, with one attempt producing only a "clatter of strange monosyllables—Dort beer, dort bloo, dort hitch, hitch beer, blue beer, beer chak, dort gatch" (2008: 90). Like Albania's remoteness, the reputed difficulty of the language remains a common trope. In his *Blue Guide to Albania*, James Pettifer introduces Albanian as "one of the least known European languages, with a reputation for difficulty and obscurity in its process of word-formation and grammatical structure" (1994: 73), while Hanbury-Tenison observes that "Albanian is a curious and difficult language, unrelated to any other and therefore hard to penetrate" (2009: 9).[2]

In many instances, however, anticipated difficulties of communication fail to materialize. "I've also been surprised not just that so many people speak English, but that they speak it so fluently," observes Tony Wheeler shortly after arriving in Tirana (2007: 51), while even when encountering non-English-speaking Albanians, Dervla Murphy finds she is able to communicate with them "despite the language barrier" (2002: 195). Nevertheless, communication continues to be perceived as a potential problem. The use of interpreters means that encounters with non-English-speaking Albanians are necessarily mediated. Robert Carver calls into question the reliability of those interpreting for him on several occasions, while Murphy finds herself wondering whether the local witnesses she talks to about Albanian customs and traditions are telling the truth or playing a role. In Pukë, an interpreter called Sokol tells Murphy that his brother was shot dead in a blood feud because he had bought a young woman a drink in a bar. Initially sceptical, Murphy wonders if "he was trying to shock me by presenting this stereotype of 'the stage Albanian'". It is an uncertainty which puts at risk the value of this encounter to her as a source of knowledge about Albanian culture. Moreover, if Sokol play-acts, then so, too, might other people: their testimony may be equally unreliable and Murphy's encounters with them equally distorted. In this instance, however, Murphy comes to the conclusion that Sokol is a reliable witness:

---

[2] This, of course, isn't true: Albanian is a branch of Common Indo-European and, as such, is related—albeit distantly—to a great many other European languages.

his "vignettes of family life in Pukë were straining my credulity yet it was impossible to disbelieve them" (2002: 216–7). The story of the brother's death can be admitted as evidence and serve to confirm her earlier assertion that violence is an inherent characteristic of Albanian culture. What was perceived as a potential barrier to encounter—Sokol's deliberate subversion of expectations and stereotype—has been removed by the 'impossibility' of disbelief and the recognition of her contact as a reliable witness.

Here, then, I reiterate my assertion that the form and outcome of any given cross-cultural encounter owes more to the competencies and skills—the *personal* circumstances—of the individuals involved than to objectively existing 'barriers' presented by the physical and cultural terrain on which it occurs. This also becomes apparent if we consider acculturative stress or culture shock.

Most commonly, acculturative stress is thought of as a relatively simple—and temporary—anxiety reaction to unfamiliar cultural circumstances and codes of behavior. Feelings of disorientation, uncertainty and of being overwhelmed attend a period between 'first contact' with a new cultural environment and a successful moment of reorientation, adaptation or socialization. According to this model, the severity and duration of the symptoms—one of which may be a resistance to engagement with the 'host' culture—will depend on the extent of the differences between the 'home' and 'host' cultures and the consequent difficulties of adaptation this presents to the traveller.

Certainly, acculturative stress can operate as an impediment to encounter. Philip Ward's *Albania: A Travel Guide* offers several examples. Despite its sub-title, this 'guide' is, in fact, an autobiographical narrative recounting a single journey through Albania in the early 1980s as part of a tour organized by Regent Travel and Albtourist. As such, it combines passages concerning the author's experiences with methodical incursions into historical, cultural and topographical information. Characterising himself as "a Briton with no axe to grind", Ward's stated aim is to represent Albania as a coherent, comprehensible and useful set of facts and observations "for the independently minded who care to look behind the Iron Curtain" (1983: 1).

In practice, however, Ward finds it difficult to maintain his self-proclaimed impartiality and detachment. Effusive responses to the Albanian landscape are matched by fierce critiques of the regime and those who live under it. The "Paradise" of the landscape in southern Albania, for example, is offset by the "living inferno" of a textile factory in Berat. His narrative, in fact, soon becomes one of disillusionment, with moments of crisis reported with a convincing intensity. In Saranda, Ward joins the evening promenade along the seafront before withdrawing to "a narrow, empty spit of beach" (1983: 86) and experiencing a claustrophobic melancholy attended by thoughts of drowning and death. Not even the natural "Paradise" which has previously restored his equanimity assuages his feeling of dislocation, his desire for a "serenity" akin to oblivion: here even the natural world—a "mob of fossil shells", roaring waves—is characterized by violence and destruction.

Other episodes recounted by Ward follow a similar pattern: periods of apparent equanimity are interrupted by an encounter with a cultural phenomenon which produces an attack of claustrophobia and/or melancholy. This, in turns, causes Ward to withdraw from the encounter, both physically and mentally, and yet the responses he reports appear disproportionate to his circumstances and suggest that his acculturative stress is not a simple anxiety reaction caused by the differences between 1980s Britain and 1980s Albania. Indeed, what he appears to be experiencing is the psychological phenomenon which Freud calls transference: the resurgence and projection of past emotions onto present circumstances (whether they are appropriate to those circumstance or not), which comes with the risk of "misunderstanding their nature and taking them to be new, real experiences, rather than reflections of the past" (2003: 205). Ward's culture shock, in other words, may be an expression of emotions attached to past experiences which resurface when prompted by associations set off in his unconscious.

The psychoanalytical anthropologist Waud Kracke understands culture shock in precisely these terms. In his paper 'Encounter with Other Cultures', he contends that cross-cultural encounter is an "intense experience which is likely to stir up fantasies and memories which otherwise would remain dormant in day-to-day life but in a situation like this (as in love and psychotherapy) will be mobilized and expressed in the form of transferences" (Kracke: 65). These transferences, he continues, offer a more satisfactory explanation of culture shock than those models which describe it as a temporary dysadaptation syndrome, a self-limiting mental disturbance, a form of mourning (for one's own culture) or a simple anxiety reaction. For Kracke these models only offer partial descriptions of the experience of acculturative stress and, he suggests, their incompleteness originates in a conceptualization of any culture as a relatively stable template or shared 'map'. I return to the possible link between culture shock and how culture is conceptualized later. For now, I cite Kracke's interpretation to illustrate that, while culture shock can have a profound effect on the form and outcome of cross-cultural encounter—distorting and interrupting exchange, leading to withdrawal or conflict—this, too, is a barrier to encounter which arises not so much from the external circumstances of the 'host' culture as from the personal psychological circumstances of those involved in the encounter. That West Europeans report instances of culture shock on arriving in Albania—or anywhere else in the Western Balkans, for that matter—does not indicate that contact with Albanian or Western Balkan culture need be inherently 'shocking' or 'stressful' to Western Europeans.

Conceptual factors

If the factors which can inhibit, distort or interrupt encounter considered so far might be classified as perceptual-circumstantial, the second category incorporates the conceptual frameworks from and into which perceptions of cultural phenomena feed. These frameworks are, like Merleau-Ponty's "world of thoughts", part of our apparatus for perceiving and engaging with "things there in front of us" (1962: 80), a set of concepts and acquired judgements which are not fixed (we have the capacity to adjust them, to learn from experience), but which nevertheless act as a filter on and focus for our perceptions and provide a structure of assumptions or template into which we fit encountered phenomena in order to make them comprehensible. Anthropologist Mary Douglas identifies a similar apparatus at work when she writes, in *Purity and Danger:* "In perceiving we are building, taking some cues and rejecting others. The most acceptable cues are those which fit most easily into the pattern that is built up." Moreover, Douglas continues, over time we become more confident in our pattern-making abilities, and although encountering new experiences and anomalous or ambiguous phenomena—which don't fit the pattern we are building—may lead to our modifying our structure of assumptions in order to accommodate them, this is not the only possible outcome: "Uncomfortable facts which refuse to be fitted in, we find ourselves ignoring or distorting so that they do not disturb these established assumptions" (Douglas 1966: 45–6).

Here, then, Douglas makes a specific link between our conceptual frameworks and our ways of perceiving or encountering the world. In accounts of cross-cultural encounter between Western European travellers and the Western Balkans, we can certainly detect traces of several conceptual frameworks which operate in this way, encouraging the filtering out of "uncomfortable facts" and the focusing in on those phenomena which fit pre-existing patterns. The most well-documented of these is Balkanism.

The particular sets of stereotypes and paradigms associated with Balkanism and its function as an ideological discourse have been identified and discussed in a range of critical studies, from Vesna Goldsworthy's *Inventing Ruritania* and Maria Todorova's *Imagining the Balkans* to Andrew Hammond's *The Debated Lands* and Božidar Jezernik's *Wild Europe*. Similar to Orientalism, as described by Edward Said, it is a phenomenon which can either be regarded as an offshoot of that discourse or as a wholly separate category. From either perspective, however, Balkanism can be seen as a way of thinking about the region which, as well as producing partial representations of the culture and inhabitants of South East Europe, derives from and reproduces a hegemonic ideological orientation towards it. In that they describe the region in terms of exoticism, traditionalism and primitiveness, Balkanist texts reinforce its 'otherness' in relation to the rest of Europe and thereby to help to maintain its liminality and subaltern status. These texts need not be overtly denigratory to produce this effect. As Andrew Hammond comments in the introduction to his anthology of writing on SE Europe, *Through Another Europe*, romanticizing the region can also serve to perpetuate Balkanist stereotypes: "On balance being considered a 'lusty peasant' is as disagreeable as being called a 'wild-looking fellow'" (2009: xix). Thus while the abusive generalizations Carver catalogues in *The Accursed Mountains* are examples of negative stereotyping, Balkanism can also manifest itself in ostensibly 'neutral' descriptions of topography, architecture, clothing, meals. In *Wild Europe*, for example, Jezernik elucidates the Balkanist assumptions implicit in apparently neutral descriptions of coffee and coffee houses (2004: 147–165). Similarly, a description of the concrete used to construct the networks of bunkers which Enver Hoxha had built across large parts of Albania as "substandard" may appear to be a technical detail, an impartial statement of fact. When it appears in the context of a travel literature which is already saturated in Balkanism, however, it feeds into and derives its authority from a discourse founded in the assumption that Albanian and SE European culture is somehow 'other' to that of 'standard' or, indeed, 'superior' Western Europe (Winchester 1999: 170).

Whether the images produced are denigratory or romanticized, then, Balkanism can be thought of as a form of anamorphosis: it distorts evaluative descriptions of SE Europe so that they become coherent only when viewed from a particular ideological standpoint. Statements such as Carver's "Albanians themselves couldn't produce but could only fake" (1998: 52) can only have meaning when they are viewed from a Balkanist perspective. Where these anamorphic distortions differ from that of, say, the elongated skull in Holbein's painting 'The Ambassadors' is that they are not presented as such when they appear in supposedly impartial travel narratives. The conceptual—and ideological—framework in which Balkanist images of Albania have been produced are denied by authors characterising themselves as empirically trustworthy. As Slavoj Žižek argues in his analysis of anamorphosis as an ideological technique, the assumptions which determine how a phenomenon is perceived are "reflected back into the perceived object itself" such that "anamorphosis undermines the distinction between 'objective reality' and its distorted subjective perception" (2001: 150). Balkanism, in other words, both produces distortions and, by providing a means of making sense of them, contributes to the transformation of subjective opinion into objective fact or knowledge.

As such, then, Balkanism operates in a similar way to the 'patterns' and 'worlds of thought' described by Merleau-Ponty and Douglas: it encourages a focus on certain kinds of phenomena and filters out those which appear to be anomalous. As is evident in Carver's denigratory catalogue, Balkanism also provides a 'safe haven', a secure terrain of supposed knowledge, onto which a traveller can retreat from encounters with phenomena or behaviors which initially appear to threaten the coherence of the Balkanist anamorphosis. Whether at the point of material encounter or interpretative re-encounter, Balkanism effectively keeps whatever is being encountered at a distance, as something 'typical' of the 'other'.

Historically, Balkanism has served as something more than a self-sustaining conceptual barrier to cross-cultural encounter. As an ideological discourse, it has also been deployed as a means of discouraging actual material encounter by locating SE Europe in a liminal politico-geographical space on the 'far' side of a division between 'civilized' (western) Europe and the 'barbaric'. Balkanism portrays SE Europe as a dangerous place to go, not just for individual West European travellers, but also for West European governments. It has, in other words, been used to justify non-interventionist policies towards SE Europe, and while this has not been consistent—since the end of communism, Western governments have occasionally needed to use Balkanist discourse to justify actual military intervention in the region and to raise questions about putative European Union accession processes—the Balkanist version of the region remains politically expedient. On the one hand, imagining SE Europe as inferior and backward presents it as being ripe for economic, cultural and political intervention; on the other, describing it as chaotic, violent and barbaric presents it as being unready for integration into the European Union. This combination of ripeness and unreadiness is not as contradictory as it seems. Serving to maintain SE Europe in an uncertain, peripheral position, the two 'sides' of Balkanism effectively prepare the ground for whatever action western governments, institutions and corporations choose to take. Either way, it implies that the future of SE Europe resides in western hands.

Since the end of communism, too, conventional Balkanism has, to some extent, been overlaid by what might be termed Ostism—an image of communism which has come to replace the one generated during the Cold War. Until 1989, communism, communist Europe and the Soviet Union were represented as a serious, imminent threat to Western Europe and the capitalist sphere of influence in general. They were seen as the source of dangerous ideas, as supporters of anti-western insurrection, as ruthlessly efficient suppressors of opposition and dissidence within their own nation-states and as possessors of a heavily industrialized and technologically advanced economy whose military-industrial complex had produced huge and well-equipped armed forces which could invade or destroy the West with only four minutes' warning (Campbell 1982: 288). As such, the threat they reputedly posed could be used to justify a Western response and, in particular, vast military expenditure: unlike Hoxha's bunkers—which are routinely dismissed as the manifestations of paranoia—the West's accumulation of an arsenal of nuclear and non-nuclear weaponry could not be attributed to paranoia because the threat was deemed to be real. Since

1989, however, the West's need to justify its response has evaporated and the hegemonic image of communist Europe has been amended. The communist regimes' reputation for exerting totalitarian control and suppressing opposition remains intact—even though, as E. P. Thompson points out, neither the Polish government nor the Soviet Union was able to suppress Solidarność (1982: 13)—but what the opening of the Iron Curtain appears to have 'revealed' is that, far from being on a par with the West, the communist economies and military-industrial complex were too primitive, crude and inefficient to present a real threat. The belief that the Soviet sphere of influence enjoyed near parity with the West has been redefined as erroneous—a product of communist propaganda and the difficulty of securing accurate information from and about the 'mysterious' East.

Even at the height of the Cold War, of course, the Western Balkans were rarely perceived as a direct military or economic threat to the West. Parts of what was then Yugoslavia were popular holiday destinations for West European tourists, and only Albania was regarded as ideologically dangerous because Hoxha's state remained an isolated enigma and Radio Tirana, broadcasting on or near the same wavelength as BBC Radio One, attempted to convince western listeners that Albania was a highly efficient, economically advanced socialist utopia in the vanguard of ongoing world revolution. Similarly, even denigratory accounts of communist Albania published before 1991, such as Eric Newby's, reinforced its reputation for being a peculiarly repressive and sinister state, while memoirs written by British SOE personnel about their wartime experiences with Hoxha's partisans emphasize the potentially threatening ruthlessness, courage and skills displayed by the communist resistance in its double-pronged campaign against the Axis forces and its royalist-nationalist rivals. For much of the post-war period, too, communist Albania had at least one ally that was perceived as being a direct threat to the West: the Soviet Union until 1961 and Maoist China between 1961 and the early 1970s. Even the more apparently 'open' (i.e. to the West) communist state of Yugoslavia could, at times, enter the category of 'threat', most notably whenever its membership of the non-aligned movement saw it allied with nations engaged in anti-colonialist (i.e. anti-Western) conflicts.

The history of communist-era SE Europe, however, has come to be rewritten since the change of regime in the early 1990s. The 'enigma' of communism, it turns out, concealed, not a highly efficient military-industrial complex, but a primitiveness, irrationality and incompetence which is all too familiar from conventional Balkanist texts. Again this is politically expedient, in that it seems to affirm the seemingly unquestionable 'victory' of capitalism, the triumphalist version of history in which communism didn't collapse because of internal contradictions, dissident protest or economic failure, but was 'beaten' by an innately superior western capitalism. This version of history not only sustains formerly communist Europe's inferior status, it also provides a pre-emptive response to *ostalgie*, which, in its retrospective reappraisal of communism as a potentially viable ideology, represents a threat to Western hegemony.

In saying this, of course, I am not suggesting that the reiteration of stereotypes and generalizations in travel writing is directly related to or has a causal effect on policy decisions about the Western Balkans made by West European governments and Euro-Atlantic institutions such as NATO. In the foreword to the revised edition of his *Balkan Ghosts*, Robert D. Kaplan reports that President Clinton's initial reluctance to intervene militarily in the Bosnian conflict arose from having read 'the history of ethnic rivalry' recounted in the original, 1993 version of Kaplan's book. Even Kaplan himself, however, concedes that, if his narrative did play a role in Clinton's decision-making, it was only one of many factors and that 'at the beginning of his term [of office], Clinton had so little resolve that he was casting around for any excuse not to act' (2005: x-xi). Indeed, as I have argued above, Balkanism and Ostism are 'pliable' discourses: they themselves and the stereotypes and paradigms they perpetuate can be adjusted or selected in accordance with geo-political circumstances and institutional priorities. They are not the sole reason West European and Euro-Atlantic institutions behave in certain ways towards the Western Balkans: it is not simply due to Balkanism and Ostism, for example, that Albania's application to join the European Union has proceeded—or not proceeded—in a particular fashion. Many other factors come into play, and the relationship between discourse and policy is, perhaps, best thought of, not as a simple one of cause-and-effect, but as a complex series of feedback loops. Discourse provides the field within which policy decisions are taken, but policy decisions—and all the other factors which may influence—can themselves adjust the field of discourse in which they occur.

Similarly, I am also not suggesting that every West European who encounters the cultural complexities of the Western Balkans can get no further than the particular sets of stereotypes and paradigms traceable to the ideological priorities of Balkanism and/or Ostism. Challenges to the prevailing image of SE Europe—and West European policy towards the region—occur, and even over the course of a single travel narrative a traveller-writer may well move beyond the constraining 'filter' offered by these readymade discourses: Carver's *The Accursed Mountains*, in fact, can be read as a prolonged attempt to test the assumptions he has inherited from hegemonic discourse against his material experiences in Albania, an attempt which doesn't always result in a clear-cut vindication of his own prejudices and generalized conclusions. Balkanism and Ostism are an ideological space to which he returns eventually, but there are moments *en route* when his encounters become less encumbered by these enduring mental habits.

Finally, then, I suggest that, beyond specific ideological discourses such as Balkanism and Ostism, the way culture itself is conceptualized is key to the progress of cross-cultural encounter. Both Balkanism and Ostism themselves, in fact, are examples of a templated model of culture. It's a model which derives from functionalist anthropology. In his introduction to *Argonauts of the Western Pacific*, for example, Bronislaw Malinowski asserts that "the first and basic ideal of ethnographic field-work is to give a clear and firm outline of the social constitution and disentangle the laws and regularities of all cultural phenomena from the irrelevancies. The firm skeleton of the tribal life has to be first ascertained." Although, as Malinowski goes on to state, "these things, though crystallized and set, are nowhere *formulated*", they can nevertheless be discovered by "drawing ... general inferences" (1922: 10–12). A culture, in other words, may be defined in terms of certain key characteristics—its traditions, continuities, behavior patterns, conventions—and emerge as "a stable, space-time isolate with a singular set of key social mechanisms" (Boon 1982: 15). Culture becomes 'superorganic', its collective institutions existing over and above—we might even say *despite*—the individual, who, in turn, can be located in relation to a shared cultural identity or national character. Cultural change remains possible, but the emphasis is on what remains unchanged for any given cultural group, the similarities which exist within it and the differences which distinguish it from others. It is these continuities, similarities and differences which are regarded as fixed points or contours on that group's cultural 'map' and which, in the case of Albania, for example, would constitute the essential characteristics of Albanian culture and Albanian identity or Albanian-ness.

Descriptions of encounters with individual cultural phenomena produced within this conceptual framework, then, tend to converge on an equally stable interpretation of those phenomena. Other possible interpretations are either rejected as inappropriate or presented as having less truth-value than the one deemed to be correct: they are designated as opinion, rather than fact. As I have already suggested, descriptions of Albania's concrete bunkers in English-language travel narratives written during and after the communist period conform to this pattern (they are routinely described as poorly constructed, ineffectual, pointless, 'crazy', 'paranoid'), while, on a broader scale, it is possible to identify a series of—usually binaristic—templates which underpin entire narratives and offer a seemingly fixed diagnosis of Albanian culture *per se*: lack/excess in Newby's *On the Shores of the Mediterranean*, chaos/criminality in Murphy's *Through the Embers of Chaos*, Stalinist/Third World in Theroux's *Pillars of Hercules*.

More so than the specific repertoires of generalizations and stereotypes made available by discourses such Balkanism and Ostism, I would suggest that it is this view, that any—and, indeed, every—culture can interpreted, understood and explained in terms of a relatively stable underlying template, which inhibits cross-cultural encounter. Paradoxically, it is the very strategy outlined by Malinowski—to get to the essential "skeleton" of a culture—which appears to distort, even prevent engagement with the ipseity of any given culture and lead to a more-or-less inevitable withdrawal (in Kapuściński's sense) from experience and encounter-as-exchange into structured, generalized knowledge and conceptual safety. If one conceptualizes culture as a template, any cross-cultural encounter will be always-already constrained by a framework which filters out the anomalous, individual and specific.

Conclusion: from template to symbol

The template model is not the only way of conceptualising culture. One alternative which can be isolated from a densely populated repertoire of such models is derived from symbolic and psychoanalytic anthropology. According to this, culture is not a uniformist entity with a singular internal architecture, but "a set of symbols and meanings *in terms of which* individuals orient themselves to each other and to the world" (Kracke 1987:

79) and "the set of interrelationships between a symbolic scheme and the diverse concerns, conscious and unconscious, of some population" (Boon 1982: 112). Rather than being a stable, continuous, superorganic structure existing *beyond* the individual, culture becomes a continually changing—although not structureless—symbolic economy in which meaning is produced and negotiated at the individual, group and population levels. Similarly, the individual is no longer regarded as the bearer of an essential cultural identity, but as an active subject who produces and reproduces, interprets, uses and adapts values, meanings and images, both according to their own needs and desires and in negotiation with other active subjects. As a result, any given culture will be as diverse as its constituent and constituting individuals, a stock of symbols whose meanings are, as Boon puts it, "rich, deep, multivocal, many layered, highly wrought, and shared but also rarifiable, subject to abstraction, exportable, often communicated: thus not substantively shared but rather *exchanged*" (Boon 1982: 121). Moreover, boundaries between individual cultures are not fixed and clear. They are porous, overlapping: meanings and symbols can be communicated across them, as well as within them. Thus, even such apparent fixities as 'Albanian-ness' are perceived as negotiable concepts open to multiple usages and interpretations. In the absence of "laws and regularities" which are not themselves symbolic formations, Waud Kracke concludes, "the process of coming to understand [the negotiated reality of another culture] is not necessarily a terminable one, any more than one fully knows anyone of one's own culture" (1987: 79).

If the templating process can represent a withdrawal from encounter, a return to a notionally fixed position, then this conceptualization of culture as a dynamic symbolic economy offers the possibility of encounter-as-exchange. Indeed, from this perspective, encounter and the exchange of meanings and values are inherent to the ongoing process of symbol formation by which culture and cultural identity are produced. The porous and overlapping inter-cultural boundaries of this model allow for these encounters and exchanges to occur both within and across them. Likewise, in the absence of a binaristic template, cultural codes and identifies are endowed with plurality and temporality, emerging as constantly shifting phenomena "always susceptible to critical and creative recombination" (Clifford 1988: 12). Descriptions of cultural phenomena as elements in a symbolic economy will be no more complete, no less partial, than those produced in accordance with the template model, but their partiality can no longer be construed as failure on the part of an individual observer to elucidate *the* correct meaning of a given phenomenon and thereby render it transparent. Instead, they can be understood as acknowledgements that cultural codes, artefacts and behaviors are open to multiple, many-layered, sometimes conflicting interpretations, some of which will inevitably remain opaque. This conceptualization of culture, in other words, allows for cross-cultural encounter with a dwelt-in world, rather than a withdrawal into (pre-existing) abstractions mapped onto an encountered materiality.

If approaching another culture from this conceptual starting point avoids some of the barriers to encounter I have identified with the template model, however, it also presents difficulties. In his analysis of acculturative stress, for example, Waud Kracke argues that the kind of debilitating disorientation and psychological transferences which he identifies as the symptoms of culture shock occur at precisely those moments when an individual perceives the culture encountered as a seemingly limitless symbolic economy. It is, in other words, one thing to conceptualize another culture as an endlessly changing, negotiated reality, and quite another to encounter phenomena and behaviors to which no single meaning or value can be readily attached. The resultant disorientation can prove to be as inhibiting to cross-cultural encounter as other perceptual and conceptual barriers—and may well result, as it does for Robert Carver and Philip Ward, in a defensive counter-assertion of a stable, but reductive templated version of the encountered culture.

Here, then, we appear to reach an impasse—and yet as Kracke goes on to argue, acculturative stress need not result in defensive withdrawal. By disrupting or forestalling the templating process, it can, in fact, make it possible to begin the process of coming to understand a culture as a dynamic and negotiated reality, a dwelt-in world, rather than as a fixed and bounded isolate, through the process of responsive encounter-as-exchange. English-language writing on the Western Balkans, in fact, contains many episodes in which the templating process is interrupted and the traveller-writer—rather than withdrawing behind a list of negative stereotypes and generalizations—negotiates a meaning or value for an encounter in collaboration with an encountered individual. Dymphna Cusack, for example, describes her meeting with a 'traditional' Albanian family in Lac who behave in ways which challenge her own templated version of the culture—and that presented to her by her officially sanctioned guides and interpreters—as "something precious" (1966: 104).

Nor is it necessarily the case that the templating process is always a defensive mechanism. Indeed, in order to reach the point at which cultural phenomena can be perceived as elements in a dynamic symbolic economy, it may be necessary to begin by locating them in a template and regarding them as clues towards a greater understanding, a closer encounter. Projecting a single, coherent meaning onto Albania's bunkers, for example, may not be the end-point of encounter, but a means of bringing them into focus prior to a more active perceptual engagement with them. A description of them as "paranoid" or "substandard" may be understood as being 'preliminary'—a point of access to a description of a more complex whole or to the recognition that the whole of any given cultural phenomenon, whether it is something as apparently simple as a concrete bunker or as evidently complex as, say, Albania's bodies of customary or *kanun* law, will inevitably remain partially opaque and that the whole being described is not the phenomenon in itself but the experience of encountering it in a specific set of historical, physical, psychological and conceptual circumstances.

Certainly, the particular templates whose effects I have identified can be read as 'preliminary' descriptions. Even Newby's seemingly inflexible lack/excess template of Albanian culture can be interpreted as such: its obtrusiveness at certain moments in his narrative allows us to see that, despite his assertions of autonomy and empirical trustworthiness, his account is partial and selective. Similarly, the temporary suspension of old/new, Soviet/Third World and chaos/criminality models in Cusack's *Illyria Reborn,* Theroux's *The Pillars of Hercules* and Murphy's *Through the Embers of Chaos* enable us to recognize that beyond what these travel writers have been able to grasp of Albanian culture, there are meanings and values which remain beyond their reach.

Undoubtedly, then, the kind of perceptual-circumstantial and conceptual barriers to encounter I have been discussing are deeply engrained. That they coincide, in many instances, with and, in their turn, reinforce the ideological discourses of both Balkanism and Ostism and the enduring geo-political division of Europe also appears to give them a resilience to change. At the same time, however, these barriers are not brute facts, but institutional ones—they have themselves been negotiated into existence—

and, once recognized, they can be renegotiated, not so much overcome and ignored as utilized as a means of entering into engagement and exchange across borders which are, after all, of our own invention.

References

Boon, J. A. 1982. Other Tribes, Other Scribes. Cambridge: Cambridge University Press.

Byron, Lord George Gordon. 1986. Lord Byron: The Major Works. Edited by Jerome J. McGann. Oxford: OUP.

Campbell, D. 1982. War Plan UK: The Truth about Civil Defence in Britain. University of Michigan: Burnett Books.

Carver, R. 1998. The Accursed Mountains. London: John Murray.

Clifford, J. 1988. The Predicament of Culture: Twentieth-Century Ethnography, Literature and Art. Cambridge, MA: Harvard University Press.

Cusack, D. 1966. Illyria Reborn. London: Heinemann.

Douglas, M. 1966. Purity and Danger. London: Routledge.

Freud, S. 2003. An Outline of Psychoanalysis. Translated from German by Helena Ragg-Kirkby. London: Penguin.

Gibbon, Ed. 1776–8. The History of the Decline and Fall of the Roman Empire Volume IV. London.

Goldsworthy, V. 1998. Inventing Ruritania. New Haven: Yale University Press.

Hammond, A. 2007. The Debated Lands: British and American Representations of the Balkans. Cardiff: University of Wales Press.

Hammond, A (ed.). 2009. Through Another Europe. Oxford: Signal Books.

Hanbury-Tenison, Robin 2009. Land of Eagles: Riding Through Europe's Forgotten Country. London: IB Tauris.

Jezernik, B. 2004. Wild Europe: The Balkans in the Gaze of Western Travellers. London: Saqi Books & The Bosnian Institute, 2004.

Kapuściński, R. 2008. The Other, translated from Polish by Antonia Lloyd-Jones. London: Verso.

Kracke, W. 1987. *Encounter with Other Cultures: Psychological and Epistemological Aspects*. Ethos, Vol. 15, No. 1, Mar, pp. 58–81.

Lear, Ed. 2008. *Edward Lear in Albania: Journals of a Landscape Painter in the Balkans*. Edited by Bejtullah Destani and Robert Elsie. London: IB Tauris/The Centre for Albanian Studies.

Malinowski, B. 1922. Argonauts of the Western Pacific. London: Routledge.

Merleau-Ponty, M. 1962. Phenomenology of Perception. Translated from French by Colin Smith. London: Routledge.

Murphy, D. 2002. Through the Embers of Chaos: Balkan Journeys. London: John Murray.

Pettifer, J. 1994. Blue Guide to Albania. London: A & C Black.

Thompson, E.P. 1982. Beyond The Cold War. London: END & The Merlin Press.

Todorova, M. 2009. Imagining the Balkans. Second edition. Oxford: OUP.

Ward, Ph. 1983. Albania: A Travel Guide. London: Oleander.

Wheeler, T. 2007. Bad Lands. London: Lonely Planet.

Winchester, S. 1999. The Fracture Zone. Harmondsworth: Penguin.

Žižek. S. 2001. Did Somebody Say Totalitarianism? London: Verso.